TEAM PARENTING FOR CHILDREN
IN FOSTER CARE

TEAM PARENTING FOR CHILDREN IN FOSTER CARE

A MODEL FOR INTEGRATED THERAPEUTIC CARE

Jeanette Caw with Judy Sebba

Foreword by Professor Robbie Gilligan

Jessica Kingsley *Publishers*
London and Philadelphia

Team Parenting® is a registered trademark describing the therapeutic fostering approach developed by Core Assets.

Figure 4.1 has been reproduced with kind permission from BAAF.
Figure 4.2 (from Delaney 1991) has been reproduced with kind permission from the author.
Figure 9.1, 9.2 and 9.3 have been included with permission from Key Developmental Assets™.

First published in 2014
by Jessica Kingsley Publishers
73 Collier Street
London N1 9BE, UK
and
400 Market Street, Suite 400
Philadelphia, PA 19106, USA

www.jkp.com

Library of Congress Cataloging in Publication Data
A CIP catalog record for this book is available from the Library of Congress

British Library Cataloguing in Publication Data
A CIP catalogue record for this book is available from the British Library

ISBN 978 184905 445 4
eISBN 978 085700 820 6

Printed and bound in Great Britain

Contents

LIST OF FIGURES

FOREWORD

Foster care is a big umbrella. It covers many forms of alternative care for vulnerable children, forms that differ in subtle or significant ways. If we think of foster care as family care then we may think of three layers – firstly, informal care arranged within family networks in moment of crisis, or in response to long-term need. It seems that this is a universal response, irrespective of culture, to the care needs of children when parents die, are ill, or for some other reason are not present. Family members step in to make alternative arrangements for the children on their own initiative, and without consultation with authorities outside the family. More recently, since the mid-1900s in many countries, there has been the emergence of official or formal foster care organised by, or with the authority of, public bodies. The authorised provider places the child in need in a suitable family. Such formal foster care has been expanded increasingly in recent times to include what is known as kinship care (or relative care), where children are placed by the public authorities, or at least with their knowledge, blessing and practical support. Yet more recently, we have seen the emergence of programmed care, where carers follow a prescribed and, hopefully, evidence-based set of practices to offer care that meets the identified needs of the young person.

What these three different layers of family placement share is a sense of collective project. The carers are at the centre of the project of foster care, but they depend on the support of others to make their effort sustainable. The authors of this book lay out with great enthusiasm a manifesto or a programme for a team-based and evidence-based integrated model of foster care: team-based parenting.

Foster care is a vitally important umbrella. It provides children at crisis point with family-based care. It does so when the alternative may be remaining in the eye of the storm in a family in crisis without physical or emotional 'cover', becoming homeless without benign adult attention, or being placed in an institution which, on the evidence from many countries and cultures, all too often may fall very far short of what is needed in terms of compassion, safety or security.

We all cheer on foster care and foster carers. But the irony is that we do so, while also knowing remarkably little about the detail of how foster carers do what they do, or about how they might best do what they do. The truth is that there are likely to be many ways of doing foster care well. We need to draw on the special gifts of each carer, but we must not be confined to those gifts as a source of wisdom and expertise. We must also draw on a deeper well of inspiration, on lessons from the experience of a wider range of carers, and from the insights of young people who have been in care. But we also need to learn from studies that try to identify critical elements that help to separate good from poor care and effective care practice from ineffective care practices. The stakes are high. We are impacting, for good or ill, on the lives of vulnerable children and their future prospects.

This book draws on a range of evidence and ideas to offer a committed, yet informed, vision of how to do foster care. It promotes one model, one vision. And it is very welcome for that. It balances passion with rigor. It sets out in detail a vision for how to do foster care, and it very honestly tries to assess the available evidence about such models, this one and other closely related. It brings an important quality in the carer, integrity, to the appraisal, openly acknowledging many times the good, and the sometimes not so good news about the evidence. Building an evidence base for foster care is a slow process – there are few 'eureka' moments. More likely, there is a slow hard slog from which insights are gradually crafted.

There are many forms of foster care and many models of foster care, not least because foster children are not one singular homogenous group. The diverse circumstances, histories and needs of fosters require a correspondingly nuanced and diverse set of responses to the needs of children in care. This book makes a valuable contribution to a much-needed body of work on approaches to doing foster care that can help respond to that diversity of need.

Read this book. Appreciate the wisdom and experience on which it is based. But also use your critical judgement. You do not have to agree with every point or every piece of guidance to find value in what the book offers. I think it is a tribute to the authors and their achievement that I find myself wishing that I could sit down and talk with them about many of the points they make. This is the sign of a valuable book, one that gets you thinking and energised. And it is very appropriate that a book on foster care should stimulate thinking and energy, since these are two important ingredients among those required in the daily practice of foster care. I can see this book helping carers at home when they find quiet moment to reflect, but I can also see the book providing useful material for training events and discussion groups for foster carers.

Professor Robbie Gilligan
School of Social Work and Social Policy,
Trinity College Dublin

Acknowledgements

I have the following people to thank for their contributions to this book:

Jane Masters (Principal Therapist, Core Assets) for her key contribution to using Team Parenting when working with the Core Assets' Sexually Problematic Behaviours Service.

Russell Dicks (Senior Therapist, Core Assets) for his assistance in developing ATTUNE groups and writing the section on it.

Gabrielle Jerome (Head of International Social Work Practice Development) and Estella Abraham (CEO Key Assets International) for writing on using Team Parenting in other cultures and countries.

Joy Kelleher (Development Manager, Core Assets) and Annette Fairhurst (Senior Therapist, Core Assets) for their central contribution to the chapter on Key Developmental Assets.

Angelia R. Wilson, Senior Lecturer, University of Manchester, for her contribution to Chapter 2.

Kate Morgan (Clinical Psychologist, Core Assets) for her professional consultation on the use of the Parent Stress Index and providing a description of the test (Abidin 1995, 1997).

Laura Cothay (Senior Therapist, Core Assets) for writing up ADAPT in manual form, which was used to contribute to the relevant chapter.

Liz Arnesen (Senior Therapist, Core Assets), Paul Hamnett (Senior Therapist, Core Assets), Russell Dicks (Senior Therapist, Core Assets), Loren Krish (Senior Therapist, Core Assets), Sylvia Jackson (Senior Education Officer, Core Assets), Kate Brookes (previously employed as Senior Education Officer, Core Assets) and Maria Bakatselos (Children's Services Manager, Core Assets) for their help in writing case studies.

Gill Boag-Munroe for assistance in editing and referencing.

Annette Fairhurst (Senior Therapist at Thames Valley, CAG) for her contribution to Chapter 9.

INTRODUCTION

'Team Parenting' is the main focus of this book. In order to understand its roots, a short personal story is told here which sets the context in which the approach developed.

Foster Care Associates (FCA) was started in October 1994 in the Midlands by a Local Authority social worker called Jim Cockburn and a foster carer named Jan Rees. Jim, in his capacity as social worker, had placed young people with Jan. He found they worked together well, with mutual respect and a shared passion for wanting to improve the lives of young people. One day, the placement of a young person whom Jim was working with, Caroline,[1] became disrupted. No other placements were available in the area and Jim was faced with moving Caroline to the south of the country to a residential unit, away from all that was familiar to her. Resistant to participating in this upheaval in her life, Jim contacted Jan and asked her to foster Caroline. Acknowledging that Caroline had many difficulties and would, in all likelihood, be a challenging young person to foster, Jim suggested to Jan that additional support would be provided, to ensure the continuity of the placement. He convinced his Local Authority to fund these additions as it made fiscal and monetary sense, keeping her in foster care as opposed to an expensive out-of-authority residential arrangement. Caroline moved in to live with Jan and her family. In this environment, Caroline thrived. Caroline is now 29 years old and in touch with Jan to this day.

This experience gave Jim an idea – that hard-to-place young people could live in a foster home. Current practice at that time was to place young people with multiple difficulties and challenging behaviours in therapeutic residential units. Jim approached Jan with his vision and together they formed Midlands FCA. From the beginning, Jan envisaged providing an integrated form of foster care, with the young person at the centre and supported by a group of

---

1   Not her real name.

professionals and carers who would work collaboratively together to meet her needs. Therapy was provided, as was educational support and a support worker. Jan perceived that for the young person, the involvement of a support worker and engagement in extra-curricular activities would be therapeutic in itself. Having fun, learning new skills and engaging in a one-to-one relationship with an adult, she believed, would be beneficial for young people's burgeoning self-esteem and confidence. In addition, having a worker who could engage the young person away from the foster home, would give the foster carers a much needed break.

Individual therapy was provided to address the deeply traumatic experiences that looked-after young people had endured and that might otherwise leave them with deep-seated emotional and psychological injuries. This therapy offered the young people a safe space to access buried memories and make sense of what had happened to them and how they came to be where they were. Education officers became involved from the point of referral. Where new placements entailed a geographical relocation for the young person, they negotiated school places for young people at the start of their move so there was no disruption to their education. In addition, they provided tuition to support young people when they were out of school or needing additional help with accessing learning and education.

From the outset, foster carers received support 24 hours a day, seven days a week. Social workers had small caseloads and were encouraged to form good, honest relationships with their foster carers. The goal was to equip foster carers with the tools they needed to look after hard-to-place young people. The surrounding support network and additional inputs were intended to ensure that foster carers were not alone in their task of caring for young people and that they received the support and rest they needed to endure the adversities that fostering could bring. However, the expectations placed on foster carers were high too: they were required to be self-reflective practitioners, consciously competent and able to consider the feelings that were evoked in them by individual young people. This reflexivity was purported to be essential to stop a reactive, unthinking response to what was essentially a behavioural communication by young people to foster carers of their emotional state.

This intensive support of foster carers and the provision of supporting professionals working together aimed to build an 'artificial family' around young people. This vision for the provision of a warm, nurturing team of people who felt positively about individual young people and wanted to advocate for their best interests to be met, is one that has been replicated across cultures both by FCA and other fostering providers. Variations on the provision may be differently labelled, for example, 'Team around the child' or 'multi-agency working', but it enables the young person to come to feel a sense of connection with the wider organisation and the staff they work with on a regular basis. Thus, even if their placement breaks down, many young people will request to remain in a placement connected to the area team, as they will have established on-going relationships with social workers, the therapist, education officer, support worker and even the administrator.

This desire to create a sense of belonging for young people is exemplified by the following excerpt from *A White Merc with Fins* which initially inspired Jim Cockburn in that it was this fundamental need he sought to address:

It was OK for the Red fucking Indians.

The Red Indians could go out into the forest for their forty nights and they knew, they knew for certain, like you know Tuesday comes after Monday, that when they came back the Tribe would still be there, camped on the plain beside the river by the ancestral burial grounds where everyone knew they were going someday, they would be there to welcome you back and take you in and listen to your stories about what you did and what secrets you learned out there, like the paramilitary prisoners in Ulster know when they've done their time, the Tribe will be waiting and the campfires will still be there for them.

We haven't got that, we have to make up our own tribe as we go, we are free to do that, that is good, that freedom is wonderful, it is what everyone wants as soon as they are given the choice, as soon as the Great Leaders die we go for freedom, but being free means you have no safety net either.

Now, if we go out into the forest, we could come back and find everyone has moved on and the tracks are dry, we could just end up sitting by the river all alone and telling our wonderful news to ourselves alone and stirring the cold ashes where the campfires were, and listening to the lost ghosts crying.

It happens.

It happens every day, it leads to the park bench, it leads to people so lost they will do anything to join a tribe, they will shoot up with needles they know are full of poisoned blood just to be allowed to sit around a campfire with people they know and hate, they will believe that a few thousand old, lost Jews who the SS somehow missed are actually running countries of 30,000,000 people, they will shout God Loves You as You are, or Eng-a-land Eng-a-land, or Allah Akhbar, or SOcialistrevolutionarygroup, they will grab any crap cheap story they are thrown, just so long as it half-hangs together, just so long as they are allowed to sit by some fireside somewhere in the cold, wandering world and not to the tribal passwords and say: We, We, We.'

(Hawes 1996, pp.165–166)

THE INTRODUCTION OF TEAM PARENTING

Whilst from the beginning in FCA therapy was provided for children and young people, over time the separation of this provision as a distinct service came to be experienced as problematic. The details of this unfolding journey are explored in Chapter 2. Suffice at this stage to say that the impetus for Team Parenting to emerge as a model in its own right was driven by dissatisfaction with the therapy service as a discrete provision which focused its endeavours on the child or young person. This practice was not exclusive to therapists within this agency. However, it was a desire to spread psychological thinking to foster carers and other professionals involved with the placement that prompted the redesign of the therapy service and the inception of Team Parenting. Believing that therapists could instil therapeutic knowledge and engender reflective practice amongst all those involved with the child or young person gave birth to the idea of Team Parenting as an integrated model that would direct its energies across all domains of the child's life. The dual wish therefore for an approach that would inject therapeutic thinking and reflective practice into every professional working with a looked-after child and that these professionals would function coherently together as a team led to the creation of Team Parenting.

Team Parenting encompasses an integrated approach that seeks to better the outcomes for looked-after children in a multitude of ways. Recognising the multi-faceted nature of human life and what can contribute to the fulfilling of potential, Team Parenting relies on a multi-disciplinary group to work with children and young people's placements ensuring the following:

- They are well looked after in a safe and stable foster placement.

- Foster carers have an in-depth understanding of the impact of complex trauma on a child's functioning across all areas.

- Foster carers are trained to be therapeutic parents who can facilitate a child's recovery from the early trauma they may have experienced.

- Social workers support foster carers to contribute to the potential of placement stability and efficacy.

- Children and young people are supported in education by their foster carers.

- Professionals in education are provided with the opportunity to comprehend the specific needs of looked-after children and how to meet these in schools.

- Children and young people's resilience and emotional well-being is facilitated by the role of support workers who support them in extra-curricular activities.

- Therapists hold a pivotal role in co-ordinating the parenting team around the child to work together as a reflective and psychological group of professionals holding that particular young person's needs in mind.

- Therapists contribute to the social worker role of up-skilling foster carers' knowledge and understanding of attachment issues, complex trauma and therapeutic parenting via consultation sessions and training.

- Therapists attend to the centrality of the healing potential that the foster carer has with a child or young person via their relationship and the quality of care on offer. If necessary, this is supported by direct therapeutic work.

- All involved are psychologically aware, emotionally literate and reflective practitioners whose goal is to co-operatively and collaboratively provide an integrated package of therapeutic fostering for children and young people.

Whilst Team Parenting originated and has been predominantly practised in its pure form within FCA, this book seeks to share the central tenets of the approach in the hope that features may be incorporated by practitioners where relevant and applicable to their context. Team Parenting does not purport to be an icon of excellence or to own the expertise on how to work effectively with looked-after children. As will be observed throughout the book, Team Parenting has been heavily influenced and shaped by other practitioners, researchers and writers in the field. The premise of this book therefore is to contribute to existing knowledge, expand the current dialogue regarding efficacious practice with this client group and explicate the underlying evidence, concept and practice of Team Parenting. The humble aspiration of the author is that what follows will inspire others to improve their understanding of the needs of children in care and to work to improve the provision for them.

An explanatory note is required regarding FCA. At the beginning of 2013 FCA rebranded and became known as the Core Assets group. This was in recognition of the fact that the agency had established new companies operating within social care but outside of fostering. Rebranding brought all of these enterprises under one roof and one name. Henceforth, in this book, FCA is referred to by its new name Core Assets.

Note: For ease of reading, the female pronoun has been used throughout the book when referring to a single unspecified person.

CHAPTER 1

CONTEXTUAL FACTORS INFLUENCING THE RISE OF TEAM PARENTING

CHAPTER CONTENTS

Setting the scene

The political and legislative context in social care

Chronology of relevant childcare legislation
Quality Protects
Care Standards Act (CSA) 2000
Choice Protects
National minimum standards for fostering
Children (Leaving Care) Act 2000
Adoption and Children Act 2002
Childrens Act 2004
Children and Young Persons Act 2008
The Munro Review of Child Protection
Implications for fostering

Other models
Multi-dimensional Treatment Foster Care
KEEP
Multi-Systemic Therapy
Functional Family Therapy
Fostering Changes programme
The Secure Base Model – Schofield and Beek
Kate Cairns – trauma model
Dyadic Developmental Psychotherapy

SETTING THE SCENE

This book describes key elements that can contribute to the recovery for looked-after young children from their early experiences. It offers a description of an integrated and therapeutic approach which has been found to be effective within one independent fostering agency. The aim of the book is to share good practice and to provide ideas for how the challenges of working effectively with children looked after both therapeutically and across agencies may be met. The author hopes that such material may be useful to practitioners and professionals across a range of settings. Different chapters in the book describe various elements of the Team Parenting approach. The interventions delineated herein can be used as stand-alone components by practitioners in their field or incorporated as a whole to inform service design and provision.

In Systemic Therapy, context is important. Similarly in Gestalt Therapy, environment and its interaction with the individual, is where the 'self' and experience is formed. In writing about Team Parenting, the historical, political, legislative and societal influences that existed at its inception should be acknowledged. As we will see, Team Parenting emerged from within an era of policy and legislative change which emphasised the need to improve outcomes for looked-after children. This, together with an acknowledgement of the challenge of looking after young people with disturbed backgrounds and disturbing behaviours, and an increased awareness of their need to become securely attached to a primary caregiver, informed the development of an array of approaches used in this country and the USA.

Team Parenting is one of these approaches. When it was created it was distinctive in its use of the professional network and its reluctance to engage young people in foster care in traditional, individual, long-term psychotherapy. These features are no longer distinctive as they have become regular tenets of practice with looked-after children. However, Team Parenting remains distinguishable by its emphasis on the need to infuse every interaction and intervention both with the young person and those around them, with therapeutic intention. Moreover, Team Parenting is perhaps unique in the breadth of its approach, encompassing, as it does, a range of interventions that span different domains of a young person's life that are brought together in a coherent and integrated whole. Finally, Team Parenting can be said to adhere to its therapeutic foundations in being a responsive, flexible approach that responds to individual clinical need as it presents and emerges.

This first chapter explores the political and legislative context within which Team Parenting emerged. It also explicates other existing models which work with children in the care system both within this country and the USA. A description of these models is considered important by the author in order that comparisons may be drawn and that Team Parenting can be situated within a theoretical and practice-based landscape as well as a political and legislative one. Subsequent chapters delineate the key components of Team Parenting as an approach, its defining features and the separate interventions that, woven together, make up the whole.

THE POLITICAL AND LEGISLATIVE CONTEXT IN SOCIAL CARE

The last 20 years have seen major shifts in child welfare practice and a raft of new legislation and policy passed by a succession of governments. Although this trajectory could reasonably be said to start with the 1989 Childrens Act, which was passed by a Conservative government, it was the major policy initiatives of the New Labour government in 1997 that set out to improve the lot of vulnerable young people in society. This goal has been taken forward by the current (2013) coalition government, albeit with a change in emphasis and terminology.

Some of the most vulnerable children in our society can be found within the looked-after system (Meltzer *et al.* 2003). New policy and legislation have sought to ensure greater protection for vulnerable young people when they live at home as well as addressing the deficiencies of the care system. Lamentable failures in the child welfare system to ensure the very survival of some young people have led to new legislation that has sought to improve outcomes. Repeated and recurring themes that run through these policies are the need for integrative, joined-up working that ensures young people are kept safe and can achieve their potential. Shortfalls in multi-agency working were found in both of Lord Laming's reports, the first (Laming 2003) following the death of Victoria Climbié in 2000 and the second (Laming 2009) the demise of 'Baby Peter' in 2007.

Frost and Stein (2009) postulate that the change of direction in child welfare practice was set in motion by two policy initiatives – the requirement for multi-agency working and the prioritisation of improving outcomes for children and young people. They elucidate that these are inherently linked as one will necessarily impact on the other. There is general agreement that greater interagency working will improve the fortunes of young people across the board. Although there is little actual empirical evidence to support this, the ramifications of not communicating or sharing information across professional disciplines is plain to see in the unfortunate and untimely deaths of children who have died in their own homes.

A consequence of these events was recognition of the imperative need to work across professional divisions. Previous to these changes, Frost and Stein (2009) argue that child welfare was organised in silos. Thus, education, health, youth work and so on all worked independently of each other. They became positioned and familiar with particular ways of working and their specific client group. However, this could not be maintained under Prime Minister Tony Blair's call for *modernisation* and *joined-up thinking* (Blair 1998, cited in Frost and Stein 2009). In a political landscape influenced increasingly by the economics of the market, social welfare clients became the consumers: 'there is a discernible movement from services led by organisational objectives towards an attempt to be led by "outcomes", a holistic approach to the child or young person' (Frost and Stein 2009, p.315).

Team Parenting emerged within this legislative and political context. Team Parenting, in its practice, methodology and philosophy, embraces multi-agency working. The cornerstone of Team Parenting could be said to be an integrative approach to working with young people, aiming to engender collaborative and co-operative practice to ensure that their needs are met in a coherent and seamless manner. Certainly Team Parenting works against the use of the 'silo' ways of working to which Frost and Stein (2009) refer. Whilst Team Parenting was born out of foster carer discontent within Core Assets, it clearly owes much of its founding principles to the values placed on joined-up working by policy makers. It is therefore an approach born of its time and as such it is useful to start this book with an outline of the legislation that influenced both its inception and its continued evolution. What follows is a chronology of childcare legislation that has directed child welfare practice in connection to fostering looked-after children.

CHRONOLOGY OF RELEVANT CHILDCARE LEGISLATION

QUALITY PROTECTS

In 1998, the Department of Health drove changes in childcare practice with *The Quality Protects Programme* (DoH 1998b). This agenda was released in response to the Utting Report of 1997 (Utting 1997) which identified and delineated the disadvantages faced by children in need. Quality Protects was intended to be a three-year programme whereby local authorities were expected to work closely with the Department of Health to overhaul the management and delivery of services to children and families. It actually ran until 2003. Quality Protects led to an investment in fostering; it aimed to improve health, education and other outcomes for all children but focused specifically on looked-after children (Sellick and Howell 2004). Within Quality Protects there were eight target areas. The ones which were particularly pertinent for fostering were: the requirement to increase the number of foster placements for looked-after children; the stipulation that care leavers receive greater support; and that the opportunities for children to access adequate health care, social welfare, education and leisure were enhanced.

CARE STANDARDS ACT (CSA) 2000

This act was passed in July 2000 and enacted in 2002. It replaced the Registered Homes Act (1984) and parts of the Childrens Act (1989) which pertain to the care or accommodation of young people. It established regulatory bodies for social care in England and Wales, and provisions for registration and standards in social care work and training. It followed two White Papers by the Government from 1998 and 1999 entitled *Modernising Social Services* (Department of Health 1998a) and *Building for the Future* (Welsh Office 1999).

CHOICE PROTECTS

The Choice Protects review was announced in March 2002. The Choice Protects review followed the findings of a Social Services Inspection called *Fostering for the Future* (Department of Health 2002). This review expressed concerns about the overall standards of foster care and its ability to meet the complex needs of looked-after children. Foster carers were asked what support they needed. They listed financial remuneration, adequate training, out-of-hours support, links with other carers and a wish to be seen as part of a team looking after the child as primary considerations. Central to Choice Protects were its ambitions to improve placement choice and placement stability.

NATIONAL MINIMUM STANDARDS FOR FOSTERING

In March 2002 the new National Minimum Standards for Fostering were published and a National Care Standards Commission was established which would bring all fostering agencies – statutory, private and voluntary – under the same inspection and regulatory system. These standards have since been updated. The following from the 2011 standards have relevance for Team Parenting and inform its practice today:

Standard 2: Promoting a positive identity, potential and valuing diversity through individualised care. Foster carers are supported to help children develop positive self-esteem and emotional resilience.

Standard 3: Promoting positive behaviour and relationships. Foster carers have high expectations, provide an environment that encourages and role models positive behaviour. Foster carers receive support and advice on managing challenging behaviour, foster carers receive training on how to manage conflict and difficult behaviour, and how to de-escalate conflict.

Standard 6: Promoting good health and well-being. Children have access to ensure all health needs are met including physical, emotional and psychological [...] as required via access to appropriate services. Children are encouraged to take part in a range of activities that promote their physical and emotional health.

Standard 7: Leisure activities. Children develop skills and confidence in areas of interest.

Standard 8: Promoting educational attainment. Education is promoted as valuable in itself and as a preparation for adulthood. Children are encouraged to fulfil their educational potential. The foster home should be a learning environment. Foster carers are to have a role in educational attainment and to work closely with the education provider. Explicit about foster carers' role saying should be in regular contact, maximise potential, advocate for the child.

Standard 12: Promoting independence and moves to adulthood and leaving care. Practical independent skills, financial skills, emotional resilience and positive self-esteem.

Standard 20: Learning and development of foster carers: 'Foster carers maintain an ongoing training and development portfolio which demonstrates how they are meeting the skills required of them by the fostering service...how they will be supported to undertake ongoing training and development...' (p.40).

Standard 21: Supervision and support of foster carers – supervision and support that enables them to foster, peer support made available, have access to other professional help to enable them to care for the child.

Standard 23: Learning, development and qualifications of staff: 'All social workers and other specialists...are professionally qualified and, where applicable, registered by the appropriate professional body' (p.47).

(Department for Education 2011a)

CHILDREN (LEAVING CARE) ACT 2000

New Labour's drive to reform the care system included their long-standing concern about young people's life chances after they left care and how looked-after children were being prepared for this major transition. The Children (Leaving Care) Act 2000 aimed to encourage local authorities and others caring for looked-after children to improve planning for young people leaving care, to prevent young people having to leave care prematurely at age 16, and to improve financial support arrangements (Frost and Parton 2009). The Act stipulated that each child should be assessed as to their readiness to leave care and that every young person would have a Pathway Plan and a Personal Advisor. The Pathway Plan would identify needs for support and assistance up to the age of 21. The Care Leavers Regulations in 2010 (DfE 2010) has since updated this Act.

ADOPTION AND CHILDREN ACT 2002

This Act replaced the Adoption Act of 1976, updated the Childrens Act 1989 and modernised the whole existing legal framework for domestic and inter-country adoption. It had three parts – part one set out the framework of adoption law in England and Wales, part two made amendments to the 1989 Children Act and part three established the Adoption and Children Act register. The Act aimed to ensure that the needs of young people were put at the centre of the adoption process, that birth parents understood the impact of consenting to adoption, that disputes were resolved early so adoption did not become a *fait accompli*, that the voice of the child was heard (directly or indirectly) through reports to the court and that there was effective case management without delay to the decision-making process.

CHILDREN ACT 2004

This Act made further amendments to the 1989 Children Act in response to the death of Victoria Climbié. The Government's response to Laming's Victoria Climbié Inquiry report (Laming 2003) was the *Keeping Children Safe* report (DfES 2003a) and the *Every Child Matters* Green Paper (DfES 2003b), which in turn led to the Children Act 2004. The Act stipulated clear accountability for children's services, better joint working and an improved focus on safeguarding. Alongside the Act, the Government published *Every Child Matters: Next Steps* (DfES 2004). This provided details of the broader, non-legislative facets that were to be taken forward to promote children's well-being. With this came the introduction of Local Children's Safeguarding Boards, replacing Area Child Protection Committees and Children's Commissioners. The commitment to integrated working was enshrined in the stipulation that Local Authorities appoint a Director of Children's Services who would be responsible for both education and social care.

The Children Act 2004 provided the legal basis for how social services and other agencies deal with issues relating to children. It provided the legal underpinning to *Every Child Matters: Change for Children* (HM Government 2004). The Every Child Matters policy applies to the well-being of children and young people from birth until they reach the age of 19 and is based on the idea that every child, regardless of their individual circumstances or background, should have appropriate support throughout their life. There are five key principles to the policy, for which the government believe children should have support. These are to:

- be healthy

- stay safe

- enjoy and achieve

- make a positive contribution

- achieve economic well-being.

CHILDREN AND YOUNG PERSONS ACT 2008

In 2006, the most recent concerted focus on improving the conditions of children in the looked-after system was launched in the form of the Care Matters initiative. This project unfolded in the context of the legislative, policy and cultural changes generated by the Adoption and Children Act 2002 and the Children Act 2004 (Every Child Matters). In 2007, the Government published a White Paper *Care Matters: Time for Change* (DfES 2007). This followed the Green Paper *Care Matters: Transforming the Lives of Children and Young People in Care* (DfES 2006). The White Paper included a commitment to amend the legislative and regulatory framework for looked-after children and care leavers as well as amending the statutory guidance and National Minimum Standards.

The areas that the Green Paper *Care Matters* (DfES 2006) attempted to address through a range of improvement programmes were: corporate parenting; family and parenting support; the experience of care placements; educational experiences and achievements; health and well-being; transition to adulthood; and the role of the practitioner. The legislative expression of this initiative was the Children and Young Persons Act 2008, the purpose of which was to reform the statutory framework for the care system in England and Wales by implementing the proposals of the White Paper (DfES 2007).

In terms of foster care, the Care Matters policy instigated a number of initiatives:

- It revised the National Minimum Standards for Adoption and Fostering, with more emphasis on improving the relationships between carers and children.

- It piloted the Multi-dimensional Treatment Foster Care (MTFC) (Biehal, Ellison and Sinclair 2012) programme to support the most vulnerable children through therapeutic interventions. It aimed to make this programme for children with complex needs more widely available to foster carers.

- It funded a national roll-out of the Fostering Changes training programme – a positive parenting programme for foster carers in all sectors on how to improve relationships and manage difficult behaviour (Briskman *et al.* 2012; Warman, Pallet and Scott 2006).

- It started a national roll-out of the Children's Workforce Development Council (CWDC 2011) Training, Support and Development Standards for Foster Care.

- It funded The Fostering Network to run a confidential advice line service for foster carers.

- It introduced a national minimum allowance for foster carers in 2007 (DfES 2006).

The Care Matters agenda also clearly stipulated the need for every child to have an attuned relationship with a caregiver who works to promote their emotional well-being and resilience (Pithouse, Lowe and Hill-Tout 2004). Enshrined in the legislation was a recognition that skilled and trained foster carers were needed if they were to be able to address the needs of young people who had experienced backgrounds of abuse and neglect.

THE MUNRO REVIEW OF CHILD PROTECTION

This review was commissioned by the Department of Education in June 2010 and published in May 2011 (DfE 2011b). It was prompted by the death of Baby Peter. Eileen Munro, the author of the review, emphasised the importance of re-introducing essential elements of social work practice that had been diluted over the years by increased focus on targets and prescriptive timescales. She called for a re-engagement with child-focused practice and argued for the central place of relationship, reflection and thinking in social work practice. Supervision as a critical practice tool was highlighted. The review suggested that clear recommendations should be made that stipulate *guidelines and rules that are essential for working together.* The Government stated that it agreed with Professor Munro that effective multi-agency working across a wide range of professionals was critical to building an accurate understanding of what was happening in the child or young person's life, so that the right help could be provided.

IMPLICATIONS FOR FOSTERING

Much of the legislative changes of the last 20 years instigated changes in social work practice which have changed the face of fostering. During the 1990s there was also a change in the type of young people being brought into care. This was due to a number of factors, including an increased concentration on preventative work and keeping young people at home, a change in policy and practice whereby young people were no longer accommodated because of poor school attendance or delinquent behaviour, a focus on rehabilitating young people back home after a period in care and decreased reliance on residential care (Warman *et al.* 2006; Wilson and Evetts 2006). The consequence of these shifts in practice was that most young people who came into care now did so because they had endured complex trauma in their early lives. The ramifications of this situation were that foster carers required more sophisticated skills and greater psychological knowledge in order to care for these young people adequately. In response to this, fostering became increasingly more regulated. Implicit in this was an acknowledgment of the move from fostering being an everyday task of looking after children to a specialist one requiring particular knowledge and skills (Wilson and Evetts 2006).

Young people who have endured histories of abuse and neglect experience emotional and psychological damage that needs to be overcome. The fact that this damage is frequently represented by disruptions in trust with early caregivers has implications for their recovery. When the natural order of things has been overturned by being harmed by those who are meant to protect you and keep you safe, opening oneself to being cared for by unfamiliar adults is a risky business indeed. In this way, foster care, whilst containing the seeds of a reparative experience for young people, is besieged from the start by their negative expectations, derived from their traumatic pasts, which they bring with them (Dozier *et al.* 2002). If foster care is to succeed, placements need skilled and knowledgeable foster carers supported by a team of professionals to ensure that placements are not derailed by the destabilising behaviours of these highly distressed and traumatised young people.

There is recognition of this dilemma in the literature – that what young people most need is also very difficult to provide as they defend against it:

> The need for effective attachment to well-trained carers who can help promote resilience in children who need to cope with adversity and not adopt dysfunctional ways to respond to abuse or neglect is perhaps the single biggest challenge to contemporary fostering. (Pithouse *et al.* 2004 p.20)

Also, 'To realize foster carer's therapeutic potential, carers require intensive support and training, especially where the goal is to sustain long-term placements of children with attachment- and trauma-related difficulties' (Murray, Tarren-Sweeney and France 2011, p.156).

Core Assets understood the implications of this for foster carers. Core Assets, one of the first independent fostering agencies to be established in the 1990s, was part of a trend that had led to a flurry of new independent fostering agencies being created. Of the Independent Agencies established by 2000, 60 per cent of these had been set up in the two years from 1996 to 1998, when Local Authorities themselves were struggling to recruit foster carers (Sellick and Howell 2004). This represented a sea change in fostering provision as the private sector emerged as a competitive provider to Local Authority fostering services. The opportunity for such a shift to occur had been provided by the Government's Quality Protects and Choice Protects agendas.

Like many fostering service providers and other independent agencies, Core Assets perceived that foster carers required remuneration for their efforts, support and training if their endeavours to facilitate healing for young people were to succeed. This conviction was supported by the literature. Studies had shown that foster carers felt more satisfied when they were treated as part of a team (Sinclair, Gibbs and Wilson 2004). Sinclair *et al.* (2004) recommended offering foster carers training, consultation and the same respect as shown to other professionals. They extemporised that doing so would lead to a committed fostering service which would in turn facilitate placement stability (Wilson and Evetts 2006). This is exactly what Team Parenting aims to do. However, accepting the enormity of the task in facilitating recovery from complex trauma for young people and in sustaining placement stability, Team Parenting is an approach that locates the achievement of these goals as being beyond the sole remit of the foster carer. Instead, the creation of a collaborative, co-operative and cohesive team working together and therapeutically with the child or young person at the centre is intended to support this endeavour and further its chances for success.

That there continues to be a need for good quality foster care is without question. Statistics released by the Department of Education indicate an increase in the numbers of children coming into care (DfE 2012). On 31 March 2012 there were 67,050 looked-after children. This is an increase of 2 per cent compared to 31 March 2011 and an increase of 13 per cent compared to 31 March 2008. The rise in numbers can be attributable to young people spending longer in the care system as opposed to simply an increase in the number entering care. A greater proportion of young people looked after are now cared for in foster care. At 31 March 2012, 50,620 young people were cared for in a foster placement. This represents 75 per cent of all looked-after children and is an increase of 4 per cent of the figures in 2008 where 71 per cent of young people were in foster care. The majority of young people (62%) who enter the care system do so for reasons of abuse and neglect. This figure has remained relatively stable since 2008.

OTHER MODELS

Before moving on to delineate the specifics of the Team Parenting approach, it is useful to consider other models that currently exist within fostering. Four of the models described below came originally from the USA. They can be conclusively described as tightly defined treatment methods due to their requirements for model fidelity, evidence-based practice, the use of clinical outcome measures, tying practice into the founding site via supervisory mechanisms and having distinct interventions. Four other approaches have been included in this discussion. Two of these, emanating from the UK, are perhaps more suitably described as approaches than models. They lack the rigid adherence to a tightly defined set of procedures that features so heavily in the models from the USA. Instead, they are characterised by theoretical suppositions and knowledge that inform their practice. They are featured here so that comparisons and points of commonality with Team Parenting may be drawn.

MULTI-DIMENSIONAL TREATMENT FOSTER CARE

Multi-dimensional Treatment Foster Care (MTFC) was developed in the USA in the 1980s as a multi-modal intervention for children with challenging behaviour (Chamberlain 2003). It is a highly structured behavioural programme, providing wraparound multi-professional support and daily communication with carers, the team and school. The key elements of the intervention are:

- the provision of a consistent reinforcing environment in which young people are mentored and encouraged

- provision of clearly specified boundaries to behaviour and specified consequences that can be delivered in a teaching-oriented manner

- close supervision of young people's activities and whereabouts

- diversion from anti-social peers and help to develop positive social skills that will enable young people to form relationships with a positive peer group.

Multi-dimensional Treatment Foster Care for Young People (or Adolescents, commonly referred to as MTFC-A) provides older children (usually aged 11–16) with a short-term foster placement, usually intended to last around a year, followed by a short period of aftercare to support the transition to a new placement or return home. Individual treatment plans are developed and regularly reviewed. Behaviour is closely monitored and positive behaviours are reinforced using a system of points and levels. Care is provided by specially trained foster carers who are supported and closely supervised by a clinical team, including a programme supervisor to co-ordinate the intervention, an individual therapist and a skills worker to work directly with the child, a family therapist to work with parents or follow-on carers, and a foster carer support worker. Additional consultancy is provided by a child and adolescent psychiatrist. In England, MTFC teams also include an education worker.

The theoretical tenets of the programme rest on behavioural principles. Each foster family works with one child at a time for 6–12 months. Foster carers and clinical staff are trained in behaviour management systems for the age group with which they will work. MTFC has three programmes:

1. MTFC-P (preschool – 3–6)

2. MTFC-C (child – 7–11)

3. MTFC-A (adolescent – 11–16).

The approach involves giving lots of encouragement and celebrating children and young people's achievements. They are helped to learn and practise new skills in a supportive environment. The foster carer is seen as a key agent of change and is supported by a clinical team who helps to make changes in other aspects of the child/ young person's life. When the children and young people move on to permanent placements, the team helps their permanent carers to continue this work.

Evidence of impact and limitations of MTFC

Biehal, Ellison and Sinclair (2012) completed the first independent study of MTFC. The authors found that the intensive fostering programme was successful in reducing re-offending, the need for custodial sentencing and delaying reconviction (Biehal et al. 2012, p.22). However, it seems that these results were not sustained after the young people left the programme. Biehal et al. (2012, p.22) conclude: 'For a number of the young people therefore, learned pro-social behaviour did not appear to be fully internalised, with the result that situational factors had a powerful effect on their behaviour once they left their foster placements.'

The authors propose that it is the highly structured nature of the programme, close supervision, boundary setting, the use of positive reinforcement and engagement in education and other activities, which are contributory factors to improved outcomes for the duration of the placement. The change in environment results in the minimisation of influences from deviant peers (Biehal et al. 2012). However, once young people return to their communities of origin these assets disappear. Therefore, on-going work is required by local community service provision if the positive results of the programme are to be maintained (Biehal et al. 2012).

KEEP

KEEP is a group which was established with the goal of keeping foster carers and kinship carers trained and supported. It emerged in the USA in response to the lack of empirical support for interventions that were being used with foster carers (Chamberlain *et al.* 2008a, 2008b). It was implemented as part of a research programme which aimed to test its effectiveness. The aim of the group was to strengthen foster carer skills: 'The objectives of KEEP are to give parents effective tools for dealing with their child's externalizing and other behavioural and emotional problems, and to support them in the implementation of those tools' (Piescher, Schmidt and Laliberte 2008, p.55)

Theoretically, it draws upon the behavioural approach found in MTFC. Its goal was to address the link between challenging behaviour and placement breakdown.

Drawing as it does on behavioural theory, KEEP teaches foster carers to increase the rate of their positive reinforcement parenting strategies over disciplinary methods. KEEP has a rule that there should be a ratio of four to one of positive reinforcement to discipline. The group follows a manual that sets out what is to be covered in each session. There is some flexibility as there are two free sessions built into the programme so that there is additional time to review topics or to explore them in more detail. There are 16 sessions in total, each lasting 90 minutes. Groups are run for seven to ten carers. At the end of each session foster carers are given homework to complete between sessions. If foster carers are unable to attend a group, the facilitators visit them at home, where they cover the same material. Incentives are offered to foster carers to attend in the form of refreshments and agreement that attendance at KEEP would contribute to their overall training requirements. Two workers facilitate each group, with one being designated the lead role.

Evidence of impact and limitations of KEEP

Chamberlain *et al.* (2008a, 2008b) carried out tests to measure the changes in behavioural difficulties being experienced at home. The measure used was the Parent Daily Report Checklist (Chamberlain and Reid 1987). As well as scoring the ratio of positive reinforcement to discipline used by carers the study found that KEEP did lead to improvements in parenting and a decrease in behaviour problems. The authors acknowledged that the decrease in behaviour problems was partly due to the increase in positive reinforcement but also could be attributable to other factors. However, overall Chamberlain *et al.* (2008a, p.25) argue that KEEP achieved its goal in the study, which was to demonstrate that 'the capabilities of foster and kinship parents can be enhanced to positively impact outcomes for the children in their care'. The consequences of this success were that there were fewer placement breakdowns and an increase in the number of young people deemed suitable for reuniting with their birth families. Piescher *et al.* (2008), reviewed this study as well as three others (Chamberlain *et al.* 2008a, 2008b; Price *et al.* 2008). Whilst they concur that initial results prove promising, their criticism of these studies is the lack of long-term follow-up. They suggest that the sustainability of the changes made needs further investigation and research.

MULTI-SYSTEMIC THERAPY

Multi-Systemic Therapy (MST) originated in the USA. It was developed by Henggeler and colleagues during the 1970s (Stout and Holleran 2012). It was originally intended for use with birth families to keep young people out of the juvenile justice system. It is now a commercially available licensed model. MST draws theoretically on a range of influences, including structural family therapy, strategic family therapy, cognitive behaviour therapy and social learning theory. Key proponents of MST hold that there are three major factors that impact negatively on outcomes for young people; these being inadequate parenting, poor participation in education and deviant peer influences (Henggeler and Sheidow 2012). The MST model is designed to be implemented with young people aged 12–17 and their families. The aim of MST is to increase young people's participation in education and minimise young people's engagement in offending or anti-social behaviour. It is an intensive, family- and community-based intervention intended for young people who are involved with substance abuse and/or violent behaviour. It is also recommended where mental health issues are a factor and where there are substance abusing parents.

How services are delivered

Therapists work in teams. They have small caseloads (4–6) and are available to work in the family home 24 hours a day, seven days a week. Each piece of work lasts approximately 4–6 months and involves around 60 sessions. The goal of the work is to equip parents with the parenting skills they need to manage their adolescent's behaviour. It is a strengths-based approach and teaches recognition and utilisation of potential resources (e.g. extended family, neighbours, friends) and removing possible 'barriers' to success (e.g. inappropriate peer relationships, drug use). The therapists engage the family by involving them in the design of the treatment plan. When the intervention proves successful, the work moves into cementing the components of this progress into a plan to ensure change is sustained. Where the intervention is not successful, the therapist engages with those involved in the work to formulate a new one, which is then reviewed once it has been implemented. Work therefore proceeds in a *recursive loop* (Henggeler and Sheidow 2012).

The nine principles
MST adheres to nine principles, which are as follows:

1. 'Finding the Fit': assessment should ascertain how young people's behavioural problems fit within a broader systemic context.

2. 'Positive and Strength Focused': interventions should emphasise the positive and focus on the strengths that currently exist in the system, utilising these to promote change.

3. 'Increasing Responsibility': interventions should encourage parents and young people to give up their irresponsible behaviours and act responsibly.

4. Interventions should focus on what is currently occurring in a family's life, involve the family in taking definable actions to redress difficulties and target distinct problems.

5. 'Targeting Sequences': interventions should identify where sequences of behaviours between systems are maintaining the problem, and act to rectify this.

6. 'Developmentally Appropriate': interventions should fit the developmental needs of the young people and their parents or carers.

7. 'Continuous Effort': interventions should require daily or weekly effort from family members.

8. Interventions should be continually assessed and evaluated by all those involved to determine whether they are being effective.

9. Interventions should be designed so that the skills and aptitudes learned can be transferred to other situations. The goal is that problem resolution is an ability that can be 'generalised' to other situations, and improvements can be 'maintained' once the programme has ended.

Fidelity to the model is important and is achieved by:

- manualisation of key components of the programme

- initial and on-going training of clinical and supervisory staff

- on-going feedback to the therapist from the supervisor and MST expert

- objective feedback from caregivers on a standardised adherence questionnaire

- organisational consultation

- intense case management

- close supervision of the therapists and supervisors.

Evidence of impact and limitations of MST

When therapists adhere to the model rigidly, then results are said to be better. When therapists go off task, then results are considerably worse. MST has been running for 40 years and boasts a robust and substantial evidence base: 'With 20 published outcome studies (18 randomized trials and 2 quasi-experimental studies) and delivery to more than 17,000 youth and families annually, MST is one of the most extensively validated and widely transported evidence-based psychosocial treatments' (Henggeler and Sheidow 2012, p.34).

Henggeler and Sheidow (2012) draw a distinction between efficacy trials and clinical effectiveness trials, the former designed to determine whether a treatment can work and the latter designed to test whether the intervention is successful in the real world. Treatment in clinical effectiveness trials is delivered by local therapists who work within the community. Henggeler and Sheidow (2012) cite efficacy studies across a range of client groups, using different outcome measures as indicators of success (Borduin *et al.* 1990; Borduin *et al.* 1995; Brunk, Henggeler, and Whelan 1987; Henggeler *et al.* 1986; Schaeffer and Borduin 2005). Similarly, effectiveness trials also point to MST's positive outcomes (Henggeler, Melton, and Smith 1992; Henggeler *et al.* 1993; Henggeler *et al.* 1997). Some of these trials have been conducted by the founders of MST themselves. Henggeler and Sheidow (2012) argue that these studies have been replicated successfully for the most part, although they accede that a study in Sweden did not demonstrate good results (Sundell *et al.* 2008). They suggest that this was due to the low fidelity of the therapist and conclude that overall the research indicates that MST can be successfully applied in community settings to treat externalising and internalising problems in young people. They cite evidence that MST does improve family functioning and decrease time spent with deviant peers (Henggeler, Pickrel and Brondino 1999; Henggeler *et al.* 2009). Henggeler and Sheidow (2012) claim that these studies highlight the efficacy of the theory of change that underpins MST – that reduced time with deviant peers and enhanced family functioning produces better outcomes for young people.

Stout and Holleran (2012) evaluated MST, along with Functional Family Therapy (see p.42), as interventions that reduced the number of out-of-home placements that were made in New Jersey following their introduction. The authors conclude: 'We found that the addition of MST and FFT programs was associated with a statistically significant reduction in out-of-home placement requests that was not offset by an increase in admissions to public acute care hospitals' (Stout and Holleran 2012, p.319).

Carstens *et al.* (2009) postulate that the set-up costs of programmes like MST can make them prohibitive. Certainly, the initial training, the low caseloads, the on-going need for supervision from the main site in the USA and the licensing fee mean that the financial outlay is considerable (Carstens *et al.* 2009). However, Stout and Holleran (2012) believe that the saving gained from not moving young people into out-of-home placements is financially remunerative as well as bringing other added benefits such as keeping young people in their family of origin and within their communities. Greenwood (2004) finds that programmes such as MST, MTFC and FFT are more cost-effective than those that target younger age at-risk children. He proposes that this 'is due to their large effect sizes, modest cost, and ability to target very high-risk youth' (Greenwood 2004, p.210).

There is, however, some disagreement in the literature about the effectiveness of these interventions. Baldwin *et al.* (2012) and Littell (2005) found that MST did not consistently produce improved results over treatment as usual. In their meta-analysis they conclude that MST, FFT, MTFC and Brief Strategic Family Therapy produce better results than the usual treatment, but that though the differences are statistically significant, they are small. Most critically, they highlight the need for further research to decipher the essential components that make for a successful intervention:

> The situation is likely a bit more complicated than that but the literature in this area is not yet sufficiently large to answer critical questions, such as is one treatment more effective than the others and on what outcomes do the family therapies have the biggest effect? Policy makers, researchers, clinicians, and patients all want answers to these more nuanced questions. (Baldwin *et al.* 2012, p.298)

Shepperd *et al.* (2009) undertook a Cochrane systematic review of mental health interventions, one of which was MST, that offered an alternative to an inpatient setting and as such were *beyond the scope* of normative outpatient treatment. The review included two randomised controlled trials carried out on MST in the USA (Henggeler *et al.* 1999; Rowland *et al.* 2005) that assessed the efficacy of the intervention over inpatient care. They found that 'Young people receiving home-based MST experienced some improved functioning in terms of externalising symptoms and they spent fewer days out of school and out-of-home placement' (Shepperd *et al.* 2009, p.4).

However, overall the authors conclude that differences were not significant. They indicate that there is no evidence to recommend this intervention over others but point out that this may be more due to the weakness of the research, which needs clearer baseline and outcome measures, rather than an accurate assessment of the individual interventions.

FUNCTIONAL FAMILY THERAPY

Functional Family Therapy (FFT) was introduced by Dr James Alexander and Dr Bruce Parsons in the late 1960s in the USA (Alexander and Parsons 1982; Alexander *et al.* 1998). The first randomised control trial was carried out in 1971. This revealed evidence that the intervention worked to reduce youth recidivism. FFT now claims a 25–60 per cent reduction in recidivism. FFT is a research-based programme that aims to work preventatively with young people aged 11–18 years old with behavioural problems, alcohol and/or substance abuse problems. The programme is short term, offering between 8–14 sessions for those with moderate problems and 26–30 sessions for those with more serious problems. The work is carried out over a period of three to six months. Work can be carried out either in a clinic setting or in families' homes. Unlike the previous models, most FFT therapists are qualified as therapists prior to their FFT training. Caseloads are moderate with a full-time therapist carrying 12–15 cases at a time. Part-time working is not encouraged. The programme aims to reduce defensive communication patterns, increase supportive interactions and promote supervision and effective discipline in families.

FFT does not purport to be a model that can be transferred across treatment groups. It is particularly designed for use with young people with behavioural problems. FFT focuses on current relationships and what is already working well. Theoretically, it is premised upon the notion that current difficulties with young people emerge from dysfunctional family relationships. The model therefore has a *strong relational focus* and interventions concentrate on changing family styles of relating and communicating (Henggeler and Sheidow 2012). Clearly defined interventions are used and these are introduced across phases. The interventions draw from other therapeutic modalities (cognitive behaviour therapy, behaviour management) but these are always delivered with an emphasis on relationships and how they function (Henggeler and Sheidow 2012).

The phases within which the interventions are delivered aim to introduce a systemised way of working even when families are in chaos.

The phases are as follows:

- Engage and motivate young people and their families by decreasing negative interactions and also by acknowledging the pervasive negative experiences to which some families are subject (e.g. racism, poverty, abuse, isolation etc.). 'The process of engagement aims to engender hope and create positive expectations' (Henggeler and Sheidow 2012, p.43). Reframing is used to shift the negative focus on young people's behaviour and ascribe a relational meaning to it instead. Therapists are required to be non-judgemental, maintain neutrality and defuse or divert negative interaction within the session.

- Change behaviour by identifying unhelpful interactional sequences and patterns of relating. Skills are taught in the sessions – for example, communication, parenting, problem-solving and conflict management.

- Changes are generalised so that families can use the skills they have learnt to change problem areas in other situations. The therapist gradually reduces session frequency and the family puts into practice new skills to ensure sustainability of the changes that have been made.

Fidelity to the model is achieved by a specific training programme and a client assessment, tracking and monitoring system that stipulates particular assessment protocol and outcome accountability. FFT operates in teams of up to eight therapists who work together on cases.

Evidence of impact and limitations of FFT

Greenwood (2004) and Stout and Holleran (2012) have evaluated FFT as producing positive outcomes. Parsons and Alexander (1973) found that FFT improved family relationships and reduced recidivism for status offences, but not criminal ones, significantly more than in the comparison groups. Henggeler and Sheidow (2012) cite additional studies which give mixed results, one demonstrating lower court involvement of young people receiving FFT in comparison to their siblings (Klein, Alexander and Parsons 1977) and another showing positive outcomes for young people engaged in serious offences (Barton, et al. 1985). However, they state that these results failed to be replicated in a more recent study with young people who were substance abusing (Waldron et al. 2001). Henggeler and Sheidow (2012, p.44) conclude that 'the efficacy findings for FFT are mixed, but certainly suggest promise in treating both status offenders and more serious juvenile offenders'.

Interestingly, Sexton and Turner (2010, p.1) claim that:

> FFT has an established record of outcome studies that demonstrate its efficacy with a wide variety of adolescent-related problems, including youth violence, drug abuse, and other delinquency-related behaviors. The positive outcomes of FFT remain relatively stable even after a 5-year follow-up (Gordon *et al.* 1988), and the positive impact also affects siblings of the identified adolescent (Klein, Alexander and Parsons 1977).

Their study in 2010, which investigated the effectiveness of FFT with young people in a community youth offending setting, obtained more mixed results. This study, the largest yet of FFT, compared the intervention with probationary services. It is the first study to be carried out by community practitioners working in the field and in this way can be classed as what Henggeler and Sheidow term an effectiveness study. Echoing Henggeler and Sheidow, Sexton and Turner (2010) note that community studies face greater challenges than clinically based trials, most notably in the co-morbidity of existing problems and in the skill level of the practitioners. The study therefore set out to test not only the effectiveness of FFT but to what extent therapist adherence aids or abets its effectiveness as in an intervention.

At first sight, the results of the study demonstrate no difference between FFT and probationary services. However, closer analysis reveals that strict fidelity to FFT yields better results: 'The results indicate that when practiced with model specific adherence FFT respectively resulted in a significant 34.9 per cent and 30 per cent reduction in felony and violent crimes and a non-significant, 21.1 per cent reduction in misdemeanor crimes' (Sexton and Turner 2010, p.9).

Model fidelity was particularly critical when working with high negative peer risk young people (i.e. those likely to reoffend due to peer influences) and with those who are also the most difficult to effect change (Sexton and Turner 2010). For this group, strict adherence to the model produced significant results, whereas for lower-risk young people, this variable disappears. The authors conclude: 'For positive outcomes to occur, FFT needs to be delivered in specific and precise ways that demonstrate the therapist adherence to the clinical model particularly with the most difficult youth' (Sexton and Turner 2010, p.11).

FOSTERING CHANGES PROGRAMME

The Fostering Changes programme was originally implemented in 1999 in the London Borough of Southwark (Warman *et al.* 2006). It was developed by the Adoption and Fostering National Team at the Maudsley Hospital with King's College, London (Briskman *et al.* 2012). In 2009, given the success demonstrated in early trials of the programme, the then DCSF awarded a grant for facilitators to be trained in 154 Local Authorities in England. The programme consists of a 12-week course delivered on a weekly basis by two facilitators. Sessions incorporate theoretical teaching and learning new skills. Carers feed back each week on the new skills they have been practising at home, before new material is introduced.

The basis of the approach is that foster carers are pivotal to change as how they respond, listen and care for young people will fundamentally affect behaviour and outcomes (Warman *et al.* 2006). Foster carers are required to engage actively in learning, reflecting on their practice honestly and openly. The possibility of this occurring is enhanced by the nature of the closed group, where carers come to trust each other and the facilitators. The Strengths and Difficulties Questionnaire (Goodman 1997) was originally used to evaluate progress with the Parenting Stress Index (Abidin 1995) being introduced later (Warman *et al.* 2006). A randomised control trial of the programme has since been completed using a wider range of outcome measures and assessment tools (Briskman *et al.* 2012). The authors of this study concluded that Fostering Changes demonstrates positive outcomes for both carers and children by reducing behavioural difficulties and enhancing the quality of their relationships (Briskman *et al.* 2012).

THE SECURE BASE MODEL – SCHOFIELD AND BEEK

Schofield and Beek, based at the University of East Anglia, carried out a longitudinal study of 52 children placed in foster care between 1997 and 2006. They used this study to analyse the factors which contributed to young people doing well in foster care. From their research they concluded that certain key elements were necessary for young people to be able to form attachments to their caregivers and to function optimally. They developed a model for foster care which would provide these central tenets. This model has evolved over time and now incorporates the following five dimensions:

1. Being available – helping children to trust.

2. Responding sensitively – helping children to manage their feelings and behaviour.

3. Accepting the child – building self-esteem.

4. Co-operative caregiving – helping children to feel effective.

5. Promoting family membership – helping children to belong.

Schofield and Beek have written extensively on both their research findings and the model that they have developed (Beek and Schofield 2004; Schofield 2001, 2002; Schofield and Beek 2005a, 2005b, 2006, 2009). The model draws upon attachment and resilience theory. Schofield (2001) proposes that the two theories connect and that there is a conceptual overlap between them.

The Five Dimensions

The five dimensions are explored in more detail below:

1. *Availability*. In their research Schofield and Beek found that young people valued the practical and emotional availability of carers throughout placement and into adulthood. They highlight that young people who are in foster carer will have had their developmental trajectory altered by their early experiences. Therefore, they may experience dependency needs for a longer period than their securely attached peers. However, they will also be affected by the normal process of maturation. Schofield and Beek (2009) recommend that foster carers adapt their parenting in order to respond to the distinct needs of the young person. In phase two of their research, they identified that young people who were doing well were more able to use their carers as a secure base. This led to more settled behaviour at home and at school (Schofield and Beek 2005b).

2. *Sensitivity.* Schofield and Beek (2006) suggest that this is a fundamental dimension as the capacity to manage one's own feelings and behaviour constitutes a protective factor against mental health issues. This dimension makes use of the ideas of mind-mindedness – the ability to understand one's own mind and that of others. Foster carers need to be able to accurately infer what is happening in the young person's mind and articulate this as a way of facilitating the young person to become aware of his or her own mental processes as well as those of other people. As well as being able to verbalise for the young person their possible emotional state, it is crucial that foster carers can respond with attunement and sensitivity. When carers were unable to reflectively consider the meaning of the child's actions, then they were prone to feel critical of the young person and of themselves. This led to disappointment in the fostering task (Beek and Schofield 2004).

3. *Acceptance – building self-esteem.* Schofield and Beek (2009) identify that self-esteem can be particularly difficult for young people in foster care due to a multitude of factors. They see that foster carers have a critical role to play in building a young person's self-esteem, and with one young person described how the foster carer, despite his challenging behaviour, was able to retain a holistic view that captured his underlying humanity: 'In Leroy's case, the carer's acceptance meant believing in his essential decency and goodness in spite of his disturbed and threatening behaviour' (Schofield and Beek 2009, p.262).

   Accepting the young person as a whole and seeing them as more than their behaviours enables them to start to feel good about who they are.

4. *Co-operation – helping young people to feel effective.* When parents and children work together to solve problems, a sense of competence and confidence is generated. However, young people who have been abused can feel powerless and in response become overtly controlling of others. Regrettably, the care system can reinforce the experience of being out of control. This is in part due to unplanned placement moves,

abrupt changes in social worker and alterations in the care plan. In their home lives it is therefore important that foster carers allow young people appropriate levels of decision making that is congruent with their developmental stage. Negotiating decisions and learning to make compromises facilitates a young person's efficacy and ability to engage co-operatively in relationships (Schofield and Beek 2005a).

5. *Family membership – helping children to belong.* Schofield and Beek (2009) argue that it is important that foster carers demonstrate a commitment to young people beyond their move into independence. Helping young people to belong to the foster family also encompasses an expressed communication and understanding of what it means to belong to different families. Foster carers should facilitate open discussion around the conflicting feelings and split loyalties young people may experience between their birth and foster family.

KATE CAIRNS – TRAUMA MODEL

Kate Cairns (Cairns 2002a, 2002b) is a foster carer who has developed a model for working with the trauma that many young people in care have experienced. She views trauma as a bio-psycho-social injury that affects every area of a young person's life. In particular, she describes it as leading to:

- regulatory disorders which impact on a young person's ability to manage their stress and emotions

- processing disorders which impede the ability to make sense of the world

- social function disorders which mean young people struggle to connect with people around them.

She describes three phases of recovery connected with these three types of impairment:

1. The need to stabilise and develop regulatory skills. She suggests this is done by establishing safety, teaching about trauma and teaching words for feelings.

2. Integrate experiences of their lives and process information accurately by converting trauma into safe memories. Recommended interventions are teaching physiological self-management, facilitating cognitive restructuring and allowing for emotional processing.

3. Become socially adaptive by teaching social responsiveness, building self-esteem and facilitating the capacity for enjoyment of life.

She describes this as a cyclical journey; so once a child has become stabilised, they can do some integrative work on their memories and previous experiences, which in turn may de-stabilise them. Each part of their recovery needs to address the physiological, cognitive and emotional effects of the trauma they have endured or witnessed. Cairns (2002b, p.103) describes this process as 'making a narrative out of terror, which enables our brains to function again'. She suggests that this can only occur in a place of safety, as it is feeling safe that 'allows us to take this little bit of memory and relive it safely, without crossing the threshold into being overwhelmed by the totality of the original disintegrative experience' (Cairns 2002b, p.103).

Cairns also utilises the concept of resilience in her work. She describes resilience as the ability to adapt well to change and challenge. Her proposition is that 'resilience protects against trauma but it is also destroyed by trauma'. She suggests that broadly people tend to be more resilient if they have a problem-solving approach to adversity, good social and communication skills and a sense of purpose and future. She suggests that resilience can be facilitated by working on the domains of:

- talents/interests
- social competencies
- positive values
- secure base
- friendships
- education.

There has not been much written critique of Cairn's work. Fairtlough (2003) reviewed her book *Attachment, Trauma and Resilience* (2002b).

She points out that the book is less a manual and more of a sense-making venture, as much for Cairns as for others, into the world of caring for children and young people who have been traumatised by abuse and/or neglect (Fairtlough 2003). Fairtlough's (2003) criticism of Cairns is that she is uncritical at times, particularly as regards the post-traumatic stress model to which she refers. Fairtlough (2003) also suggests that Cairns can be homogenous in her descriptions. All children's responses to attachment, resilience and trauma are lumped together and diversity issues such as race, disability, ethnicity and so on, and political factors like war, persecution, poverty and violence are ignored. However, overall Fairtlough (2003) concludes that Cairns provides a valuable exploration of the core principles of therapeutic fostering which could be useful for foster carers and professionals alike.

DYADIC DEVELOPMENTAL PSYCHOTHERAPY

Dyadic Development Psychotherapy (DDP) is a treatment model that has been developed by Dan Hughes (1997, 2006, 2007, 2011) in the USA. It is an approach that is used to address trauma and loss. DDP draws upon attachment theory as well as work by other practitioners and theorists – for example, Allan Schore (1994), Ann Jernberg (1979), Daniel Stern (1985) and others. It is a family-based model and includes foster carers or adoptive parents in the work. DDP is a directive approach that operates differently from more traditional non-directive therapeutic ways of working with children. Dan Hughes proposes: 'Traditional child psychotherapeutic approaches for the poorly attached child are often insufficient. They have neither the intensity nor the comprehensiveness needed to elicit therapeutic change' (Hughes 1997, p.49).

The initial goal of DDP is to create a safe enough space for the young person to explore and integrate traumatic memories that carry with them powerful emotions of shame, fear, sadness and/or rage. Safety is created within the therapy by the therapist adopting 'PACE' as a therapeutic stance. PACE stands for playfulness, acceptance, curiosity and empathy. With this position as a backdrop for the work, the therapist encourages the child to delve into memories and experiences that may have been previously denied or avoided. Whilst such recollections may lead to the child becoming dysregulated, the therapist uses PACE to re-establish regulation and connection with them, enabling a further round of exploration. The basis of DDP is that the creation of a coherent life-story facilitates a child's ability to form a secure attachment to their caregiver as well as being a protective factor against mental ill-health.

DDP is carried out within a clinical setting with the carer present. Their presence, witnessing the creation of the child's life-story and participating in the therapeutic process, amplifies the burgeoning attachment between them and their child. Being part of the therapy also enables the foster carer to learn from the therapist's approach with the child and creates the opportunity for the therapist to coach the carer in responses that are embedded in PACE. Whilst DDP is a psychotherapeutic approach, its intention is also to spill over into the child's home life, where the foster carer is encouraged to parent using PACE whenever possible. In the therapy room and at home, DDP has two central endeavours, which are to co-regulate the child's affect and co-create meaning with them. The ability to achieve both of these contributes to emotional well-being and optimal functioning on all levels.

DDP draws on theoretical suppositions that inform psychotherapeutic practice. As a psychotherapy, practice proceeds in a reflexive feedback loop. Certain key principles are adhered to in the work but the tempo and direction are altered to fit with the client's needs and capacity. In this way it is less of a tightly defined model than some of the other treatment methods that have emerged from the USA – for example, MST or MTFC. These features mean that it is easily integrated into Team Parenting, which is also a therapeutic approach whose strengths lie in its recursive clinical practice as opposed to formulaic implementation of set interventions.

Evidence of impact and limitations of DDP

DDP has received criticism for its lack of a clear evidence base (Allen 2011; Chaffin, Hanson and Saunders 2006; Mercer *et al.* 2010; Pignotti and Mercer 2007). Mercer *et al.* 2010 criticise Becker-Weidman and Hughes (2008) for their assertion that DDP is an evidence-based treatment and dispute this. Mercer *et al.* (2010) draw a distinction between Evidence-Based Practice (EBP) and Evidence-Based Treatment (EBT), the latter being more robust due to the use of *controlled clinical trials* and *replication of results*. In contrast, Sackett *et al.* (2000) note that EBP is not a static state of knowledge but rather represents a constantly evolving state of information (Mercer *et al.* 2010).

They suggest that when EBP and EBT are confused, the result can be that research into therapeutic interventions makes bolder claims than can be supported by their methodology. Mercer *et al.* (2010) question Becker-Weidman's research (2006a, 2006b) along these lines, disputing the validity of their outcome and diagnostic measures, their data analysis and the independence of their replications.

Pignotti and Mercer (2007) had previously criticised DDP after the publication of Becker-Weidman's original research and letter (2006a, 2006b). They described DDP as a 'poorly defined intervention' (p.516) and questioned the extent to which it was really based on Bowlby's (1969) attachment theory, given that 'the commonalities are limited to a few vocabulary terms' (p.517). Allen (2011) concurs with this, proposing that Bowlby's attachment therapy (1988) was designed for adults to form an attachment to the therapist and the links between DDP and attachment theory are rudimentary at best. He, like Pignotti and Mercer (2007) suggests that there is no evidence for attachment therapy being replicated safely with children. Rather, he objects that the danger of a child forming an attachment to the therapist is that when the work ends she will experience abandonment all over again.

There have been other criticisms of DDP. Chaffin, Hanson and Saunders (2006) are critical of attachment therapies that include physical restraint, enforced regressive techniques and other invasive, intrusive interventions with children. Whilst they point to a *paradigm shift* (p.382) that has occurred in attachment therapies – from a more confrontational approach to one that engages in emotional regulation and attunement with the child – they remain suspicious that practice has not been transformed. Instead, they propose that behind closed doors malevolent practices continue to exist. They include DDP in this as 'holding' was originally recommended by Dan Hughes (1997). Becker-Weidman (2006c, p.379) responds to some of these criticisms, clarifying that responding to a child's developmental age is very different from 'forcing a child to engage in some activity'. His argument is that 'treating a child on the basis of the child's developmental age is not only indicated but also is an essential part of appropriate parenting and treatment'.

Becker-Weidman and Hughes (2010) respond to the criticisms of their work, acknowledging their epistemological and ontological base. They state a preference for EBP over EBT, suggesting that the former more adequately reflects the broad-ranging, complex and different needs of a clinical population as opposed to 'university research-based populations' (p.6). More importantly, they point to the therapeutic elements of DDP which are broadly acknowledged in research to be fundamental to a therapy's effectiveness, citing the work of Lambert and Ogles (2004). These are the presence of empathy, the therapeutic alliance and, increasingly with regards to parent and child, relationships and the importance of intersubjectivity (Stern 1985).

In the USA providing clear, robust evidence of the efficacy of medical and therapeutic interventions is essential if these are to be funded by health insurance companies. However, by virtue of the endeavour of psychotherapy to *fit the client* (Flaskas 1997), conducting randomised control trials and replicating these is strewn with difficulties. The interventions that have demonstrated the best evidence base (Leve *et al.* 2012) are those grounded in social learning theory and behaviourism and which include a manual from which to work. They are therefore more prescriptive and, although therapeutic by nature, are not psychotherapies. Whilst the necessity of moving towards a clearer evidence base for DDP and all psychotherapies cannot be denied, the difficulties in achieving this should not invalidate what they can offer.

In this chapter the origins and concept of Team Parenting have been introduced. An historical perspective on key legislative and policy changes has been set out in order to provide the wider context in which the development of Team Parenting has occurred. Other approaches to intervening in the lives of children who have suffered from neglect or abuse are critically appraised with respect to the evidence of their efficacy. Chapter 2 goes on to provide a detailed description of the Team Parenting model.

THE EMERGENCE OF TEAM PARENTING
DEFINITIONS AND PRACTICE

CHAPTER CONTENTS

THE ORIGINS OF TEAM PARENTING

The specific concept 'Team Parenting' began its journey in Core Assets in 2002, although other models of multi-agency work existed before and have been developed since. As we have seen in the previous chapter, it arose within a context of a variety of factors that were impacting on social care at the time. These factors emerged from a number of different domains which, whilst distinct, had overlapping influences on each other. They came from the following:

- The political and legislative contexts of the late 1990s and early 2000s when improving the lives of one of society's most vulnerable groups, looked-after children, was high on the government's agenda.

- A burgeoning awareness that the difficulties that affected looked-after children were often specific to them as a result of their traumatic, early experiences and an increasing acceptance that these difficulties were broad and multi-faceted – spanning cognitive, psychological, physical, emotional, behavioural and social areas of functioning.

There was a realisation that for any or all of these to be addressed effectively, a multi-disciplinary approach would be needed.

- A freshly grasped acquiescence that for many of these children the origins of their psychological difficulties were embedded in their formative relationships with their primary caregivers. This knowledge emanated from a renewed enamour with attachment theory at the start of the 1990s. Attachment Disorders as a clinical presentation grew from the theoretical tenets of John Bowlby's attachment theory (Howe and Fearnley 1999). Clinicians and practitioners had started to write about the features of such a presentation during the 1990s (Delaney 1991). In 1994 Attachment Disorder was accepted in the DSM-IV (American Psychiatric Association 1994) as a diagnosis in its own right – 'Reactive Attachment Disorder'.

- Changes in therapeutic practice with this client group. Recognition of the specific challenges these young people faced, particularly with regards to their attachment relationships, gave rise to a new era in clinical practice. The dominance of the therapist as 'expert', privileged with the knowledge to be able to help individual children, was replaced with acknowledgement of the importance of the wider network. In particular, the pivotal position of the foster carer being able to effect changes for the child, due to their role as potential attachment figure, entered centre stage (Archer 2003; Delaney 2006; Hughes 1997; Sprince 2000; Thomas 1997).

- A shift in focus from the drivers of service design. Research in the field, both in the USA and in the United Kingdom (e.g. Ciccheti 1989; Gilligan 1997; Schofield 2001) generated an interest in outcomes for looked-after children. Government policy started to demand a relationship between outcomes and service delivery. No longer could service design be based on organisational objectives and priorities alone (Frost and Stein 2009). Social work practice needed to improve the lot of looked-after children and evidence this improvement with clear measurable outcomes. Services began to review their *modus operandi* with this in mind (Frost and Stein 2009).

Initially at least, most independent fostering agencies sought to offer something different from Local Authority fostering services, setting out their stalls as niche providers of placements for older children who were more difficult to place due to their more challenging behaviours. The original vision of Core Assets was to meet the needs of troubled young people in an integrated way. The intention was to reverse a familiar trend where being removed to a 'place of safety' and coming into care was no guarantee of a better life (Leve *et al.* 2012; Swick 2007).

Some fostering providers, including Core Assets, sought to make individual therapy available to all children and young people. Psychotherapists worked individually with some of the children and young people, aiming to offer them a containing space (Bion 1971) where via play, art, or other means they could express and articulate their experiences. Whilst the child or young person might not understand the hidden communication their play revealed, the therapist would look for meaning and symbolisation that could act as windows to the young person's inner world. With this understanding, the therapist would tentatively offer to the young person interpretations that would connect their external activities and behaviour with their internal representations and experiences. Such offerings could be for the young person the beginning of insight – the start of understanding the tumultuous feelings they experienced in their body and sought to distract from via avoidance and extreme behaviour. The therapist did not demand from them an explicit conversation, although this was welcomed and facilitated when it occurred. More, it was hoped that an implicit knowing could start to be generated and a connecting for the child of past and present, internal and external, emotion and behaviour (Hunter 2001).

The case study below demonstrates the type of work that would be undertaken during individual psychotherapy. Usually children attended weekly therapy sessions with a therapist. Therapists worked using a non-directive approach, so that the child led the session. Art, play and other creative approaches were favoured to facilitate the child expressing themselves without having to rely on words or logical sequencing. The therapist joined the child's play and was directed by them to fulfil certain roles. Alongside this participation the therapist would speculate with the child what their play might represent and how this might connect to their past and present experiences. In the case study below the therapist, Annie, responds to Jon and his use of the therapeutic space. Foster carers were not included in these sessions and often the work could be on-going over a number of months or even, as in this case, years.

CASE STUDY

The therapy room was set up in such a way that it offered a wide variety of opportunities for the child (Jon) and the therapist (Annie). It was possible to be comfortable (on soft cushions), to build opposing 'camps', to fire on the enemy (with soft balls/bow and arrow/used corks), to paint/draw/model, to dress up, to read/be read to, to build with Lego®/scrap materials, to knock things about/down (balloons, bubble wrap, strong cardboard boxes), invent games with and without rules, to push the boundaries within limits of personal and physical safety, to play alone or with Annie.

In the sessions, Annie aimed to follow Jon in his explorations of the room and of his inner world, working hard to pay attention to themes and details within his play. She tried to link thoughts and actions, and to reflect (both aloud, and to herself) upon what she noticed and how she felt.

The early work was characterised by much vigorous physical activity, many changes of ideas/direction, and a sense of there being overwhelming danger and violence very near to the surface. Jon would often defend himself by denying his difficulties, and 'attack' Annie rather than think about what felt to him like 'unthinkable things'. As time went on, he became better able to use the physical and psychological boundaries, within the therapeutic relationship and the room, to explore the anxieties he felt about so many aspects of his life.

The bulk of the work was to form and maintain a secure enough attachment to enable exploration of such themes as betrayal, hurt and damage, fear/disappointment, being passed from hand to hand, feeling friendless and like a loser. It was important that Annie survived jealous 'attacks' and did not punish or retaliate. It was essential for Annie to receive regular clinical supervision, which helped her to maintain enough distance between 'her stuff' and 'Jon's stuff' so that sessions were able to be Jon's and not hers. Many times Annie found her feelings running so high that thinking became difficult.

In the work, which spanned three years, Jon showed Annie that he needed, and could use, a safe and secure place where he could be a tyrant, separate from home and school, with someone who was not part of either of those systems.

Towards the end of the work, Jon was able to show Annie that behind the tyrant was a person who felt small and desperate, betrayed, mixed-up and lonely. This was particularly painful for him, and he would often deflect her acknowledgement of his pain by criticising her talk as 'soft', and therefore beneath contempt.

Sometimes this work could be painstakingly slow and the therapist would find themselves on the receiving end of the young person's projections (Cashdan 1988; Ogden 1982). Such work, drawing on the central principles of psychoanalysis, preserved the young person's confidentiality. This was done in the interests of ensuring that the young person experienced therapy as a safe space where what they 'told', talked about, expressed, revealed or shouted about would go no further (unless their safety was at risk). Maintaining boundaries of confidentiality, would, it was hoped and believed, instil in the children and young people a confidence that they could safely explore issues in the presence of a non-judgemental and interested adult.

Excluded from the therapy room but required to bring their foster child for therapy, foster carers within Core Assets, began to express dissatisfaction with this arrangement. At this time (1995–2002), therapists were employed as sessional therapists rather than being permanent, contracted staff. Organisationally therefore, they were detached and slightly separate from the main body and functioning of the fostering provider. They entered the office building to conduct sessions with young people and they left. This meant that not only were therapists set apart from foster carers in their work with the young person behind the therapy room door, but structurally they did not inhabit the same office space as the rest of the team. Opportunities for shared reflection or possibilities for conversation were limited with both the wider professional team and supervising social workers[1] involved with the child and the foster carers.

---

1   'Supervising social worker' refers to the social worker whose role it is to supervise and support the work of the foster carer. In this book the 'Local Authority social worker' refers to the social worker who has statutory responsibility for the child or young person in foster care.

For the foster carers caring daily for the young person, this system was not always satisfactory. Foster carers found themselves caring for children and young people who presented them with challenges and difficulties they may not have encountered before, or had encountered but not to such an extreme. Confounded by the young person's bewildering behaviours – encompassing a whole range including ingratiating, aggressive, controlling, superficial, rejecting, self-punishing behaviours and more – foster carers felt de-skilled and uncertain how to proceed. Yet the 'expert' who might hold some of the answers was out of range, in a room, with their foster child.

Added to this situation was the experience of some foster carers who gleaned from the child's therapist that the confusing behaviours she experienced at home, were not being presented in the therapy room. With no theoretical framework to refer to, no knowledge to make sense of such a dichotomy, foster carers experienced anger, disbelief and self-doubt. The predicament they found themselves in seemed 'crazy making'. How could their foster child, so troublesome at home, be so different elsewhere? (Dent with Brown 2006; Price 2003; Stott 2006). Either they needed to know what magical skills the therapist was employing or they must be truly failing in their role.

Differences in the professional priorities between the foster carers and the therapists were thus starting to combine to undermine a coherent approach to care provision. The ramifications of these differences between the individual therapists and the foster carers were that what might be occurring in the home was kept separate from and not addressed in therapy. The therapeutic boundary, designed to preserve the child's confidentiality and instil in them a sense of trust in the therapeutic process, could be and was interpreted by foster carers as an implicit criticism of their own work with the young person. Thus, what might support the child and therapist's relationship had the potential to be damaging to the relationship between the carer and the child.

Similar dynamics were noted by practitioners to be occurring in the services of other fostering providers. Sprince (2000) wrote convincingly in her formative article 'Towards an Integrated Network' of the dangers of excluding foster carers and social workers from the therapeutic process. She suggested that individual psychotherapy could act to absolve others in the network of any responsibility to consider or make sense of the child's inner world. This could, at first sight, be appealing, given the messiness and pain that invariably had to be encountered when delving into these young people's early experiences. However, it also left social workers and foster carers with a sense of emptiness and meaninglessness, feelings of jealousy at being excluded from knowing intimate details and fears of inadequacy at not being 'skilled' enough to share the knowledge that the therapist was gaining of the child via their work. The result was often an emerging rift in the network, with the therapist and child being identified together and the foster carers and social workers inhabiting a different space with feelings of unexpressed resentment and envy. Ultimately, this was likely to undermine the stability of the foster placement, and, as Sprince (2000, p.425) points out, 'once-weekly psychotherapy is a poor substitute for a stable home'.

Providing stable foster placements for children and young people was and still is one of the primary goals of fostering providers in the independent and public sector alike. Foster placements which break down are likely to further compromise the young person's emotional and psychological well-being. Research reiterates the importance of stable placements (Macdonald and Turner 2005; Pithouse *et al.* 2004). Informing and supporting foster carers to understand and manage the challenging behaviour they encounter with looked-after children, as well as their own emotional response to such behaviour, can add to the stability of foster placements. The importance of stability in foster care cannot be underestimated (Barber and Delfabbro 2003; Clausen, Landsverk *et al.* 1998; Landsverk and Slymen 2004; McCauley and Trew 2000; Rubin *et al.* 2007). Experience from foster carers demonstrates that fostering impacts on the family as a whole – carers as well as their own children living in the household. Foster carers perceive their own children to be fostering too. When their needs are overlooked and their well-being threatened by the challenges of the foster young person's behaviours, then the future of the foster placement is invariably put in jeopardy.

With this in mind four interacting factors were identified which could contribute to placement breakdown:

1. Threats from the confidentiality boundaries of individual therapy.

2. Lack of information being shared across the care network.

3. The impact of fostering on carers and other family members.

4. The impact of, and repetition of, attachment difficulties.

Addressing these factors within Core Assets gave rise to redesigning therapeutic provision and the development of a therapy service which was integrated into the wider team. This integration of therapy via imbuing every intervention with therapeutic thought and understanding, as well as ensuring a collaborative approach, became known as 'Team Parenting'.

THE NEW INTEGRATED THERAPY SERVICE AND TEAM PARENTING

Taking into account the existing research that demonstrated the importance of placement stability to young people's well-being, the mediating factors of a young person's behaviour and the quality of support to the placement, it was recognised that ignoring foster carers' needs had resulted in a failure to address the crucial objective of the agency – to sustain placements. In arriving at Team Parenting, a structure for the therapy service was identified that recognised:

- the central importance of the *young person in placement*

- the need for good teamworking with a greater openness and clarity regarding the therapeutic task. This was to include professionals from other agencies

- the importance of practical advice and guidance to foster carers and social workers.

Therapy was identified within Team Parenting as being pivotal. Therapists were required to embrace the philosophy of teamworking. There was a move to increased accountability and awareness of evaluating outcomes as it was expected that therapists would make explicit their evidence base and which theoretical models they used. Therapists were expected to see their 'client' not as the child but as the 'child in placement'. The therapeutic task was to give central importance to the relationship between the child and the foster carer. In this way, the relationship with the carer was fostered and the carer received practical suggestions on how to manage challenging behaviour. This work was deemed to run alongside and never replace the work of the supervising social worker with the carer. Indeed, it was considered that in some circumstances it would be beneficial for the supervising social worker to join sessions with the foster carer and therapist to ensure seamless, joined-up working and a consistent approach. The therapy service thus became an integrated part of the whole service delivery of Core Assets' Team Parenting approach.

A DEFINITION OF TEAM PARENTING

It has been difficult to arrive at a succinct definition of Team Parenting, due in part to the fact that the practice of Team Parenting encompasses so much. Team Parenting straddles social work and therapeutic practice and incorporates within it the goal of improving educational outcomes for looked-after children in order to construct for them resilience, confidence and a future. Team Parenting recognises that 'therapeutic' does not just mean time spent with a therapist, but that the foster carer, by virtue of their position as a possible attachment figure, has the potential to offer the young person the most healing and therapeutic relationship of all. Moreover, Team Parenting perceives the therapeutic task of fostering as being wider than the usual intra-psychic, interpersonal goal of therapy. It includes within the therapeutic endeavour of the placement the activities and resources provided by the support service – for example, parties, social events, holidays, clubs, fun – all with the purpose of enabling the young person to heal and trust in self, others and life.

Hek *et al.* (2010, p.39) usefully summarise Team Parenting in the following way:

> The team parenting model aims to improve placement stability and provide a therapeutic environment for the child in which they are able to thrive in terms of their physical and emotional well-being, achieve in terms of educational outcomes, feel comfortable with their own identity and grow in self-confidence. The team parenting approach is a multidisciplinary approach with social workers, support workers, educationalists, therapists, psychologists and foster carers all working together closely as well as with colleagues from local authorities and other services. The approach relies on all of these parties reaching understanding and agreement from the start of a child being looked after about respective roles and responsibilities and reviewing these throughout the placement. The approach is attachment based but also incorporates resilience and strengths based approaches.

TEAM PARENTING IN PRACTICE
UNDERLYING PRINCIPLES OF TEAM PARENTING

Team Parenting holds several critical assumptions which connect and inform each other. It purports that a foster care placement should provide stability of care within which supportive professionals can work together, therapeutically with young people. Its belief is that realisation of this goal will enhance the ability of young people to form secure attachments to their foster carers and that this in turn will lead to improved longer-term outcomes for them. Team Parenting acknowledges that every support person involved with the young person holds different information and has different experiences of that young person and that when working together they can create a cohesive full picture of the young person. Such collaborative working is seen to be in the best interests of the young person and to further their overall well-being. Team Parenting also acknowledges that children and young people with histories of trauma, abuse or neglect and/or attachment difficulties often require therapeutic input to enable them to make use of the care and attachment relationships on offer with their foster carer. It believes that where relationships work well between the foster carer and the young person, the latter's psychological, emotional and developmental needs will be met in an optimal way. As far as possible, this replicates a secure family model.

Core Assets developed Team Parenting as a systemic, resilience- and strengths-based therapeutic approach centering on the needs of the young person in placement by considering the whole placement context as a dynamic process of family/professional interactions and relationships (Becvar and Becvar 2009; Carr 1991; Carr 2006). Team Parenting provides a joined-up approach to parenting fostered young people. Taking into account the complex needs of young people with histories of interpersonal trauma and/or attachment disorders, Team Parenting recognises and respects the professional roles and care interventions of all those working with the young person (Blower et al. 2004; Bowlby 1969, 1979; Golding 2003; Richardson and Joughin 2000). While each support service may provide particular expertise to meet the specific needs of the child, the Team Parenting model brings each service together for a comprehensive, integrated approach where services complement each other and weave together a helpful network of care provision focused on understanding and caring for the child in an integrated context. Team Parenting provides joined-up care for a young person where a family of services communicate clearly with each other about the individual needs of the child and communicate with the young person in order to listen and respond effectively.

Central to Team Parenting is the move from the young person as the 'client' in any therapeutic work, to the 'child *in* placement' as the 'client'. This shift acknowledges the critical role of the foster carer as the predominant agent of therapeutic change in the child's life, and as such recognises the primacy of the daily caregiving dynamic between foster carer and child. However, the phrase 'child *in* placement' encompasses all those involved in the placement. Whilst the relationship between the carer and the young person is central, given the foster carer's potential as an attachment figure, all the other relationships and roles are seen to be important to the overall well-being of the young person. Everyone involved in the child's placement holds different information and experiences of that child, and when brought together can hold the child together and create a cohesive full picture of the child, their strengths and their needs.

The interlocking and inter-relational nature of Team Parenting is depicted in the flower diagram below. The young person and his/her foster carers at the centre, surrounded by professionals who influence, and are influenced by the child, the carers and one another.

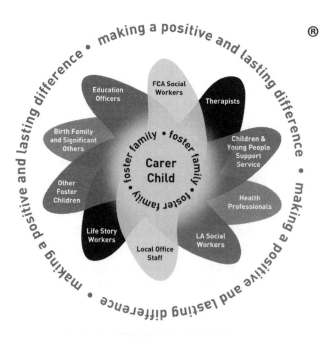

Figure 2.1: Team Parenting

Team Parenting aims to provide:

- a holistic view of the young person's needs

- relevant therapeutic support for the young person, carers and other Team Parenting professionals

- relevant additional educational or other support work for the young person

- evidence of communication between Team Parenting members regarding the child or young person's needs and issues regarding placement stability.

WHAT IS INVOLVED?

Team Parenting is about bringing together those professionals involved in the young person's life in order to provide a cohesive full picture of the child and as a result maintain stability and encourage well-being. The young person is surrounded by foster carers and professionals who aim to work collaboratively to understand and support the emotional and developmental needs of that young person.

These include the following:

- Foster carer/s.

- Young person if appropriate.

- Supervising social worker.

- Local Authority (LA) social worker.

- Education officer.

- A representative from school[2] (e.g. teacher, teaching assistant, school nurse).

- Speech and language therapist.

- Support worker.

---

2   Where teachers and schools are referred to throughout this book, it should be taken to include the Virtual School in England. Local authorities in England have a statutory responsibility to make sure that they promote the educational achievement of the children they look after, regardless of where they are placed. The virtual school led by the virtual school head which is now a statutory role is one of the key ways in which this responsibility is discharged.

- Child and Adolescent Mental Health Services[3] (CAMHS) worker (i.e. therapist, psychiatrist etc).

- Life story worker.

- Birth parents – if agreed that their witnessing of, or contributing to, the meeting would be valuable to the young person.

- Guardian.

- Youth Offending Service (YOS) worker.

Team Parenting is a fluid, flexible and adaptive approach which aims to fit the needs of the individual child in his/her placement. Whilst there are central assumptions that underlie its practice, certain key individuals whose presence is required for its optimal functioning and a range of identified interventions, it is not prescriptive or sequential in its operation. To this end, there has been some debate as to whether Team Parenting is an approach, model, framework or philosophy. However, despite the bespoke nature of its delivery, Team Parenting does incorporate some tangible elements in terms of its service design. These are the range of interventions available and the phases through which a placement might best make use of these interventions.

Team Parenting makes use of four integrated services, which work together seamlessly to ensure young peoples' needs are met in placement. These services are the social work service, the therapy service, the education service and the support worker service. These four services share the same office space and work closely and cohesively together on placements. They can be seen as internal facets of the Team Parenting approach. External services such as YOS and CAMHS are integrated into Team Parenting via Team Parenting Meetings, which are discussed in detail in Chapter 5.

The therapy and education service both contain a range of interventions that can be offered to a placement at any one time. Some

---

3   In the U.K. CAMHS provide psychiatric, psychological, psychotherapeutic, social work, occupational therapy, art therapy and clinical nursing support for children from the age of 4 up to 16 or 18. There are regional variations regarding which inputs are available. Most CAMHS teams work with issues of conduct disorder through to self-harm, eating disorders and psychosis.

placements may require all of the interventions, some only one or two. Interventions are not fixed in terms of their duration, although they are regularly reviewed to ensure a reflexive feedback loop constantly examines whether the best intervention is being used and whether improved outcomes are being achieved. New interventions can be introduced at any time to add to those already being provided, or to replace some that are no longer deemed necessary. The triangles in Figures 2.2 and 2.3 demonstrate the interventions that comprise the therapy and education service. The interventions at the bottom of the triangles are the ones that are most commonly used by each service. As we go up the triangle, the interventions become more intensive and specialist in nature. It is useful to think of this range of interventions as a menu, where one dish may be chosen or a course of dishes, according to individual requirement.

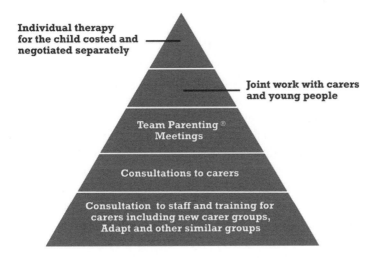

Figure 2.2: Therapy service interventions[4]

---

4   ADAPT is an acronym that stands for 'Attachment Difficulties and Parenting Therapeutically'. It is a carer group run for foster carers who are looking after young people long term who have attachment difficulties. It is described in more detail in Chapter 7.

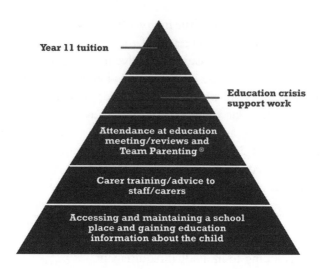

Figure 2.3: Education service interventions

In every placement, every child and young person follows their own unique pathway. However, there are phases that have been identified as being helpful in working towards ensuring placement success for the young person. It is recognised that these phases will not necessarily occur in sequence or follow an organised progression. They represent areas of work that will enable the young person to settle into their placement and begin to integrate their internal and external worlds. Delineating these stages is helpful in providing both workers and foster carers clear guidelines as to what might be the primary goals to be worked upon. Clarity and certainty in an area of work often rife with emotional upheaval and confusion can be facilitating for professionals and foster carers, giving them some sense that their efforts are being directed in a beneficial direction. These four phases are not unlike Kate Cairns' three phases of recovery (Cairns 2002b) that she recommends for traumatised children (described in Chapter 1).

The four phases

Phase 1 – Stabilising the placement within the agency. One of the fundamental principles for effectively helping young people who have experienced complex trauma and have significant attachment difficulties is the establishment of a safe, consistent and secure caring environment. For children and young people who can no longer live at home, a stable and loving foster care placement often becomes the primary setting for addressing their challenging issues. In Phase 1, the carers will have a basic understanding of how the child or young person has been experienced in their former home and within their birth family and the abuse and/or neglect they have endured. This gives the grounding to start to look at how this particular foster family can be supported to become the agents for change for this particular child or young person.

Within Phase 1 interventions and support include the following:

- Supervision with social worker.

- Initial Team Parenting Meeting.

- Education liaison attending Personal Education Plan (PEP) meetings.

- Consultations with therapist.

- Some support work may begin.

- Training.

- Key Developmental Assets[5] (KDA™).

Phase 2 – Providing appropriate responses to the young person's emotional distress. When stability and security have been established, appropriate attention to the child or young person's affect can occur. This can be facilitated by enhancing the caregivers' ability to focus on the child's emotional distress rather than their behaviour. The carers will learn about trauma and the effect this has on the brain, which will allow their care to take into account the physiological impact of trauma and how to manage emotional distress and behaviours.

Within Phase 2 interventions and support include the following:

---

5   'Key Developmental Assets' or 'KDA™s' may be described as opportunities, factors, achievements, activities, capacities and strengths that provide a young person with the best possible chance of fulfilling their potential. Extensive research undertaken by the Search Institute in the United States has demonstrated that the more exposure to and experience of these 'assets' that a young person has then the 'better' their potential outcomes and achievements are likely to be. The Core Assets Group has adapted these and developed a related 'web'-based recording tool which aims to measure a young person's progress and development against the 20 identified assets. This is described in full in Chapter 9.

- Supervision with social worker.

- Team Parenting Meetings.

- Education support.

- Consultations with therapist.

- Support work sessions with child.

- Joint child and carer sessions.

- Specialist training.

- Therapeutic carer groups.

- KDA™.

Phase 3 – Modelling appropriate emotional responses. This allows the foster carer/s and the whole team to demonstrate appropriate responses to the young person's emotional distress. This can take place via a process of re-labelling, using increased emotional literacy, support and building emotional resilience. In this phase, Team Parenting Meetings are crucial, to ensure that all members of the professional team understand the work that is being undertaken and can implement it in their own settings with the young person.

Within Phase 3 interventions and support include the following:

- Supervision with social worker.

- Team Parenting Meetings.

- Education support.

- Consultations with therapist.

- Support work sessions with child.

- Joint child and carer sessions.

- Specialist therapeutic parenting training.

- Therapeutic carer groups.

- KDA™.

Phase 4 – Building resilience. This phase ensures that all members of the team are able to teach and support the young person in developing positive, healthy and functional methods of avoiding and/

or overcoming maladaptive behaviours (e.g. sexualised behaviour, assault, drugs and alcohol) and/or victimisation.

Within Phase 4 interventions and support include the following:

- Supervision with social worker.

- Team Parenting Meetings.

- Education support.

- Consultations with therapist.

- Support work sessions with child.

- Joint child and carer sessions.

- Specialist training.

- Therapeutic carer groups.

- KDA™.

It is not expected that these phases are followed in sequence or that one should be completed before another is begun. Instead, as is consistent with the philosophy of Team Parenting as a whole, it is envisaged that they will interweave and inform each other. Team Parenting is an inherently therapeutic approach and this means that the work that is done at any particular point in time with any individual child/placement must fit the therapeutic need. Thus, with these phases, it is likely that foster carers, professionals and young people within placements may begin one phase only to have to return to it/re-visit it at a later date. Undertaking work in one phase may herald the initiation of work in another. For example, once feeling more stable than before, a young person may start to have the emotional capacity to recall and remember earlier traumatic or distressing events. Without support, she is likely to initially express emotions linked to such memories via her behaviour. This behaviour will need to be worked on in Phase 2. It might also lead to a periodic destabilising of the placement for either the foster carer or the child or both (Cairns 2012). Thus, working in Phase 2 might entail a need to revisit Phase 1. In this way, it is useful to consider working through these phases as figures of eight, with each new loop progressing in a new direction and also requiring time to go back and re-integrate the learning of the previous one. Thus, the placement is providing opportunities for learning and healing without end.

In this chapter the underlying principles of Team Parenting have been explored. The origins of Team Parenting have been identified, the professional membership of teams has been described and the four phases of work set out, acknowledging that these may not take place in a set order. Chapter 3 moves on to consider key features of Team Parenting including integrated working, the central role of the foster parent and the contribution of Team Parenting to placement stability.

CHAPTER 3

KEY FEATURES OF TEAM PARENTING

CHAPTER CONTENTS

Having discussed the underlying principles of Team Parenting, it is useful to explore particular key features in more depth. These facets initially helped in the formulation of the model and informed its identity, development and progression. They have continued to be hallmarks of Team Parenting. They are as follows:

- Integrated working.

- Foster carers as primary agents of change.

- Placement stability as a primary goal.

INTEGRATED WORKING

It is important to be clear about definitions and terminology intended when referring to integrated, multi-agency and multi-disciplinary working. Here multi-disciplinary working refers to the coming together of professionals from different disciplines within Core Assets to form part of the parenting team. Although these professionals (the supervising social worker, education officer and therapist) and the foster carers will have the most contact with each other due to belonging to the same organisation and using the same office space, the parenting team also consists of those professionals who exist outside of the agency. These are teachers, health visitors, school nurses, CAMHS teams, Connexions workers, learning mentors and others. Incorporating these staff into Team Parenting consolidates it as a multi-agency and interagency approach.

Team Parenting recognises that looked-after children often experience a fragmented style of care in contrast to their contemporaries living at home with their birth parents. For birth children still living in their families of origin or even in blended families with one of their birth parents, a coherent and meaningful history of their lives is usually contained in the mind(s) of their parents. Thus, a narrative of their cognitive, behavioural, educational, social and emotional development can readily be constructed. Such narratives are useful in terms of helping others to understand the needs of the child, particularly at key transitional life stages – for example, when he or she starts school or moves to secondary school. They are also crucial in enabling the child to develop a comprehensive and lucid sense of self. Maya Angelou (cited in Cozolino 2010, p.151) says: 'There is no greater agony than bearing an untold story inside you'.

However, for many looked-after children, it is not only that the story is untold but that it is unknown, even to themselves. As Cozolino (2010, p.367) states: 'Stories connect us to others, prop up our fragile identities, and keep our brains regulated'. When working with young people who are not in care in a mental health setting (e.g. a CAMHS team), it is common practice to include the family – at least in the assessment session and often in subsequent sessions. They can provide valuable information regarding all aspects of the child's life and experiences as well as insight into what may be occurring for the child in family interactions. For looked-after children, their 'family' consists of a complex network of individuals and organisations residing in different places and with split areas of responsibility. Legal responsibility for their care is located with the Local Authority and this is discharged in daily practice by their social worker and her team manager. Those in charge of their daily and practical care are their foster carers.

The result of this multiple-layered system of care is that information about the looked-after child and their histories is not centralised in a parent's mind but kept in disparate parts. Thus, their educational history may be logged in school records, their medical records – infamously difficult to obtain (Ward *et al.* 2002) – are mostly held with health visitors and G.P. practices, and their social care history is located in Local Authority files. When the young person has experienced multiple moves, the situation is made even worse, with the likelihood of numerous changes of worker, school and placement meaning that information is lost along the way. Building a coherent narrative and understanding of the child's life with the aim of being better able to meet their needs becomes a challenge indeed. It is this situation that the interagency aspect of Team Parenting sought to address. It took guidance from practitioners in the field, who, experiencing similar dynamics and tensions, made clear recommendations that 'we have an obligation to learn to work more effectively with that larger family' (Sprince 2000, p.431).

Team Parenting aims to militate against the fractured experience of care for looked-after children by bringing together all those involved in a young person's life to form a parenting team. Regular meetings draw these people together to facilitate amongst them a shared and comprehensive story of what has happened for the young person so far. The forum for these meetings are Team Parenting Meetings and the detail of these is described in Chapter 5. The purpose of this section is to identify integrative working as a key feature of Team Parenting and to locate its primacy in Team Parenting practice within the recent literature.

A range of research evidence points to the need for interagency working, particularly with regards to children's services such as fostering (Cocker and Scott 2006; Coulling 2000; Kelly *et al.* 2003):

> The interconnectedness of mental and physical health problems with social and educational difficulties experienced by looked-after children necessitates coordinated multi-agency interventions which systemically address the multiple factors contributing to their mental health and behaviour problems. (Kelly *et al.* 2003, p.333)

Sloper (2004) has reviewed the literature and noted that there were consistent findings on what acted as facilitators to multi-agency working:

> Clear aims, roles and responsibilities and timetables that are agreed between partners; a multi-agency steering group, commitment at all levels of the organisation involved and good systems of

communication and information sharing…support and training for staff in new ways of working is needed. (Sloper 2004, p.571)

Specifically, Sloper (2004) identified the need for interagency working to be supported at all levels of the organisation, particularly by the senior managers and executives. Commitment to this should be found within the organisation's strategic planning if interagency working is to be successful. This is echoed elsewhere in the literature (Nelson, Tabberer and Chrisp 2011; Sprince 2000).

Team Parenting demonstrated this degree of commitment. Following its inception in 2002, road-shows and workshops were delivered to staff across the country, training staff in the principles of the approach and clarifying the expectation that working as a parenting team, across disciplines and with other agencies, was now an expected requirement for the effective operation of Team Parenting. The concept of Team Parenting as a therapeutic approach sharing psychological understanding across agencies and disciplines was enshrined in the training.

This training of staff was necessary to instil what initially seemed like innovative and unfamiliar practice. Despite having co-existed with professionals of different disciplines before, Team Parenting required a greater degree of collaboration and co-operation. Hitherto, services within Core Assets (particularly the therapy service), had existed discretely of each other and intervention from a particular discipline could only be implemented after a referral had been made and allocated to a worker. Team Parenting envisaged an integrated team working together, with no separate services, no referral system and no waiting lists. Identification of need for an input required mutual decision making and planning as opposed to being the sole province of a particular specialism. For example, in deciding what should happen regarding a child's school placement, this was no longer a consideration left to the education officer alone but one which was required to be thought about together with the supervising social worker, therapist, foster carer and Local Authority social worker.

Obstacles to this new method of integrated working did exist within the agency. In the early days Team Parenting and its methodology represented a major challenge to the existing culture for social workers, education officers, therapists, support workers and foster carers alike. Used to referral systems, waiting lists and discrete services, not receiving what they initially requested in terms of 'therapy' to 'fix' the young person led to some initial frustration until the benefits of Team Parenting and working together collaboratively came to be appreciated. This need to ensure that change in practice is embraced ideologically at all levels of the organisation is found in the literature. Cocker and Scott (2006, p.21) state that 'the mere creation of structures – too often seen as a cure-all – will not of itself change professional cultures, working methods and practice'.

Sloper (2004, p.572) reiterates this: 'Multi-agency working requires changes at the level of individual practice, within agencies and at the multi-agency organizational level.' Additionally, in order for interagency working to be implemented effectively, studies reveal the need to recruit members of staff with comprehension of the value of this way of working and some previous experience. Sloper (2004, p.576) refers to a 'new type of "hybrid" professional' that can facilitate this way of working. A cultural shift was required before Team Parenting could start to operate optimally. The organisation needed therapists who acknowledged, understood and embraced the need to work with the network around the child. It was the therapists who were required to cement the original training received by staff in Team Parenting by cascading down the vision of an interagency approach that would seek to meet children's needs via a coherent and co-operative parenting team. At the beginning of this century, working systemically with the network as a therapist was still a relatively new idea and it took time for therapists to be inducted into their role. Often, therapists – more familiar with perceiving therapy to be a one-to-one activity that took place in the therapy room – struggled to perceive that interagency working and the effective formation of the parenting team was in itself a key therapeutic endeavour. As a result of this initial hurdle, therapists were trained in Systemic Therapy to give them the theoretical structure and technical expertise to deliver this new way of working.[1]

The actual practice of Team Parenting was greatly enhanced by the creation of 'team attached' therapists and education officers. Therapists and education officers moved to share office space with the

---

1   Systemic Therapy can be seen as an approach within the overall modality of Family Therapy. Viewing families as inter-connected systems became popular in the 1980s. Particular techniques are utilised within this approach (Carr 2006; Cecchin 1987). Since then, family therapy has continued to evolve. Its usefulness for Team Parenting exists in its view of the client not being a single individual and its focus on relationships and how they connect with 'the problem'.

supervising social workers. This meant there were more opportunities for communication and discussion regarding placements. Informal conversations could take place regarding a placement over the kettle or in the corridor. Therapists, overhearing social workers speak on the phone regarding a placement, could offer their thinking and knowledge once the phone call had ended. By virtue of inhabiting the same office space, information between team members was shared quickly and easily, mutual understanding was enhanced and the opportunities for misunderstanding, blame and frustration amongst team members greatly reduced (Robertson 2006).

Once the culture of Team Parenting was accepted, barriers to effective integrated working occurred most often outside the agency. Staines, Farmer and Selwyn (2011, p.322) in their review found that the supervising social workers were positive about Team Parenting: 'Collaboration with other agencies is essential. The IFA [independent Foster-care agency] team parenting approach works well when everybody knows what they're doing.'

The weaknesses in the effective operation of interagency working lay at the *intersection* with the Local Authority (Staines *et al.* 2011). Delays in decision making could lead to important services not being provided to the young person. Staines *et al.* 2010 recommend working hard with other agencies to promote interagency working and the benefits of it. At times, when a young person is placed out of the authority, the Local Authority social worker has to travel long distances to engage in Team Parenting Meetings. For busy and stressed Local Authority social workers, attending Team Parenting Meetings can seem like just another meeting, with much the same membership present as those who will be part of the looked-after child's review. However, if they can be induced to attend, experience has shown that they appreciate how these meetings operate differently and the value they can make. These meetings are run as therapeutic spaces (more of this in Chapter 5) and being together with other members of the parenting team – sharing, supporting and learning – collectively engages Local Authority social workers and offers them a way of working they may not have experienced before.

Leve *et al.* (2012) criticise multi-agency working for focusing too much on organisational and structural change with not enough emphasis on content. They ask for consideration of the 'what' as well as the 'how' in interagency working. In Team Parenting it is the therapeutic and systemic elements which lead to enhanced understanding, greater co-operation and increased skills amongst all those who are part of the network. It is this imparting of therapeutic knowledge, theory and skills that form the 'what'. Therapeutic intervention is at the heart of fostering for Team Parenting (Staines *et al.* 2011) and this is brought to the young person by taking a systemic approach, viewing the child not as 'the client' on their own but as their needs being interwoven with the relationships and context of their placement. Thus, the 'client' is the child *in* placement. With this approach, therapists engage not only with the young person but also provide relevant support and consultation for other members of the Team Parenting group. Such an approach draws attention to the importance of engaging the whole network involved in a placement and embedding within it a psychological, emotional and behavioral understanding of the needs of each young person (Golding 2003; Golding and Picken 2004; Macdonald and Turner 2005). The ultimate aim is to lead all workers to a more positive engagement with the inner world of the children with whom they are involved.

BENEFITS

The benefits of interagency working are well documented in the literature. Hek *et al.* (2010, p.3) state:

> An identified benefit of the support team approach advocated in many of the studies was the exchange of information brought about by a network of people supporting the child coming together, face to face, on a reasonably regular basis. Each team member was seen to bring valuable information about different facets of the child. This provided a fuller picture of the way the child relates to different people in different situations.

Interagency working in Team Parenting leads to the formation of a co-operative team who are joined together by a shared endeavour – to improve the outcomes for the young person concerned. Working collaboratively means they can agree a plan of action and strategies for addressing the young person's difficulties. Having all the key people involved with the young person ratify this plan and means it can be put into place across all areas of their life and reinforced by the many different people with whom they come into contact. Robertson (2006, p.190) refers to 'meaningful communities of practice' who, when working well together, are more likely to implement interventions uniformly. Whilst she is specifically discussing assessment interventions, Team Parenting takes this wider, using the creation of a coherent parenting team to 'uniformly implement' therapeutic strategies in all spheres of the young person's life.

Multi-agency working can and sometimes does reduce the stereotype views that professionals have about each other (Sharland and Taylor 2007). Such stereotypes and pre-judgements can exacerbate misunderstandings, make communication a hazardous process and contribute to splitting[2] (Sprince 2000) amongst the team. Splitting at its worst can make teamworking a minefield, where the needs of the young person become lost amongst interagency warfare, different agendas, misconceptions and competing priorities. When such dynamics are at play, the likelihood of the young person receiving a co-ordinated, considered and planned package of care is limited. Team Parenting seeks to minimise the chances of this occurring by promoting respect, valuing and understanding of each other's roles. Regular Team Parenting Meetings create the opportunity for the sharing of both information and experience. This means that there is time for the perspectives that underlie the different positions of key professionals to be understood. Understanding engenders a non-blaming culture as the dilemmas and difficulties that various team members confront are explored. Time given in this way to the creation of a thinking space facilitates mutual empathy, support and mentalisation (Fonagy *et al.* 1991). When we are able to mentalise for ourselves and others the capacity for relationships to work well is greatly enhanced. Working well together in this way ensures that the young person remains the focus of the efforts of the parenting team.

---

2   'Splitting' is a psychoanalytic concept which Klein (1959) introduced. Splitting can refer to the way in which an infant organises her experiences or a defensive mechanism where ambivalent experiences are separated out into good and bad (Lichtenberg and Slap 1973). 'Klein saw splitting as the natural way of managing the strong but opposing feelings of love and hate felt by an infant towards his or her primary object, the mother' (Stott 2006, p.49). Klein held that these feelings centred on the breast, which when available was experienced as good and nurturing, and when unavailable experienced as bad and hateful. Unable to integrate these conflicting experiences, the infant splits her mother or the breast into good and bad. Developmentally, Klein believed that infants would come to be able to integrate these experiences. When working with looked-after children who may not have been able to achieve this integration, it is as if their internal splitting is projected into the system around them. Thus, professionals and agencies become split into 'good and bad, helpful or neglectful, rescuing or abandoning' (Stott 2006, p.50).

Nelson *et al.* (2011) identify similar elements that lead to successful integrated working. In their investigation of interagency working in children's centres they find that it functioned optimally where there was 'trust between all parties based on a clear understanding of the different roles and how they could work well together' (p.307). Obstacles to integrated working included suspicion between professionals and lack of understanding of each other's roles and what they could offer.

Team Parenting is designed to provide the motivation, structure and therapeutic framework to overcome potential barriers and to facilitate informed communication between workers. This creates the forum for a parenting team to positively negotiate together the complexity of care for young people in foster care. It allows the opportunity for a team of professionals and foster carers to collectively think psychologically and deeply about the young person's past, its impact on their present and the possibilities for their future. Engaging professionals from other agency contexts in this work creates the possibility that all the child or young person's carers will become knowledgeable of how to interact with them with therapeutic intent, holding in mind the trauma they have experienced and that they need to develop the resilience to overcome it. In this way Team Parenting seeks to embed amongst all those involved in caring for and working with the young person its belief that looked-after children have specific needs due to their early experiences. The intention is that each professional or carer will moderate their practice in ways which take this understanding and new knowledge into account. Sprince (2000, p.434) calls this 'a network of carers who interest themselves in a child's inner world, and who see it as part of their job to make sense of it'.

If this can occur, then young people can experience metaphoric therapeutic communities around them whilst continuing to live within, and benefit from, family and community life.

THE ROLE OF A KEY CO-ORDINATOR

Sloper (2004) highlights the challenges for families in negotiating a multi-agency system. She describes the difficulties for families of having to manage multiple agencies and professionals, a lack of comprehension and clarity as to their roles and where to go for what, with the danger that each will offer conflicting advice leading to a high probability that the young person's needs 'will fall into gaps between different agencies' provision' (Sloper 2004, p.572). She pertinently points to parents' views which requested a single point of contact to provide a co-ordinated package of care. Yet, despite this having been recognised as far back as 1976 in the Department of Health and Social Security (1976) Court Report, this has rarely been achieved (Sloper 2004). Whilst her comments pertain to birth families and parents, the same frustrations are inevitably experienced by foster carers in a multi-agency system. As stress undermines foster care quality, minimising the frustrations of negotiating a clear pathway between different agencies will not only lead to a better, more co-ordinated package of care but, one hopes, also to improved, more emotionally available foster care.

The co-ordinating role of the therapist within Team Parenting Meetings goes some way to achieve this. The therapist becomes the repository or container (Bion 1971) for the system, both in terms of linking and making sense of psychological experiences and behaviours and in the practical sense of co-ordinating the coming together of the parenting team. Once the team has come together for a Team Parenting Meeting, the therapist facilitates the space. She has responsibility for drawing the meeting to a close and agreeing with those present a range of actions that will seek to address the young person's needs as they have been identified in the meeting. This open and visible planning of interventions is reviewed each meeting, encouraging amongst team members a commitment to enact their agreed task. In between meetings, the therapist often becomes the point of contact for professionals struggling with the young person's behavioural or other issues. This method of working means that young people in foster care receive a more co-ordinated service, tailored to meet their particular needs, and improved access to other agencies via the therapist (Sloper 2004). For example, CAMHS teams, often difficult to access, having been part of Team Parenting Meetings and having developed an effective and mutually beneficial relationship with the therapist, are likely to be much more responsive to requests for advice:

> Effective team working was characterized by clear objectives, high levels of participation, emphasis on quality, support for innovation and clear leadership. A diverse range of professional groups working

together was also associated with higher levels of innovation in patient care. (Sloper 2004, p.575)

In summary, Team Parenting recommends the following as Key Principles in Interagency working:

- Some common foundation of knowledge.

- A proper understanding of individual roles.

- A broad awareness of important issues.

- A collaborative practice.

- An ability to contribute expertise effectively.

- Understanding and respect for the expertise of others' reflective practice.

- Comprehensive approaches to complex problems.

- Challenging norms.

- Preparation for change.

FOSTER CARERS AS PRIMARY AGENTS OF CHANGE
FOSTER CARERS' PRESENCE AS ATTACHMENT FIGURES

Taking into account that disruptions to their early attachment relationships had resulted in profound psychological damage, Team Parenting moved to a position of considering that the young person's most pressing emotional task was to be able to form secure attachments to their caregivers. Informed by attachment theory, Team Parenting, as we have seen, moved away from viewing the therapist as the expert with the potential to exert therapeutic change to considering that the foster carer, by virtue of their presence as an attachment figure, was best placed to affect the healing of the child. It was understood that for young people with attachment disorders or difficulties, what they feared and resisted most was a close, dependent relationship with a caregiver. Previous experiences of depending on an adult for their well-being had resulted in pain and fear. Thus, many of these young people who had endured neglect, abuse or trauma at the hands of their caregivers developed survival strategies to manage the situations in which they found themselves. These survival strategies were aimed at controlling their environment to the greatest possible degree in the hope of minimising the occurrence of any further trauma or hurt. A whole range of behaviours could be deployed, from being aggressive and attacking to being overly compliant and non-communicative. Inevitably, their early experiences had led to the formation of fundamental, unconsciously held core beliefs which in a new situation prevented them being able to make use of the good quality care on offer.

These core beliefs have been categorised and written about in different ways: John Bowlby (1973, 1979) referred to a child's internal working model; Daniel Stern (1985) conceptualises them as *representations of interactions that have become generalized* (RIGs); and William Bucci (1997) writes about *emotional schemas*. In drawing upon attachment theory, Team Parenting mostly alludes to Bowlby's internal working models. Comprehending that young people who have been maltreated are likely to have formed assumptions that they are not lovable, other people cannot be trusted and the world is not a safe place to be, shifted the focus of the therapeutic endeavour. It came to be perceived that what these young people most needed was to form a trusting relationship with a carer wherein they could experience themselves as lovable and deserving of nurturing parenting. However, of course, due to their current distrust and internal beliefs, they would resist the development of this relationship at all costs. After all, previous experience had demonstrated that trusting and depending on others was a risky business.

It was perhaps this dynamic that had contributed to the difficulties between foster carers and individual therapists written about in Chapter 2. Trusting a carer was threatening for a young person in foster care, forming a relationship with a therapist who was only seen for one hour once a week was less so. Thus, the relationships young people formed with their therapists were often not littered with the complex difficulties and challenges that foster carers experienced with them at home. However, what now came to be understood was that the behaviour that was presented to the foster carers was an attempt to keep the relationship at a distance due to the perceived dangers that such a relationship could impose. Ironically, many young people were successful in the strategies they employed, for unable to manage their behaviours foster carers did withdraw and ultimately, defeated and despairing, sometimes ended the placement. Sadly, this could only confirm for young people their original core beliefs – that they *were* unlovable, other people could not be trusted to care for them and the world was an unsafe and unpredictable place to be (Cameron and Maginn 2008; Delaney 2006; Macdonald and Turner 2005; Price 2003).

Young people needed to experience a different style of relationship with a caregiver from the one(s) that had characterised their early histories. If this could occur, then healing could take place. Team Parenting drew its assumptions and beliefs from research, and these viewpoints have continued to be reflected in the literature over the last 20 years. Craven and Lee (2006) consider that foster carers are in a *unique position* to help the child recover by virtue of their position as care providers. They recognise that looked-after children have experienced their attachment relationships and affectional bonds being broken, often time after time. Foster carers, however, can provide warmth, nurturing and understanding. They can help the young person to make sense of what has happened to them and the multiple losses they have encountered in their short lives. Looked-after children need to be able to trust and experience some security with those who care for them. Craven and Lee (2006) argue strongly for the foster carer to be involved in the child's healing, stating that it is imperative that foster carers have an understanding of the young person's attachment style, attachment disorders in general and how to work to facilitate emotional recovery.

This unique position of foster carers as potential therapeutic agents of change was recognised by the new approach of Team Parenting. Team Parenting saw foster carers as the primary agents of change for the young person, not the therapist. However, in order for foster carers to become primary agents of change, they would need to be trained and supported to become therapeutic foster carers. The focus of the work for the therapist therefore shifted from the young person to the foster carers. Therapists were now to work through the foster carers to reach the child. It was deemed more important that the young person formed a trusting relationship with their foster carer than with the therapist. The ways in which foster carers were supported to take up their positions as therapeutic foster carers are explored in detail in Chapter 4. For now, it is important to identify this feature of identifying the foster carers as the primary agents of change as being one of the hallmarks of Team Parenting.

BENEFITS

This radical change in outlook and approach had unforeseen benefits. Utilising foster carers as specialists in their own right coincided with contextual shifts in the wider fostering world. Improved preventative work on keeping children out of care for longer and the decreased use of residential units meant that the type of young people entering foster care often came with histories of abuse and neglect and the consequent multiple needs that go with such experiences. Added to this, the increased regulatory framework of fostering with the National Minimum Standards in 2002 meant that fostering began to be perceived as a more specialised task with skills beyond the ability to look after children being required (Warman *et al.* 2006; Wilson and Evetts 2006). Foster carers themselves, given the nature of the task they increasingly faced, wanted recognition of the skills and expertise they brought to fostering. This then became a recursive loop, with greater skills and training for foster carers required by agencies expecting them to become therapeutic in their fostering, and carers, once functioning in this way, requiring greater recognition of the role they played.

As a result, Team Parenting practice, via a number of interventions, taught and coached foster carers to understand the psychological positions of the young people they fostered and to know how to intervene to promote their overall well-being. This process resulted in two benefits: First, foster carers enjoyed their learning and development and consequently became more satisfied with the fostering task. Second, when they could put what they had learnt into practice to good effect, they found they enjoyed their relationship more with their foster child. These two factors have been found to have a reciprocal relationship to each other (Whenen, Oxland and Ushington 2009). However, the writers of this paper acknowledge that forming satisfactory relationships with young people in the care system is very challenging due to their attachment difficulties and the externalisation of their emotional conflicts. Therefore, foster carers need on-going support and training in order to facilitate them in their task as primary agents of change.

Yet, when this could be achieved, there were also benefits to the children and young people in placement: 'When carers were emotionally and practically available to young people throughout their placement [...] the relationship assisted with overcoming a range of difficulties in the young person's life.' (Hek *et al.* 2010, p.3). Hek *et al.*'s (2010) pronouncement that effective, good quality, attuned, involved and emotionally available foster care produces better outcomes for children and young people is found elsewhere in the literature (e.g. Robertson 2006; Warman *et al.* 2006). Robertson (2006) argues that when foster carers have access to information/ training they are better equipped to meet the child's needs and more confident to advocate for the child. Cocker and Scott (2006) go so far as to boldly state that in their view the only interventions that work are those delivered with and through foster carers. Leve *et al.* (2012) reviewed a number of interventions with looked-after children and found that with appropriate training and support foster carers can be taught to develop relationships with young children which enable them to form secure relationships to their caregivers, regulate their behaviour and manage their emotional responses. Additionally, they identified that some of the programmes they reviewed for children of primary school age were successful in teaching foster carers positive management of challenging behaviour. They conclude from this that improving the emotional and psychological well-being of looked-after children has to become a primary goal alongside the focus on placement stability and safety, which previously have occupied centre stage. They say that 'when foster families receive support aimed at improving home-based experiences that addresses behavioural and neurological underpinnings and placement capacity, children do better' (Leve *et al.* 2012, p.12). By moving foster carers to the heart of the therapeutic endeavour with looked-after children in an attempt to address their attachment difficulties and previous trauma, this is exactly what Team Parenting sets out to do.

TEAM MEMBERS

An interesting by-product of elevating foster carers to primary agents of change was a reconsideration of their status. This review was occurring elsewhere within fostering albeit heavily influenced by the independent fostering agencies that were caring for children/young children who had higher levels of need and required greater skill from their foster carers in meeting these needs (Wilson and Evetts 2006). There has been some debate about whether foster carers have the capability or are prepared for the extra responsibility that comes from being seen as a member of the professional system around the young person (Robertson 2006). However, in Team Parenting, membership of the parenting team was expected and, research shows, was welcomed by foster carers (Staines *et al.* 2011). In their research Staines *et al.* (2011) found that Team Parenting did have the effect of engendering a sense of belonging to the parenting team in foster carers. They stated that 'many carers commented on the inclusive and respectful nature of the team [...] We are always discussing things together and we all make decisions on how to meet the child's needs. We always feel equal' (Staines *et al.* 2010, p.323).

There are many sources citing foster carers' desire to be seen as part of and included on the multi-disciplinary team who were caring together for looked-after children (e.g. McDonald, Burgess and Smith 2003; Pithouse *et al.* 2004; Wilson and Evetts 2006). Sinclair *et al.* (2004) found that foster carers felt dismayed and disillusioned when their views were overlooked and their expertise unrecognised. They wanted to be kept informed and empowered by social workers to use their own discretion in making decisions and judgements in their care of the young person. It seems that foster carers relished being treated as equals (McDonald *et al.* 2003) and that this, together with other factors, could greatly improve their satisfaction with the fostering experience. Robertson's (2006) premise is that more attention should be paid to the person with whom the child has *the most secure relationship* as a source of information. Logically this makes sense although historically, despite their far greater knowledge of the young person by virtue of them living together, the views of foster carers have often been discounted. Team Parenting sought to counteract this, valuing foster carers for the demanding and unrelenting task they undertook with young people who often rejected the care that was on offer. Supporting and training foster carers to work with this, resisting the induction to reject the young person, and find subtle inroads into enabling a trusting relationship to be formed is part of the ambition behind making foster carers primary agents of change:

> It is important that agencies understand the crucial part that foster carers play in nurturing and supporting children and realise that support to carers links to issues of stability, permanence and militates against placement breakdown. Nonetheless, the status of carers is a hotly contested issue. (Hek *et al.* 2010, p.3)

PLACEMENT STABILITY AS A PRIMARY GOAL

Research has consistently indicated that recurrent changes in placement are correlated with poorer outcomes for looked-after children (e.g. Leve *et al.* 2012; Macdonald and Turner 2005; Pithouse *et al.* 2004; Rubin *et al.* 2007). Placement breakdown negatively impacts on a young person's emotional and normative development, leading to negative psychological consequences that further exacerbate the risk of future breakdown. This dynamic is neatly described by Macdonald and Turner (2005, p.1266), who explicate how children whose placements end unexpectedly:

> are likely to experience more rejection and to develop ever more defensive ways of managing an unpredictable world. They are less likely to establish intimate relationships with subsequent carers, and more likely to exhibit behaviours which keep carers (and others) at arm's length.

Placement disruptions not only damage a young person's psychological and emotional resources but have far-reaching effects into other areas of their lives. Invariably the end of a placement signals not only the loss of an on-going relationship with a foster carer but also the termination of peer relationships both in the community and at school, discontinuity of school experience (which disrupts education) and loss of belonging to a particular area of which the young person has been a part (Cocker and Scott 2006; Leve *et al.* 2012; Price *et al.* 2008). All of these factors will injure a young person's developing sense of self and their identity. By contrast, stable care in a family environment can provide the opportunity for an on-going, warm, nurturing relationship with a caregiver and continuity of experience both in education and with peer and social relationships. When foster care placements are stable, they can mediate against some of the adverse experiences which young people have endured before they came into care (Price *et al.* 2008).

Whilst it is acknowledged that placement instability has a negative impact on young people in foster care, the precise role this has had in reducing well-being has been difficult to measure given a large number of other variable factors at play. Rubin *et al.* (2007) conducted a study to identify how placement instability affected behavioural outcomes. They singled out other contextual factors which could contribute to placement stability and instability – for example, the age of the child at the time of placement, the types of behaviour being exhibited at the time of placement, previous care experiences and mental health issues on the part of the birth parents. However, they found that, even taking these into account, stability tended to demonstrate greater well-being for young people at follow-up 18 months into placement. Thus, placement stability plays a part in reducing poor outcomes irrespective of what attributes the child brings, although behavioural difficulties at placement are also a strong predictor. This demonstrates the importance of working to enhance placement stability as it is clear that doing so will lead to improved outcomes for young people entering care. Rubin *et al.* (2007, p.341) argue that there is *compelling evidence* for this, concluding that:

> Regardless of a child's baseline risk for instability in this study, those children who failed to achieve placement stability were estimated to have a 36 per cent to 63 per cent increased risk of behavioural problems compared with children who achieved stability in foster care.

Studies consistently report that there is strong association between placement disruption and challenging behaviours on the part of the young person (e.g. Chamberlain *et al.* 2008a, 2008b; Leve *et al.* 2012; Macdonald and Turner 2005; Rubin *et al.* 2007; Price *et al.* 2008). Chamberlain *et al.* (2008a, 2008b) found a correlation between behaviour problems and placement instability with every additional challenging behaviour over six in a 24-hour period, resulting in a 17 per cent increased risk of placement breakdown over the next 12 months. Externalising behaviours on the part of young people present a risk to foster carers in terms of their own stress levels, well-being and satisfaction with the fostering task. Chamberlain *et al.* (2008a, 2008b) cite psychological difficulties of looked-after children and the resulting behavioural challenges as one of the prime reasons for foster carers exiting the role.

Thus, increasing placement stability would play a major part in improving outcomes for young people on all levels. Achieving placement stability thus became one of the predominant goals of Team Parenting. The feedback loop between behavioural difficulties, placement stability, foster carer well-being and foster carer-effectiveness was recognised. Therefore, Team Parenting directed its efforts to improve placement stability by targeting its interventions at foster carers. The intention was to improve foster carer skill and capacity in managing behaviour via training, support and therapeutic intervention. Improving placement stability as a goal of Team Parenting thus drew upon one of the major premises of the approach detailed above – that foster carers should be and are the primary agents of change.

The range of interventions offered to foster carers to assist with this endeavour is detailed more thoroughly in the following chapters. Suffice to say that these interventions aimed to:

- improve foster carer skill and technique in managing behaviours

- augment foster carer understanding in the emotional meaning of these behaviours with the intention of reducing them

- enrich the quality of the foster carer/child relationship with the assistance of theoretical knowledge regarding the importance of attachment and attuned and sensitive caregiving

- strengthen foster carer resilience

- intensify support to foster carers

- increase foster carer satisfaction with their role and impart a sense of their contribution and expertise being valued as well as the demands of the task being understood.

This wide-ranging set of objectives goes further than some of the interventions described in the literature. Chamberlain *et al.* (2008a, 2008b) point to research that has correlated externalising difficulties with poor parenting techniques. They highlight that there is an evidence base that suggests that improving effective parenting will result in reduced challenging behaviours. Their intervention is thus a parenting intervention and focuses on positive reinforcement as a technique to reduce externalising behaviour. Whilst they find their intervention achieves positive results, they acknowledge that this only accounts for partial amelioration of the behaviours. They hypothesise that other facets that weren't measured, such as the attachment relationship between child/carer, could play a part. Team Parenting aims to operate on a multi-faceted level, directing interventions in a range of different ways to assist in stabilising placements for young people. There is some support for this in the literature. Pithouse *et al.*

(2004) argue that foster carers need to provide warm, attuned and sensitive caregiving and respond to behavioural challenges with understanding and not rejecting the child. They postulate that prior experience and training on its own are not enough and that continuity of support and the quality of the foster carer/supervising social worker relationship are important. They conclude that adequately supported and skilled foster carers can reduce placement disruption.

This does seem to be borne out by the experience of foster carers who have been part of the Team Parenting approach. Staines *et al.* (2011, p.321) find that the majority of carers who provided written comments about the success or otherwise of their placements felt that Team Parenting practice was key to placement success, especially the support offered and the teamwork approach:

> From the beginning things would only get better, improved parenting and people working together has made him a joy to care for […] The fact that we are very understanding. We have learnt a lot on IFA courses helping us to understand, the fact that we are supported by the parenting team.

DEFINING TEAM PARENTING AS AN APPROACH

Hek *et al.* (2010) postulate that social work practice is made up of both theoretical ideas and models of delivery. The theory provides a conceptual framework to a set of ideas. Theories seek to explain, describe and sometimes predict change. Team Parenting is influenced by a number of theories, most predominantly attachment theory (Bowlby 1969), systemic theories from Family Therapy (Carr 2006; Cecchin 1987), social learning theory and resilience theory (Gilligan 1997, 2001, 2008; Rutter 1999; Schofield and Beek 2005b). It draws these theories together into an overarching framework of delivery. Models can be used by 'different people in different contexts' (Hek *et al.* 2010) and often draw on a range of theoretical bases. With this in mind it would seem plausible that Team Parenting could be described as a model. However, it is not a model in the way of MST or MTFC. It is not prescriptive or sequential and it does not demand absolute fidelity in delivery. Instead, it operates from within a therapeutic domain where each chosen intervention is designed to fit the presenting clinical need.

It is the interplay of social work and therapy within Team Parenting which perhaps causes some confusion regarding its status. Whilst social work is drawn to models, therapy is traditionally engaged in contemplation of the unfolding process of what is occurring between client and therapist to effect change. Team Parenting is an inherently therapeutic model – its whole design is premised on the fact that it sees fostering as a therapeutic task (Staines *et al.* 2011), that young people with histories of trauma will have needs that can best be addressed via therapeutic parenting and that an understanding of emotional and psychological forces (the provinces of therapy) will assist all members of the parenting team to adjust their practice and hone their skills. Reducing ways of working to technical tasks *seriously undercuts* the complexities of needing to constantly engage the 'client' in an on-going process in order for therapeutic change to be achieved (Flaskas 1997).

Given this need for therapeutic *fit* (Flaskas 1997) between the presenting need and the intervention delivered, a strict adherence to a tightly defined model would undermine the therapeutic basis of Team Parenting. When working with individuals, couples, families or groups, therapists tend to operate within a constant feedback loop, where they assess continually the intra-psychic and interpersonal dynamics before them. They utilise their observations and connect these with their theoretical knowledge to inform them of the best way in which to proceed. Noticing the impact of their chosen intervention allows for a further period of assessment and observation before they intercede again. Team Parenting works in this way and it is this therapeutic intent that gives rise to its fluidity, flexibility and adaptive delivery style.

SUMMARY – KEY COMPONENTS OF TEAM PARENTING

Team Parenting suggests the following:

- A looked-after child should be 'surrounded' by carers and professionals who understand his/her emotional, cognitive, behavioural, social, educational and developmental needs.

- This network of carers and professional will lead to the creation of a metaphoric 'therapeutic community' around the young person.

- Each member of the parenting team comprehends the depths of the psychological need of the young person and interacts with him/her, within their own role, with therapeutic intent.

- The impact of early, relational traumatic experiences is likely to impede a young person's ability to form attachments.

- A child's attachment difficulties are often central to their inability to fulfil their potential.

- Looked-after children have specific therapeutic needs because of their history and experiences.

- A young person's behaviour may be an expression of survival within their history of trauma and poor attachment.

- A young person's early experiences are likely to be 'acted out' again at a later date, either by them or by the wider system.

- Foster carers should be supported within a process of understanding, empathy and non-blame, given the enormously challenging task they undertake.

- Foster carers, due to their potential presence as attachment figures for the young person, are best placed to be the 'primary agents of change'.

- A systemic approach that works to combat the fragmentation and fracturing of the lives of looked-after children, will promote placement stability and cohesive care.

- A dynamic, vivid and experiential appreciation of how a child has come to be the way they are is essential for professionals and carers if they are to intervene effectively.

- 'Emotionally intelligent' team members should be willing and able to consider how they interact with and impact on the system and vice versa.

In essence, Team Parenting is about bringing together those professionals involved in the young person's life in order to provide a cohesive, full picture of the child and as a result maintain stability and encourage well-being. The young person is surrounded by carers and professionals who aim to work collaboratively in order to understand and support the emotional and developmental needs of that young person.

In this chapter some key features of Team Parenting have been set out. These include integrated working between those involved, the role of foster carers as primary agents of change, the priority given to placement stability as the key outcome and why Team Parenting is described as an approach rather than a model. Chapter 4 moves on to therapeutic interventions in Team Parenting, including attachment theory, re-enactment and therapeutic parenting.

THERAPEUTIC INTERVENTIONS IN TEAM PARENTING

CONSULTATION WITH FOSTER CARERS

CHAPTER CONTENTS

Support for foster carers

Knowledge
    Attachment theory
    Re-enactment/projective identification
    Complex trauma and neuroscience

Skills
    Therapeutic parenting – attunement
    Therapeutic parenting – reflective function
    Therapeutic parenting – self regulation/affect regulation

Case study

Young people in the care system are amongst the most, if not *the* most, disadvantaged and vulnerable children in our society. This has been evidenced by the study of Meltzer *et al.* (2003). Looked-after children have often experienced an early history of deprivation, trauma, neglect and abuse. The consequences of such experiences can lead them to struggle in their relationships, experience cognitive-processing impairments and be unable to regulate their emotions adequately. The latter can make them particularly difficult to care for as their unprocessed emotions are expressed messily and loudly via their behaviour. Behaving either in defensive, aggressive and controlling ways or in submissive, withdrawn and non-engaging ways is liable to alienate those who endeavour to look after them. The risks inherent in this fragile situation reach calamity when what could have been a sound and nourishing foster placement breaks down. Faced with repeated rejections and placement moves, young people invariably act to protect their already delicate self-esteems and invest less with each repeated attempt. The end result of this bleak and emotionally empty landscape is that looked-after children are far more likely than the rest of the childhood population to experience mental health difficulties, become homeless, misuse drugs or alcohol, engage in offending behaviour and find themselves in prison (Cameron and Maginn 2008; Hart and Thomas 2012; Macdonald and Turner 2005).

Given this situation, it seems imperative to militate against these outcomes, and ensure that looked-after children are provided with the opportunity to flourish in a nurturing environment with caregivers who can facilitate their optimal development and healing from past trauma. This is what Team Parenting aims to do, and in working towards achieving these objectives, it recognises that foster carers are in the best position to reach these goals. This prioritising of foster carers as the primary agents of change for children is recommended in the literature. A study by Rushton and Minnis (2002) found that the only interventions that could be evidenced to reduce behavioural problems of looked-after children were those that were delivered by foster carers. Cameron and Maginn (2008, p.1154) state that:

> emotional well-being, social adjustment and educational attainment are inextricably linked and that it is only by experiencing good parenting and appropriate emotional support […] that children and young people in care will be able to enhance their personal, social and intellectual development.

Hart and Thomas (2012) echo this, claiming that where attachment issues are paramount, indirect work with parents may be more effective than direct work with children. The premise for their position is attachment and the central role this plays in a child's social competence, resilience, emotional regulation, self-reflective capacity and executive functioning. However, in order for foster carers to be best placed to succeed at such a task, they need to be well equipped to face the challenges that these young people present to them. Placements can all too easily be derailed when foster carers lack sufficient armoury to endure the baffling and confusing dramas that are played out in their own homes. Ensuring that foster carers are best placed to manage their role involves providing them with the knowledge, skills and support they need to undertake this task.

Consultation with foster carers by therapists is one of the therapeutic interventions provided within Team Parenting. Consultation aims to achieve the furnishing of foster carers with support, knowledge and skills. Team-based therapists meet with foster carers once it has been identified that they and/or their placement might be in need of additional input. The frequency of these sessions, their location and the duration of the work are decided between the therapist and the foster carers. In the initial meeting the therapist will informally assess the areas which most need to be worked on and adjust her intervention accordingly. Usually, all three areas – support, knowledge and skills – are covered. They might not be delineated so clearly to the foster carers, and often the overlaps in subject matter and material mean that moving from one area to another runs seamlessly and indistinguishably. However, for the purpose of clarity, it is useful to separate them out here and discuss each one in turn.

SUPPORT FOR FOSTER CARERS

It is very difficult to describe adequately the havoc that a traumatised child can wreak in one's previously intact and functioning home (Cairns 2002a; Howe and Fearnley 1999; Ironside 2004). Despite being forewarned of the behavioural challenges they are likely to encounter both through the assessment process and their initial training, many foster carers feel bewildered and confounded when faced with some of the behaviours which children in the care system present. People train to be foster carers for different reasons (Beek and Schofield 2004; Sebba 2012). However, regardless of their initial and primary motivation, the majority of people who become foster carers do so with the intention of making a positive difference to the lives of the children who enter their homes. Faced then with a baffling array of destructive behaviours – lying, stealing, hitting, soiling, wetting, hurting pets, hoarding food, absconding – to name just a few, foster carers can quickly become disillusioned, despairing and debilitated by the situation in which they find themselves.

Ironside (2004, p.39) calls this 'living a provisional existence'. In fact, the literature is saturated with dense descriptions of the struggles that foster carers experience (Cairns 2002a; Howe and Fearnley 1999; Hughes 2006; Ironside 2004.) The dilemma that foster carers find themselves in is described with empathy. Howe and Fearnley (1999, p.24) describe how frequently the more love that is offered, the more rejecting the child becomes. In fact, 'all attachment-related issues seem to lead to arousal and aggression, none of which appears to make sense to well-meaning others, especially new, loving carers'.

Ironside (2004, p.40) describes how such experiences can lead to a dismantling of the sense of self, so that '…it is the foster carer's experience of the loss of a comfortable sense of themselves and the description of the loss of hope and the sense of inner decay that is so resonant and absolutely pertinent to their situation'. She delineates graphically how foster carers become enmeshed in a frightened and frightening state of mind where the child they care for seems to have the ability to *penetrate their psychological defences*. This pernicious state of affairs needs some urgent support if all those involved are not to experience further emotional wounding.

When foster carers come for consultation with therapists, the damage done to their sense of selves can leave them in a place of emotional sterility and profound vulnerability. Clearly, as people, foster carers express their experiences in different ways, some with more openness and awareness than others. Cairns (2002a, p.7) expresses the hurt that foster carers may feel openly: 'It is intensely painful to live with a child who does not trust you, though you have never done them any harm or offered anything but loving care.'

Some foster carers describe feeling de-skilled and uncertain, that they are failing and that they are experiencing an inexorable erosion of their confidence and goodwill. However, others will not be able to identify this awareness so clearly and may defend themselves against this painful knowledge by behaving defensively and blaming the child. Either way, it is imperative that the therapist works hard to establish a safe and sound working alliance with the foster carer in consultation before any real work can be done.

Consultation is not therapy; its purpose is not the therapeutic healing or transformation of the foster carer's own material, but a space to allow the foster carer to come to think about the foster child in different ways, thus transforming their practice. However, for this process to be able to take place, foster carers need to feel safe and feel that they can be heard within a non-judgemental and trusting relationship. Given that most foster carers come to consultation when they are struggling with their child in placement, it is highly probable that they are not feeling safe. We know from attachment theory (Bowlby 1969, 1973, 1979) that when we do not feel safe our stress system is aroused. In situations of stress, we focus on survival (this is usually psychological, not physical, survival) and our exploratory system closes down (McCluskey, Hooper and Bingley Miller 1999). Under stress we reduce the range of strategies available to us (Chimera 2010) as we fall back on habitual and ingrained ways of coping. In order for foster carers to be able to take in new information and fresh thinking, they need to be free enough of stress to engage in an exploration with the therapist of the meaning behind the behaviour they are finding so difficult. It is the therapist's responsibility to create the conditions for this to occur and this will be primarily via the working relationship.

Thus, the therapist needs, in the first instance, to listen to the foster carer and to encourage open exploration of their feeling and thinking states of mind. This can only be achieved by offering a reflective space, where feelings can be heard and considered without the fear of being judged. Therapists need to impart to foster carers an understanding that it is accepted and natural that they will experience highly aroused and intense emotional states when caring for foster children. It is helpful for foster carers to know that therapists want to know about these emotional states and that they offer a containing, soothing presence and space where these overwhelming feelings can be thought about. This process offers not only relief, but also an opportunity for understanding. Bohart and Greenberg (1997, p.5–6, cited in McCluskey et al. 1999, p.83) suggest:

> being able to name an experience first makes the previously implicit explicit, thereby providing an improved sense of facilitation and comprehension of how one knows what one is experiencing. This in and of itself provides some clarity and relief from earlier confusion.

Being able to have different thoughts creates the possibility of different actions. When foster carers can think in new ways about the behaviour they are presented with, there is the potential for them to respond differently. This in turn opens up the way for children to behave differently too. It is, as Bateson (1972) said, the difference that makes the difference.

Hart and Thomas (2012) speak of the necessity of creating for carers a secure base with the therapist, from which they can explore what is occurring in the placement. They refer back to the Rogerian core conditions – empathy, congruence, warmth – and argue that these should be features of the therapist's relational style with the carer. They found that when this state existed, not only did it allow for a space to be opened up where the child's needs could be at the forefront of everyone's mind but that the carers the therapist worked with mirrored the therapist's style with the children: 'A cyclical model emerged in which the parents were consistently mirroring with the children the emotional contact and analytic framework embedded within the therapeutic work undertaken between the adults' (Hart and Thomas 2012, p.314).

Of course, establishing safety within the consultative relationship can only ever be temporary. Foster carers will find themselves repeatedly destabilised by the behaviours they encounter. McCluskey *et al.* (1999) describe the therapeutic process as having a cyclical existence. Empathic attunement or the 'intuitive grasp of the underlying emotional state' (McCluskey *et al.* 1999, p.84) to the foster carer's experience leads first to relief and then to the opportunity for understanding and thinking. Once this storm has been quelled, there is the opportunity for the introduction of new material. The exploration of fresh subject matter may initiate another period of emotional disquiet and disturbance. It is the therapist's role to manage the emotional arousal of the foster carer during these cycles so that thought can be applied to the difficulties being presented. Being able to reflect on the struggles being presented in a coherent and meaningful way allows for the foster carer to assume a meta-perspective to the difficulties in which they can otherwise feel embroiled. As the foster carer and therapist work together in this way, an attachment forms. This attachment (recommended by Hart and Thomas 2012) mirrors the careseeking, caregiving partnership Bowlby described as a feature of secure relationships (McCluskey *et al.* 1999). It is this partnership in consultation that enables foster carers to feel supported – even in their darkest moments – and able to engage in the fostering task honestly and with their whole selves.

KNOWLEDGE

This section explores three vital areas of knowledge that are covered during consultation with foster carers: attachment theory; re-enactment/projective identification; and complex trauma and neuroscience.

ATTACHMENT THEORY

Part of Team Parenting's operating therapeutic principles rest on attachment theory. Attachment theory was introduced by the psychoanalyst and psychiatrist John Bowlby in the 1960s and 1970s. Observations of infants in a nursery during the Second World War and reflections on the behaviour of delinquent boys led John Bowlby to his formulation that we now know as attachment theory. Bowlby's student, Mary Ainsworth, gave this theory empirical and scientific rigour by the use of her Strange Situation Test (Ainsworth *et al.* 1978).[1] This test appeared to demonstrate with some clarity the three different attachment styles that Bowlby described: secure, insecure ambivalent and insecure avoidant. Attachment theory has been added to over the years and the concept of a disorganised attachment style came into existence in the 1990s. This form of attachment is thought to most accurately reflect the style of those children and adults who may have an attachment disorder. George, Kaplan and Main (1985) have also utilised attachment theory to produce the Adult Attachment Interview. This interview tests adult attachment styles according to the coherence of adults' answers to a set of questions about their life story. Interestingly, Main (cited in Bowlby 2010) found an 86 per cent correlation between mothers' attachment styles when they were interviewed during pregnancy and their infants' attachment styles post-birth, using the Strange Situation Test.

It is useful to draw upon attachment theory during consultation with foster carers. The one-to-one nature of consultation gives the opportunity for therapists to check with foster carers their understanding of attachment theory and its practical application in their parenting of children and young people. There are certain key assumptions which attachment theory makes that are necessary for foster carers to know. These are:

- Attachment theory is an evolutionary concept (Schofield and Beek 2006). Its assumption is that our need to attach to a primary caregiver is based on a vital biological and instinctive

---

1   The process of the Strange Situation involves an infant (approximately 12 months old) being confronted with several stressful situations. She is introduced with her mother to a strange room where she plays for a while with some toys. A stranger then enters the room. A short while later, her mother leaves. Later, her mother returns and they are reunited. Then both the stranger and the mother leave the room, meaning that she is on her own. The way that she manages these separations and reunifications denote her attachment style.

drive to survive. Seeking proximity to a caregiver will ensure our survival. This is true for all species but especially so for human beings as our infants are particularly vulnerable at birth:

> This little scrap of humanity is […] utterly dependent for her very survival on the goodwill of those who nurture her […] Yet right from birth the baby does show behaviours which actively contribute to her own survival. When placed under stress such as hunger, discomfort or fear, the baby produces distinctive activity which serves to draw the attention of a caregiver. We call this activity attachment behaviour. (Cairns 2002b, p.48)

- Our need as human beings to form attachments to others lasts a lifetime. As we grow older, we form new attachment relationships that may become more figural for us than our primary ones. However, the primary ones, if good enough and secure, are not replaced. Therefore, during adolescence, attachment to the peer group becomes important and in adulthood attachment relationships within a sexual partnership become appropriate life-stage goals. However, these relationships co-exist with the early attachment relationships and it is not unusual for happily married/ partnered adults with children of their own to turn to their parents in times of stress. 'These long-term relationships identify the strongest attachments. The continually changing nature of such lifetime bonds helps individuals achieve a strong sense of identity, self-worth and responsibility' (Fahlberg 1991, p.23).

- Attachment forms over a period of time between an infant and a caregiver, when a caregiver is able to recognise, understand and meet the infant's needs. This process of needs being met is best delineated by the arousal/relaxation cycle which demonstrates how infants experience a frequent and shifting awareness of need. In the early days this is usually physiological as they come to grips with their own physical system existing independently and needing to function separately from their mother's body. Later, their needs will become emotional, cognitive and psychological.

Figure 4.1 demonstrates the eternal flow of awareness of need, expression of need, satisfaction, rest and then on into a fresh awareness of new need.

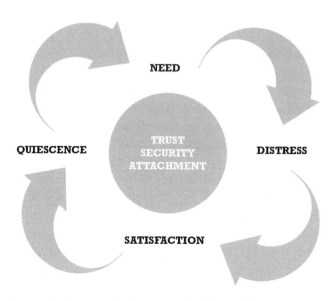

Figure 4.1: The arousal relaxation cycle (from Fahlberg 1991, p.33)
Source: Reproduced with kind permission from BAAF.

- When this cycle is mostly what the infant/child experiences, then she will grow up to have a positive view of the world. Bowlby (1973) used internal working models to delineate how children and young people with different experiences of their early attachment relationships will view the world in opposing ways. Thus, a securely attached child is likely to grow up believing that she is lovable, that other people can be trusted to take care of her and that the world is a safe place to be. By contrast, children and young people with insecure attachment styles may grow up feeling unlovable, that other people cannot be trusted and that the world is an unsafe and frightening place to inhabit. It is imperative that foster carers can vividly imagine how different life and relationships can feel to a child or young person whose trust has been broken at an early age and whose formative years have been about survival and not about growing up, thriving, exploring, learning and loving.

- Children and young people who are not brought up by adults who can attend to and meet their needs most of the time will find ways of managing the situation in the best way they can. Those who endure unmet needs as well as being abused, harmed and/or not protected by those who look after them will add further strategies to promote their optimal survival. This is known in the Gestalt Therapy literature as a creative adjustment (Clarkson 1989; Hycner 1991; Mackewn 1997; Perls, Hefferline and Goodman 1951; Yontef 1993). As living organisms, our instinctive drive to survive ensures that we adapt to our circumstances in ways that ensure the likelihood of our continued existence. This can mean that children and young people with insecure attachment styles or a disorganised attachment style use extreme forms of behaviour for self-protection. Thus, some of the behavioural features of a child or young person with an attachment disorder can be a compulsive need to control others, oppositional and defiant behaviour, intense lying even when caught in the act, a lack of eye contact, indiscriminately charming and friendly behaviour, easily replaced relationships, lack of empathy, poor understanding of cause and effect, poor communication skills, pervasive shame, all-or-nothing thinking, habitual disassociation or hyperarousal and vigilance. It is the place of consultation to unpack the meaning behind these behaviours and comprehend their survival value to the child or young person when they lived in more hostile surroundings. This knowledge is vital if the foster carer is to be able to move from perceiving the child or young person as 'naughty' and 'ungrateful' to utilising old coping methods to manage what they perceive as a threatening and dangerous world.

In recommending an understanding of attachment theory and comprehension of how a child or young person's behaviour can change when their attachment needs are inadequately met, it is necessary to be aware of the limitations of this theoretical map. Attachment theory is a theory and not a truth; it is important not to confuse the map with the territory. Certain schools of thought, such as social constructionism, would balk at the definitive language and presumptions made by such a theory. Indeed Barth *et al.* (2005), whilst not denying attachment theory's usefulness, warn against the predictive way it has been used in the literature. They explicate that a child or young person's early history is not a definitive predictor of future outcomes. Rather, early traumatic experiences are liable to lead to the development of neural pathways that are likely to be associated with adult pathology. Moreover, they stress that while attachment difficulties may *predispose* a child to behavioural problems, their current environment needs to be considered too (Barth *et al.* 2005). They criticise the unilateral direction of change recommended by some of the attachment therapies in the literature (Dozier 2003; Cairns 2002b) and cite Steele (2003), who believes that the concept of attachment disorders is a dubious one.

These criticisms bear weight as negatively predicting outcomes for a child or young person based on their early experiences has the potential to be damaging, limiting and unhelpful. Moreover, such a tendency would be to fly in the face of the premise of therapeutic interventions and the recent findings of neuroscience, both of which point to an optimistic recognition of the capacity of human beings to change and adapt to their new circumstances. It is pertinent that Barth *et al.* (2005) suggest that any intervention to assist a foster or adopted child should take into account their foster carer's family ecology and history. Hart and Thomas (2012) echo this too, stating that it must be acknowledged that carers bring their own attachment histories to the equation and these should be considered as well. The expected direction of change, therefore, should not be one way. Moreover, it is often foster carers who will have more capacity to adapt their responses than foster children or young people, who, still hyperaroused, fearful and distrusting of new relationships, will have limited ability to change their behaviour for some time. Thus, even though foster carers may not have caused the initial problems in the child or young person's behaviour, it is through changing their parenting style that further difficulties may be militated against.

Consultation with foster carers by a therapist creates the opportunity for exploration into parenting styles and strategies to take place. The next section on skills and therapeutic parenting (see p.114) explores some of the approaches that may be used by foster carers in their endeavour to become therapeutic parents. Team Parenting, though, while recognising that the jury is out on whether the actual diagnosis of attachment disorder exists, still makes use of the concept. This is primarily to help foster carers to make sense of the varied and bewildering behaviour they are likely to encounter during their careers. In addition, it is also to free them from inhabiting a defensive, self-critical position and to lead them to one where they can engage empathically with the child and young person's brave and courageous struggle to endure the harshness of their early existence.

RE-ENACTMENT/PROJECTIVE IDENTIFICATION

When foster carers understand the function of some of the challenging behaviours they encounter with the children or young people that they foster, it is easier to comprehend the meaning of their alienating and pernicious behaviour strategies. Keeping a low profile in a violent family, learning not to expect nurture and warmth, and seeing oneself as unlovable and undeserving are ways of avoiding disappointment for children and young people who have been neglected and abused (Macdonald and Turner 2005). It is also a way of arriving at some kind of formulation as to why they have received the treatment they have (Macdonald and Turner 2005). However, these adaptive strategies do not disappear upon entry into a foster home where good quality care is on offer. For the foster child or young person, new relationships are as much a source of threat to them as previous ones, for what they have learnt is that other people are not to be trusted to behave predictably or in ways that will keep them safe. They therefore employ similar behavioural tactics with their foster carers to protect themselves from what they imagine will be further harm. Price (2003, p.52) calls these repetitive behaviour patterns that looked-after children revert to, *roadmaps*, and says that 'traumatised children create multiple, internal attachment models; under stress they appear to revert to the 'roadmaps' relating to their original caregivers'.

It is sometimes difficult for foster carers to comprehend how children and young people continue to perceive them as potential purveyors of harm, when all they want to offer is good quality care and a home. Schofield and Beek (2006) describe how all of us have pre-verbal, unconscious, procedural memories stored in our brains. These create felt memories of situations. A sense of being loved and well cared for or a sense of fear and unpredictability could inhabit these memories. These memories create a flavour for us of what the world is like. They engender within us a predictive strategy where we remember and expect to see our previous experiences repeated. This mechanism means that we see what we expect to see. It is easier to fit our expectations of others into boxes than use new information to change the boxes (Schofield and Beek 2006). Living in this way imbues the world with some certainty and predictability. As Cairns (2002a, p.8) says:

> our fundamental assumptions about the world are not just beliefs, but are taken by us to be facts. We cannot distinguish between experiential facts – the three-dimensional presence of the table on which my computer sits – and our core beliefs about the universe as we perceive it.

Acting upon their beliefs and expectations that caregivers are a potential source of harm, children and young people continue to engage in the behaviours they utilised to promote their survival in previous abusive situations. Whilst these destructive behaviours were needed in the past to keep them safe, invariably with foster carers such behaviours can set up a repetitive cycle that further decreases the likelihood of them experiencing stable, accepting and life-affirming care. According to Macdonald and Turner (2005, p.1226) 'believing you are unlovable and that everyone rejects you can eventually lead to patterns of increasingly "testing" behaviour that can indeed defeat the most determined carer'.

Behaviour problems are correlated with placement breakdown leading to further experiences of reflection and defensiveness (Macdonald and Turner 2005). Without awareness of the likelihood of this repetitive cycle, foster carers and foster children and young people can find themselves locked into a vicious pattern. This plays out where a child or young person's self-protection strategy leads them to disengage from the care on offer and resist the warmth and nurture they are offered. Experienced as being rejecting of the efforts and goodwill of the foster carers, they are then rejected in turn. This situation can easily arise with foster carers who are not prepared for the strength of feeling that looking after such hurt and damaged children and young people can induce in them.

Consultation with a therapist gives foster carers the opportunity to express how they feel, being at the receiving end of extremes of behaviour which can threaten their self-confidence and goodwill. However, it also provides the forum for foster carers to begin to appreciate that such behaviour has, in the past, been a way for children and young people to manage the trauma they experienced and remain in control – thus, one hopes, decreasing the likelihood of further injury or harm (Cameron and Maginn 2008; Howe 2005). This understanding is particularly crucial for foster carers when they are faced with a child whose behaviour can be 'perceived as deliberately vindictive and hurtful and who may frequently reject/spurn/exploit acts of carers' (Cameron and Maginn 2008, p.1167). Achieving a visceral appreciation of the bleakness of the inner worlds of children and young people whose trust has been destroyed can help foster carers achieve a state of empathy and depersonalise the battles that are fought in their own homes. Perceiving that a child 'may feel that his inner world is irretrievably in ruins and may do his utmost to reduce his outside world to an equally devastated state' (Kegerreis 1995, p.103) can allow foster carers insight into the psychological processes at work.

This psychological process that leads foster carers to want to reject their foster child in the way that they feel rejected by the child is known as 'projective identification' in the psychoanalytic literature (Cashdan 1988; Ogden 1982). Richard Delaney (2006) wrote about this process with specific reference to foster children and called it re-enactment. The theoretical construct behind this process is that we recreate in the present our experience of the past by virtue of our current behaviour. Thus, if our expectation of others is that they will reject us, we are likely to behave in ways that makes fulfilment of this belief more probable. For example, we may be withdrawn and disengaged or we may seek to reject others first and behave dismissively and aggressively. This process is believed to occur in individual psychotherapy, where the therapist can feel induced to behave in complementary ways to her client's early experiences. If the therapist unconsciously responds *behaviourally* to the induction, then this is projective identification.

Ogden (1982) delineates four types of projective identification: dependency, power, sexuality and ingratiation. Delaney's (2006) theory of re-enactment bears striking resemblance to that of projective identification. He describes how a foster child may behave in a challenging way which is likely to induce a critical, punitive response from the foster carer. This response confirms for the foster child that she is unlovable and that other people can't be trusted to care for her safely. Having her internal working model confirmed leads the foster child to behave in more extreme ways as the need for self-preservation kicks in. Delaney (2006, p.47) neatly delineates this process in the form of a diagram, reproduced on the following page:

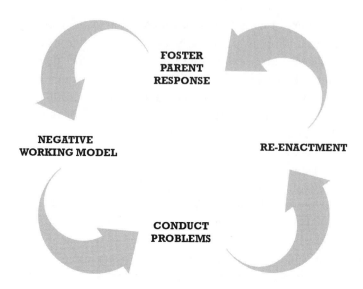

Figure 4.2: The re-enactment cycle (from Delaney 1991)
Reproduced with permission of the author.

When such a process is at work, foster carers can find themselves feeling and responding in unfamiliar ways:

> Foster and adoptive parents feel [...] unsettling levels of rage, depression, frustration, anxiety, ambivalence, confusion, inadequacy, sexual attraction, revulsion and/or withdrawal. They often wonder if they are going crazy and they might even fear they would abuse the child. In addition, dormant, unresolved issues from their own past may be re-awakened by the presence of the disturbed child in their midst. (Delaney 2006, p.60)

Foster carers have talked about unrecognisable feelings and urges in themselves in response to their foster child's behaviour. This is Ironside's (2004) *provisional existence* and can lead foster carers to feel unhinged. It is important therefore that they understand that they are receiving a non-verbal psychological communication from their foster child. If they can recognise the invitation to behave in a certain way, for example to reject the foster child, and *not* act on it, then therapeutic parenting can begin. However, for this to occur they will need the support of a therapist to debrief their own emotional experience and to be able to cognitively analyse the processes at work.

When there is not the opportunity for this consultation to take place, the placement faces very real danger of breaking down. Delaney (2006, p.42) states: 'Many foster, kinship, and adoptive parents feel trapped in déjà vu – unwitting prisoners of their foster child's past. To them it feels like they have become reluctant actors in a recurring drama written during the child's earliest years and replayed in their home'.

Dozier *et al.* (2001) have found such processes at work even with infants, where foster carers unconsciously mirror the baby's attachment style. Infants with rejecting and disengaging behaviours induce in their carers less responsive and lower warmth care. They conclude that foster carers need training to understand this dynamic and to be able to respond differently and therapeutically to their charges. Within Team Parenting it is the role of the therapist to provide such training via consultation sessions where therapeutic parenting strategies and approaches can be discussed.

COMPLEX TRAUMA AND NEUROSCIENCE

Before moving on to explore the strategies employed by therapeutic parenting, it is necessary to consider one further domain of knowledge that it is useful to share with foster carers in consultation. This is the expanding body of knowledge in relation to our understanding of complex trauma and the field of neuroscience. Whilst there is some debate about the usefulness of the concept of attachment disorder, it is increasingly accepted that many, if not most, looked-after children will have suffered complex trauma and it is the necessity of ending this experience that has brought them into care. The word 'trauma' is used to describe events that are distressing, perceived as dangerous, harmful or life-threatening, that overwhelm a person's capacity to cope and that have a long-lasting effect and could not have been prevented or controlled (Cairns 2002b; van der Kolk 2005). Complex trauma differs from trauma *per se* by virtue of the fact that it is likely to be chronic, that is on-going and repeated. It is also endured at a time of life when the cognitive capacity of the brain is not yet fully developed and is therefore unable to process the events involved in the trauma as they unfold. In addition, complex trauma impacts on the normal trajectory of development and affects the emerging structure of the brain. Due to their dependency needs, children and young people are particularly vulnerable to complex trauma. Complex trauma is invariably inflicted on its victims by those who purport to care for them. With looked-after children this is often parents or carers or other adults in positions of trust or authority.

Consultation for foster carers is essential in order to create within them an understanding of the impact of complex trauma on a developing mind. Team Parenting does not require foster carers to become neuroscientists or experts in the field of neural psychology. However, it is necessary to comprehend the emotional, psychological, physiological and cognitive ramifications of complex trauma. We know from attachment theory that, when aroused or stressed, children seek proximity to their caregiver. If the caregiver can offer comfort and soothing, then the child's emotions will be regulated and they can return to their play and exploratory behaviour. However, when the source of the arousal *is* their caregiver, this places them in a psychological dilemma. Howe (2010, p.28) calls this 'fear without escape, fright without solutions' while Archer (2003, p.80) articulates this as 'an inescapable paradox within which the youngster must seek vital comfort and security from the very source of his distress'.

In this situation children are unable to modulate their arousal and this 'causes a breakdown in their capacity to process, integrate and categorise what is happening. At the core of traumatic stress is a breakdown in the capacity to regulate internal states' (van der Kolk 2005, p.403). The impact of such experiences is long lasting and multiple, leading to:

- difficulty regulating affect and impulses
- problems with memory and attention span
- distorted sense of self and self-perception
- difficulties in forming and maintaining relationships
- somatisation (physical symptoms)
- inhibited reasoning and understanding
- inability to evaluate external stimuli
- inability to verbalise traumatic episodes
- reduced reflective function.

Trauma affects various aspects of the brain. Improvements in imaging techniques (Cameron and Maginn 2008; Cozolino 2010) have been able to provide visual evidence of impairments in brain function in children who have endured complex trauma. Associations have been found between high cortisol and attachment disorganisation in infancy, which has been demonstrated to affect the brain's fronto-temporal areas, leading to mentalising deficits (Archer 2003).

What this means in practice for foster carers is that they are parenting children and young people who have reduced capacity to manage stress, who possess poor self-regulation skills and yet who are more likely to feel emotionally aroused than their securely attached and non-traumatised peers. The damage done to their developing neural networks, combined with the experience of repeated trauma and stress, will leave them in a position of being either hypervigilant or disassociated (Archer 2003; van der Kolk 2005). Hyperalert to the possibility of the repetition of traumatic events, they are unable to make use of their cognitive or emotional perceptions but instead respond to imagined threat rapidly, utilising their 'fight/flight/freeze' stress responses. Furthermore, trapped in an over-reliance on their state-dependent memory, very low levels of stress are required before 'an entire, neurobiological chain reaction is set off over which the child has gained little conscious control' (Archer 2003, p.86). This means they exhibit extreme reactions to what may appear low-key events. They are primed for survival mode and they are unable to make use of the soothing, containing care of foster carers to regulate their emotions. Thus, as van der Kolk (2005, p.403) states: 'Many problems of traumatized children can be understood as efforts to minimize objective threat and to regulate their emotional distress'.

Foster carers need to understand that the structures of children and young people's brains are affected by complex trauma. They will have less access to their thinking brain (the pre-frontal cortex) and be more reliant on impulsive, instinctive reactions. They will behave in ways that are out of proportion to the actual event and they will perceive threat where there is none. For children and young people who have suffered complex trauma, their neural networks will take a different shape to children and young people who have known a life of safety, consistency and predictability. Authors such as Gerhardt (2004), Perry *et al.* (1995, 2002a, 2002b), Schore (1994), Schore (2003), Siegel (1999) and Sroufe (1997) are clear that our brains are experience dependent. This means that our brains are shaped by our environment and that heavily traumatic experiences will lead to certain neural networks being privileged over other ones in order to ensure survival. However, once removed from danger, these neural networks continue to operate. If foster carers can comprehend the structural impact of early trauma on the brain, they can come to appreciate the extreme challenges that the children and young people in their care have endured and that their perplexing, rejecting behaviour emanates from a lifelong struggle for survival.

However, whilst the optimal window for the development of our brains is the first three years of life (Gerhardt 2004), they do remain plastic across our lifetimes. This means that the possibility for new neural networks to be laid down remains ever present. With therapeutic parenting it is possible for traumatised children and young people to learn new ways of being in the world. Foster carers need to assimilate a degree of knowledge about how this process occurs. This is necessary, for such information will provide them with understanding as to the nature of the task ahead of them both, in its complexity but also in the potential for optimism. One hopes that if foster carers can comprehend the nature of the brain's plasticity and its responsiveness to the environment, they can also grasp the role they have to play in enabling new neural networks to be formed. Incorporating this knowledge into their practice will explicate the long-term nature of the endeavour as well as the crucial role they have to play in re-parenting the traumatised children and young people who populate the care system.

SKILLS

This section discusses the skills foster carers need if they are to become therapeutic parents. The three skills described here as components of therapeutic parenting are: attunement, reflective function and affect/self-regulation. These can be taught as part of foster carers' consultation sessions with therapists.

THERAPEUTIC PARENTING – ATTUNEMENT

Foster carers need to become therapeutic parents if they are to assist in repairing the damage children and young people have sustained before entering the care system. While parenting may appear to come naturally, the uncomfortable truth is that our parenting style emerges from pre-verbal experiences that occurred before our autobiographical memory came on line. 'When people speak to me about looking after babies they often talk in terms of "common sense". I ask them to consider the phrase: common sense is what you learned before you were two' (Cairns 2002b, p.47).

For the vast majority of parents engaged in parenting their birth children, this situation works adequately and optimally. However, children and young people who have suffered traumatic and abusive experiences in their early years will need a different quality of parenting (Cameron and Maginn 2008). As we have seen above, children and young people who have been rejected are likely to feel anger and resentment. Yet, they will probably bury and deny their painful emotions in order to protect themselves. They may therefore be emotionally unresponsive and consequently unrewarding to care for. Foster carers need to communicate warmth, acceptance and affection to children and young people, despite this situation. Their ambition should be to set about becoming a positive attachment figure for the child or young person (Cameron and Maginn 2008). By virtue of their everyday presence and their potential to offer a secure base to the child or young person, foster carers are in a far more promising position to facilitate recovery for traumatised children and young people than professionals outside of the home. It is how foster carers respond to the child or young person that contains the healing ingredient (Rocco-Briggs 2008).

Therapeutic parenting requires a twin-track approach of skilled, sensitive, attuned parenting to be offered alongside clear, firm boundaries. Cameron and Maginn (2008) recommend an authoritative style of parenting which incorporates boundaries, high expectations and warm, responsive care, with the aim of helping children and young people to feel accepted and validated. Attunement is a central quality of this type of parenting and is a relational style that comes naturally for most people in relating to babies. Cameron and Maginn (2008, p.1158) describes attunement thus:

> Underpinning secure attachment appears to be the key child-rearing process of 'attunement'. This occurs when a caregiver is not only aware of his or her emotions, but can also recognize how his or her child is feeling and can convey this awareness to the child. An attuned relationship is a prerequisite to the development of both security and empathy in the young child.

Fonagy, Bateman and Bateman (2011) call this process *marked, contingent mirroring*, when the carer can communicate verbally and/

or non-verbally an understanding of the child's emotion without becoming immersed in the same feeling state herself.

Attuned and sensitive caregiving provides children and young people with the opportunity to develop empathy, become self-reflective and process their traumatic experiences. It is crucial that foster carers appreciate their role in this and receive consultation and advice on how to facilitate this process. Foster carers need to feel comfortable embracing the emotional content of the child or young person's memories of their early, abusive experiences. Consultation with a therapist should work towards equipping them to be able to engage in appropriate conversations regarding memories and some of the distress children and young people feel, for, 'Mental health is not the absence of psychic pain, far from it. It is the ability to encounter it, tolerate it and develop through it. The children's difficulties are not caused solely by the overload of such pain, but rather by the attempt to avoid it' (Kerregies 1995, p.107).

Therapists can teach foster carers how to focus with the child on their affect when recalling certain events. Hughes (2004) suggests that Stern's (1985) *intersubjective sharing of affect* between mother and infant is the same concept as foster carer and child contemplating the same event, with the foster carer attuned to the child's affect. Attuning to the child in this way helps to regulate emotions which may be aroused by recalling traumatic memories. Living with the child provides opportunity for *countless moments of attunement* (Hughes 2004).

In this way, attuned foster carers can facilitate a process of emotional literacy whereby children and young people develop an awareness of their feeling states which are likely to have been hitherto unknown to them. Foster carers can do this by naming emotions and by role-modelling expression and management of their own emotions. This process is important as 'those who find it difficult to recognize and regulate their emotions rapidly get into social difficulty [...] Mental health is based on the ability to recognize, understand and regulate emotions' (Howe 2005, p.14).

Conversations about emotions may be initiated following behavioural outbursts. When the child or young person is calmer and more able to access their thinking, the foster carer can attune to them and wonder with them how they were feeling. For the child or young person, talking like this creates the opportunity to connect their feelings and behaviour. It also sows a reflective seed that suggests to children or young people that who and how they are now will be affected by the experiences they had in the past. Providing such an environment means that the children or young people can learn about trauma and how it may have affected them and at the same time have their arising feelings contained by the foster carer (Cameron and Maginn 2008). When children or young people are unable to articulate their memories, it is probably that they are pre-verbal, procedural and not linked to specific people or events. When this occurs, foster carers need to help the child or young person make the connections (Schofield and Beek 2006). They can wonder with the child how she may feel and how this might be related to historical events.

Foster carers need to initiate these conversations to demonstrate to the child or young person a willingness to engage with painful, emotional material. Being available in this way imparts a clear message to the child or young person that their foster carers are strong enough to withstand psychic pain and traumatic memories. It is these *everyday encounters* that offer the chances for reparative parenting (Cameron and Maginn 2008, p.1167). Hek *et al.* (2010) found that when carers are emotionally available in this way, children can be helped to overcome their difficulties. However, Team Parenting recognises the enormity of the challenge for foster carers in remaining attuned and sensitive to children or young people, given their often extreme and rejecting behaviours. This is why regular consultation with therapists is needed in order to offer non-judgemental, emotional support as well as impart skills in therapeutic parenting.

THERAPEUTIC PARENTING – REFLECTIVE FUNCTION

Foster carers' ability to offer attuned, sensitive care will greatly enhance a child or young person's ability to achieve reflective function. Reflective function, both of the self and others, is fundamental in navigating social relationships successfully. Primarily, as infants and young children we come to know ourselves by observing the responses of others to us. As Fonagy *et al.* (1991, p.203) explain:

> Our capacity to conceive of our subjective state is thus the consequence of our observations of the mental activity of others and our awareness of being observed. The mind, then, or at least the reflective self, is inherently interpersonal; and it evolves in the context of the infant–caregiver relationship.

Infants who receive attuned caregiving are able to develop a mental representation of their own psychological functioning as they grow older (Fonagy *et al.* 1991). This assists with affect regulation, empathy, mind-mindedness and mentalisation. However, children and young people who have suffered complex trauma at the hands of their previous caregivers (usually their birth parents) frequently have not been offered this quality of care. Instead, overwhelmed by their own vulnerabilities and dependency needs, these parents are incapable of mentalising for their infants and assisting them in developing a coherent sense of self. Instead, when faced with their child's unmet need they themselves collapse inwards into unbearable feelings of being out of control. Lacking the resources to manage their own affect in these circumstances, their reaction is often disorganised and aimed at quelling the source of their disturbance as soon as possible (Howe 2005). This is when abuse can occur. For these children and young people, the formation of their mind is fundamentally affected by their previous caregiver's incapacity to attune to them as separate beings with their own wishes, feelings, thoughts and intentions, and 'the child's reflective self develops in response to the psychic capacity of the caregiver' (Fonagy *et al.* 1991, p.207).

If our minds are formed in interaction with others (Howe 2005), then these children and young people grow up to perceive themselves as frightening individuals whose needs and wants engulf the coping capacities of their parents. Their parents, unable to mentalise for themselves or for their children, lack the capacity to attribute psychological meaning to their child's behaviour. This inability exacerbates their feelings of being out of control when faced with their child's behavioural expression of need or emotion. They are liable to misinterpret this and perceive their child as attacking and persecutory. The resulting position for the child is an unmet need, sometimes with the addition of a frightening and punitive parental response. In such situations they fall back on the types of defensive coping strategies that are typical of children who develop attachment disorders (Fonagy *et al.* 1991). In these circumstances, it is highly unlikely that the parent(s) will be able to comprehend that she/he may be the cause of the child's distress and adaptive behaviours.

When a parent has been able to be curious and interested in the child's developing mind, then the child will have the capacity to be curious about the minds of others and develop a coherent sense of self, self-esteem and efficacy (Howe 2005). However, for maltreated children whose caregivers have lacked the capacity to mentalise in this way, the self remains confusing and unknown, that is:

> where children are not receiving sensitive care in the early years of a kind that promotes the capacity to take the perspective of others and to be co-operative, children remain overwhelmed and muddled about their own and other's minds, often assuming the worst (that other people are hostile) when anxiety remains high. (Schofield and Beek 2006, p.20)

Feelings and emotions come to be associated with terror and unmanageable affect. They are therefore disowned and projected on to others in a bid by these children and young people to divest themselves of their feelings.

With this milieu as the backdrop for their early upbringing, children will be unable to identify, let alone reflect, on their feeling states or those of other people. This situation severely limits their capacity for social interaction. Emotions are exigent for us as social beings – they give us 'fast, unconscious responses to the unexpected and provide us with scripts for social interactions' (Howe 2005, p.12). Children and young people who are emotionally literate and can recognise their own emotions and those of others are socially competent. When one's own feeling states and those of others can be thought about and reflected upon, information becomes available which can guide behaviour and actions and be used to regulate the self. For example, children who are able to imagine how they would feel if their hair was pulled or their toy was grabbed, will be able to empathise with other children should that happen to them. Moreover, they will be able to use that information to manage their own behaviour, stopping themselves from acting inappropriately – no matter how great the impulse – due to imagining the other children's consequent feelings (Schofield and Beek 2006).

Given the lack of reflective function provided for them by their birth parents, foster carers will need to provide reparative and mentalising experiences in order to build for children and young people a reflective self which can function in relationship with others. This often means retracing developmental stages and attuning to children and young people in the way one would with an infant or toddler, mirroring their affective states and commenting upon them. This process has been called emotional scaffolding. In order to achieve this, it is necessary that foster carers are able to mentalise for themselves and for others. 'A caretaker with a predisposition to see relationships in terms of mental content permits the normal growth of the infant's mental function' (Fonagy *et al.* 1991, p.214). Mentalisation capacity in foster carers will also build an older child's mental function.

Schofield and Beek (2006) suggest teaching 'mind-mindedness' to foster carers to assist this process. They argue that foster carers need to develop the ability to see things from the child's point of view. In addition, they suggest that sensitive and available carers' minds will also help the child think about her own mind and that of others. Foster carers need time to practise their reflective function and mentalising skills. Consultation offers space for them to learn these skills, review their progress, receive feedback from therapists and integrate this into their practice. These sessions therefore provide an on-going learning environment where new skills and knowledge can be taught and then implemented in the home (Macdonald and Turner 2005).

THERAPEUTIC PARENTING –
SELF-REGULATION/AFFECT REGULATION

It has been referred to earlier in this chapter that fostering children and young people is liable to raise strong feelings in their caregivers. It is essential that foster carers are able to manage these strong feelings (Walker 2008). This is particularly poignant as the extremes of behaviour children and young people exhibit following early histories of abuse and neglect can deregulate the most composed of carers. Given this, it is critical that foster carers have resolved their own issues of trauma and loss. In addition, they need to have reflected on their own attachment systems as they will need to rely on the optimal functioning of these when faced with the destabilising behaviours they may be presented with when caring for children and young people with attachment difficulties (Hughes 2004). If foster carers are unable to manage their own painful feelings, they will be incapacitated in enabling foster children and young people to make sense of theirs (Walker 2008).

When foster carers are able to self-regulate, they are likely to respond warmly and sensitively to the children and young people in their care. In addition, they will be able to play a central role in facilitating affect regulation in children and young people. Affect regulation is widely accepted as being central to good mental health (Walker 2008). It can be defined as 'the ability to modulate or control the intensity or expression of feelings and impulses' (Walker 2008, p.2).

The ability to regulate emotions is believed to arise as a result of the type of care received in the early years. When infants and toddlers express their needs via their affect and their parents offer an attuned, containing response, then they will feel soothed and calm. Eventually, this process becomes internalised so that children grow up being able to self-regulate when away from their parents, even in moments of distress. However, when this process has not occurred adequately, children are liable to turn to other maladaptive ways to modulate their arousal. Such coping methods most commonly encompass aggression, acting-out behaviours, substance misuse, self-harm, eating disorders and hyperactivity. Faced with such behaviours, it is imperative for therapeutic parenting that foster carers are able to remain regulated. They will only be able to do so if they are comfortable with a wide range of emotions in themselves.

When foster carers are able to remain regulated and attuned even when confronted by provocative behaviours, the opportunity for therapeutic parenting occurs. Wilson, Petrie and Sinclair (2003) give a case study of just such a situation. The foster carer they describe is able to make use of difficult situations and turn them into healing encounters. Her reflective capacity means that even after behavioural challenges she is able to think about what has occurred with her foster son. Her ability to reflexively think about these episodes creates in him a curiosity regarding his behaviour and a burgeoning beginning of his own reflective capacity. The foster carer's skill in remaining calm and contained adds a healing element to their interactions, as evidenced by the fact that 'when responding to his difficult behaviour her voice tone is consistent, she remains near him, providing him both with a consistent presence and also an unhurried one' (Wilson et al. 2003, p.9).

Her understanding and empathy means that she is not personally hurt. Freed from a defensive position, she is able to help her foster son begin to understand his own feelings so he can, in the future, anticipate his own moods and alter a previous uncontrollable sequence of behaviours. This teasing out of the meanings behind behaviour with a foster child enables him to think reflectively (Schofield and Beek 2006). What previously may have been experienced as confusing and baffling behaviour now starts to make sense to him. The ability to interpret one's feelings in this way leads to the power to make different behavioural choices. This process facilitates the kind of 'cognitive restructuring' Cameron and Maginn (2008) recommend, where the child's strengths, resources, self-esteem and efficacy are built upon with the assistance of his foster carer. Wilson *et al.* (2003) see such work as the premise of good foster care, stating that looked-after children have problems with attachment, behaviour and self-esteem, and foster carers need to be able to address this effectively.

CASE STUDY

After 12 placement failures, Matt's carers were determined to see things through with Matt. However, they never expected it to be quite such a Herculean task and they needed regular consultation to sustain hope and resilience in the face of turbulent and baffling rages. By age 11, when Matt had been with his carers for a year, it had been necessary to call the police several times to contain his violent and threatening behaviour. But police meant nothing to Matt who had experienced police suddenly storming his birth parents' home to raid it for drugs, as well as prostitution and paedophilia with all its consequent commotion and brutality. Who was good and who was bad would have appeared quite a muddle to the small three-year-old Matt. Now aged 11, the police only seemed to disturb and excite him further.

I spoke with Matt's foster carers about how chaos and violence were more familiar to him than being emotionally reached and understood. We explored ways of how his carers might offer verbal containment to his hyperaroused state of mind. I encouraged them to speak to the part of Matt that remembered nobody being able to stop bad and terrible things from happening at home – except maybe with great force – and how he felt he had to fight to the death now to ensure he wasn't going to be cruelly and brutally treated himself. After reaching him in this way, and when calmed, they could then talk with him about how quick he was to feel his carers wanted to control and boss him about when trying to set limits, and how much he believed they just wanted to make him feel small and insignificant.

Matt's foster carers found it very difficult to understand how a child who had been 'rescued' at the early age of three-and-a-half would remember anything. They needed a lot of time and help to imagine and understand how his body could remember what his mind could not; what it would have been like living with a confused lack of structure, where Matt had to fight for physical and psychical survival. Given these circumstances, how could he possibly recognise what caring about or interest in him was? Perhaps he only knew what hostility was and how you had to fight to live.

Matt's big, strong male carer in particular would discuss with me how horrible it felt to be verbally abused and name-called 'paedophile' and 'abuser', and how threatened and frightened he felt by young Matt. We reflected how it made him feel very vulnerable and anxious and how him feeling this prevented Matt from feeling the frightened and powerless one. Because Matt's foster carer was open about his feelings, we were able to think about how Matt was getting rid of his own fears by pushing them onto his carer for him to feel instead. That way, Matt could feel the big, strong one in charge and not helpless anymore. We thought of various ways to respond meaningfully, including how much Matt believed his foster carer wanted him there just so he could crush and humiliate him.

After a great deal of time and painstaking effort processing and reflecting the emotional anxiety behind many an incident, Matt's dangerous and threatening behaviour began to subside and finally, after 18 months, it had disappeared at home and at school. I felt much moved to hear how grateful he felt to his carers for sticking with him and how now at last he felt he had a family of his own who really wanted him. This was marked and celebrated each night by his foster carers sitting together and naming each person belonging to their family – with Matt grinning from ear to ear when his name was mentioned. The fight had been worth it!

This chapter has explored consultation with foster carers as a therapeutic intervention and support for them in their role. The individual components of this consultation have been described. Chapter 5 goes on to discuss Team Parenting Meetings and their place within the overall Team Parenting approach.

THERAPEUTIC INTERVENTIONS IN TEAM PARENTING

TEAM PARENTING MEETINGS

CHAPTER CONTENTS

Team Parenting is an integrative and therapeutic model of care that embraces a holistic approach and multi-agency working. In many respects, Team Parenting Meetings are the epitome of Team Parenting. They are the forum where a group of professionals and carers come together to form the 'parenting team' that endeavours to care for each particular child in their placement. However, as Canavan *et al.* state (2009, p.380), '"Doing" integrated working is by no means simple or straightforward; it can be a complex process where a number of potential difficulties can serve to undermine or completely inhibit it from occurring'.

Team Parenting Meetings suffer from the same challenges that besiege any multi-disciplinary attempt at joint working. Yet the need of a multi-agency group to tackle the wide-ranging degree of difficulties faced by looked-after children are recognised in the literature and by policy makers. Fernandez (2008, p.1299) speaks of the 'overlapping domains of need' which children and young people in foster care are beleaguered by, and Craven and Lee (2006) suggest that multiple systems of care are needed if the complexity and breadth of the issues that inflict on children and young people in the care system are to be adequately addressed. These needs must be considered jointly across agencies if duplication of services and a splintered, fragmented package of care are to be avoided.

It is worth specifying that Team Parenting, whilst it is an interagency model, is more than bringing together a group of professionals to work collaboratively with looked-after children. Team Parenting is a therapeutic approach and, as such, each of its interventions is infused with therapeutic theory and intention. The same is true for Team Parenting Meetings. These are more than 'team around the child' meetings or a version of wraparound care. They are therapeutic spaces that aim to enhance psychological understanding and knowledge of the difficulties of each particular child and to embed reflective practice amongst the professionals present. Team Parenting Meetings are therapeutic interventions in and of themselves. This is particularly important to impart when convening a busy and already over-committed group of professionals to meet for the first time. Initial reluctance to attend yet one more meeting with frequently the same membership as looked-after-child reviews needs to be overcome to ensure attendance at the first meeting. Experiencing the therapeutic and reflective space that these meetings offer, together with the opportunity for true collaborative working, usually dispels any doubts as to their value, even in a tightly packed diary.

The next section will explore the practice of Team Parenting Meetings – in particular, their theoretical roots, the crucial role of the therapist in facilitating these spaces to ensure they remain useful, co-operative forums in which therapeutic work can take place, and their therapeutic benefits.

THEORETICAL ORIGINS

Any good practice is embedded within a clear theoretical framework that provides guidelines for delivery as well as goals for the work. Team Parenting, in its practice, draws substantially from attachment theory and systemic family therapy theory. However, other theoretical components inform its delivery too. Team Parenting Meetings sit at the crossroads of psychoanalytic and systemic therapy theory and practice. This is reflected by the endeavour of the facilitating therapist to shuttle backwards and forwards between an exploration of interaction and relationships in the here and now, to an investigation of the child and young person's past and its impact on their present. In Team Parenting, both ventures are equally important and indispensable. It is necessary to be mindful of the ecology of this child's particular network of relationships in *this* placement. It is also imperative to bear in mind how the child's history is likely to manifest itself and be replayed amongst this newly grouped constellation of professionals and carers. Both systemic therapists and psychoanalysts have shown an interest in working therapeutically with the network (Fredman 2007; Larner 2000; Rocco-Briggs 2008; Selekman 1997; Sprince 2000). Although there has historically been an estrangement between these two modalities, due to family therapy's reluctance to consider the unconscious and a lack of fit between the circularity of systemic practice with the hierarchical approach of psychoanalysis, the gap is narrowing (Flaskas 2009).

Both psychoanalysis and family therapy are evolving therapies that have changed over time. Whilst inhabiting very different theoretical roots, there is an increasing convergence of practice and interest in what each modality has to offer the other. A competitive element, where each modality claimed its territory, has all but disappeared. Thus, systemic therapy's previous insistence on seeing families together has shifted to seeing individuals in narrative therapy and exploring the client's constructs of their relationships with each other (Larner 2000). Likewise, psychoanalysis has moved from an expert, topographical position to a more relational position that embraces uncertainty (Larner 2000). This is good news for therapists facilitating Team Parenting Meetings as both modalities provide a wealth of theoretical material which can guide intervention in these fora.

Working as a therapist in Team Parenting Meetings is a novel enterprise. Most therapists train to work either with families or individuals (adults or children). Of course, group analysts train to work with groups, but there are few such therapists employed in the fostering services. In Team Parenting, therapists work by offering consultation to foster carers, individually, as a couple and sometimes with their social worker in attendance; they hold joint therapeutic sessions with children and young people and carers, and they facilitate Team Parenting Meetings. It is perhaps the latter that provide the greatest challenge of all in terms of how to ensure that these are therapeutic spaces that are meaningful to the network.

It is for this reason that it is necessary to utilise theory to inform the practice of Team Parenting Meetings and to consider what they aim to achieve. One of the major ambitions of Team Parenting Meetings is to engage fellow professionals and foster carers in reflective practice with each other. Reflective practice can improve individual practice when professionals engage in a reflexive feedback loop, considering how they impact on the work and how the work impacts on carers. Canavan *et al.* (2009, p.381) describe reflective practice thus: 'Reflective practice has at its theoretical core a major emphasis on the acting individual and his/her capacity to reflect and learn on an on-going basis so that practice improves, leading ultimately to better outcomes.'

Reflective practice can also aid integrative working, particularly when the reflection is taken by the group together. However, facilitating this can require some skill. There can be a reluctance to engage, professional envy and a reticence to divest individual thoughts and feelings regarding the work (Canavan *et al.* 2009). Engaging in reflective practice can be anxiety provoking as we fear judgement from others (Argent 2008), particularly where a kind of professional hierarchy exists. However, keeping our private thoughts about cases to ourselves defeats the purpose of interagency working. It also leads us into dangerous territory where we can come to see our thoughts or beliefs as 'true' and based on fact while others are erroneous and flawed (Selekman 1997). Working openly together and becoming a *shared mind* (Selekman 1997) has the potential to reduce isolation, increase knowledge and diminish the crushing feelings of sole responsibility that can easily reside with cases that have multiple challenges to overcome. How to create a space that is safe and co-operative enough for professionals to work together in this way is the role of the facilitating therapist in Team Parenting Meetings.

THE ROLE OF THE THERAPIST

Given the challenges of effective multi-disciplinary working, it is understandable that the commitment required for its optimal achievement can feel rather onerous. However, 'That children and families benefit from services working together has been evidenced, widely accepted, and enshrined in government guidance' (Nelson *et al.* 2011, p.308). Given the advantages, therefore, it is worth getting it right. In order to ensure its success, a degree of personal and innovative practice needs to be employed (Canavan *et al.* 2009) if it is not to become merely a tick-box exercise that professionals engage in because it is recommended by their organisation. In Team Parenting Meetings, it is the therapist's role to ensure that this does not happen. The success of Team Parenting Meetings can be influenced by pre-meeting planning. Convening meetings in an optimal way requires considering whom to invite, reflecting on the emotional position that each attendee might bring and also where to position each participant in the room (Fredman 2007). It is helpful to send out invitations with clear information regarding what to expect from a Team Parenting Meeting. Clarifying the expected length of the meeting and sticking to time should allay any anxiety for professionals with other commitments to go to.

Setting up the room and environment so that participants feel welcomed and nurtured is important too (Fredman 2007; Selekman 1997). Drinks should be on offer and attention paid to any specific needs. Summarising at the start of the meeting how it will work will help to set the scene and focus people's minds. Being clear that attendance at meetings will not entail extra work being assigned also relieves over-worked professionals' minds, and consideration as to the venue for future meetings demonstrates an understanding of restricted availability and freedom of movement within various job roles. This latter point particularly pertains to teachers – often they are only able to attend if Team Parenting Meetings are held at school.

As Team Parenting Meetings are therapeutic spaces, the intention is that they should not be formulaic or prescriptive, but should respond to emerging clinical need as presented by the parenting team. However, given that working therapeutically with the network will be unfamiliar to many and it is important that the meetings get off to a good start, certain guiding principles are important to bear in mind. Having convened the meeting, the therapist should ask those present to introduce themselves. Team Parenting Meetings usually have present the Local Authority social worker, the supervising social worker, an education officer, a support worker, a member of staff from school, the foster carer(s), a health professional and any other professional involved with the child. Asking each member to situate themselves in their professional context and to describe the history of their involvement with the child or young person and placement is useful (Fredman 2007; Selekman 1997). These introductions, taken in turn, also set the pace, style and tone of the meeting – that participants should listen to each other with mutual respect for, as Fredman (2007, p.207) states so clearly, 'meetings are more fruitful when people are involved in mutual listening, appreciation and respect rather than defending, controlling, counter-justifying or blaming'. In addition, unpacking jargon, asking for explanations of key phrases and working to understand different professional cultural contexts, all assist in reducing the barriers to interagency working (Selekman 1997).

Essentially, the ethos of Team Parenting Meetings is to create a collaborative, co-operative team that seeks to work together to provide a coherent and integrated package of care to the child and young person in placement. Working in this way requires recognition of the unique contributions of each individual. According to Canavan *et al.* (2009, p.381), 'while all participants may bring something to the table, it should be appreciated that all are equally valid and valuable to achieving the best outcomes for children'. It is important that the therapist works hard to create a balance for each participant between talking and listening. She needs to hold in mind every member's presence, ensure that each person has their say and that every contribution is valued, even if there are differences of opinion. In addition to this, therapists need to intervene with therapeutic intention. Therapeutic interventions are aimed at shifting perspectives, cognitions, emotional positions and relational stances. The therapist therefore plays a dual role, facilitating the contributions of others and intervening therapeutically. Sometimes, sharing theoretical thinking can be useful to encourage members to hold lightly their own beliefs and to disengage from battles over ownership of the 'truth' or the most valid perspective (Cecchin 1987).

One of the ways to engender an atmosphere of mutual respect is to positively connote each member and what they bring to the parenting team (Fredman 2007). This can help those present to understand each person's position and the lens through which they might perceive the issue being discussed. It also assists in generating an attitude of appreciation where each team member is seen as a *potential ally* (Selekman 1997). Being seen as an ally and seeing others as allies brings forth a spirit of co-operation where the team can begin to experience themselves as having an identity and working together on shared objectives. Begetting a milieu of belonging and mutual mission also facilitates the growth of trust. Where there is trust, openness and acceptance, teamworking is primed to succeed. This is a goal that needs to be continually worked towards by the facilitating therapist as multi-agency groups are easily derailed by suspicion, presumption and misunderstanding. If a team identity can be established and relationships put onto a good footing, then the foundations are present for long-term, effective alliances to be built between professionals and carers.

Coupled with the technique of positive connotation, a position of curiosity can reduce blame and fixed ideas of what is happening and what needs to change (Cecchin 1987). When blame enters the multi-disciplinary arena, defensiveness, criticism, hostility and a closing down of mutuality are not far behind. Therapists can model positions of curiosity by focusing on co-creating new meanings and encouraging an acceptance of multiple truths. It is tempting, when taxed by what seem to be overwhelming difficulties, to look for causes and explanations. These can seem alluring as we can be lulled into a false sense of security – that if we understand why something happened, then we will know how to fix it. Sadly, with human relationships, this is rarely the case. Instead, linear causality risks arriving at premature conclusions that foreclose further exploration of meaning (Cecchin 1987). Even though uncertainty can feel uncomfortable, it is often open discussion of possibilities and ideas that allow for new insight and change to emerge.

It is the role of the therapist to lead the way into temporarily 'not-knowing'; to demonstrate that 'possibilities of […] knowing […] are opened up by moments of not knowing, of letting go cherished notions and theories about the patient in favour of attentive listening' (Larner 2000, p.67). Creating such a space allows new meaning to be co-constructed amongst the parenting team, where each member has a voice and each view has credence. This limits blame, for it can come to be accepted that whilst one team member (e.g. the school) may have no problems with the child who is being discussed, another (e.g. the foster carer) may be at their wit's end. A belief in the multiplicity of perspectives allows for an open exploration of this situation. Questions can be asked, such as: 'What is it about school that the child may find easier? What function does it serve if the school and foster carers experience the child differently? How does this pattern mirror the child's earlier experiences?' Discussions in which professionals and carers share their thinking can lead to an exchange and an expansion of knowledge and understanding.

Curiosity, multiple perspectives and open exploration all invite participants to take a meta-perspective to the issue being discussed. It is the therapist's responsibility to invite non-judgemental reflection.

Inevitably, though, there will be times when one or more team members are thrown off course by the deeply felt impact of events in the child and young person's life on them. Professionals can become hooked by the child or young person's history, feeling enraged on their behalf and critical of how they continue to be let down by services. Allowing these feelings expression *and* sustaining a co-operative and respectful atmosphere can be formidable for even the most skilled therapist. Unless high emotions can be adequately contained and thought about, there is a risk of deep rifts emerging in the multi-disciplinary team. It is necessary that therapists are able to discern when to shuttle between the domains of soothing strong feeling and inviting reflective thinking to the process that is occurring. Remaining calm, not being drawn into a particular position, regulating one's own emotion in the face of others' strong feelings, being aware of one's own process and deciding on a suitable intervention to create shift are the hallmarks of good therapeutic work.

Moments of destabilisation for the team are not catastrophic in themselves. Rather, with therapy, uncomfortable periods of bewilderment can be fruitful and open the way for new work to occur (Cozolino 2010; McCluskey *et al.* 1999). However, for this to be achieved, the therapist needs to manage the situation carefully. Too much discomfort and *unsafe uncertainty* (Mason 1993) will lead to a closing down of thought and to protective positions being assumed. Enough containment, though, will allow for safe uncertainty (Mason 1993), in which enough 'not-knowing' exists to be curious but not too much, which might send team members scurrying back into their defences.

Change can occur, therefore, when there is enough safety but not too much. Being too comfortable can be as paralysing as too much discomfort, as participants can then huddle together in an agreed position of conviction from which there is great reluctance to move. Later, this can lead to being stuck, feelings of paralysis and loss of interest (Cecchin 1987). Therapists need to guard against this too, and through their interventions facilitate continual and on-going thought and movement in the Team Parenting Meetings. As much as the therapist needs to ensure a safe enough atmosphere for new thought to emerge, she needs to introduce enough instability for the meeting not to become static. This sits well within the therapeutic domain, which is neatly described by Flaskas (2009, p.3) as 'the relationship of conscious and unconscious experience, and the territory that lies between languaged stories on the one hand, and the not-yet-said and the perhaps "unsayable" on the other'.

Selecting which questions to ask can influence the tempo and culture of Team Parenting Meetings. Therapists need to be able to take a meta-position to the meeting and to be able to move nimbly, choosing their intervention selectively, depending on what is being presented at the time. When descriptions of the child or young person have become problem-saturated, asking questions that focus on appreciative enquiry can help shift perspectives. Questions from appreciative enquiry can help modify fixed views that are dense with despair and see the situation as immutable. Such enquiries focus on and might typically include questions such as: 'What has been working well? Who has noticed it has been working well? Who noticed first? Who was most pleased? What does it say about X that they have achieved Y?' In addition, introducing ways of talking that concentrate on the thoughts, feelings and behaviours of children and young people – as opposed to fusing problems with their character or personality – can expand the team's range of thinking (Fredman 2007). Therefore, rather than making a statement such as 'she is aggressive', enquiring as to 'what she does when she feels angry' separates the emotion and the behaviour from the person, allowing the person to have actions and feelings that do not wholly characterise their personality.

Therapists need to act with intentionality in Team Parenting Meetings. Asking intentional, reflexive, strategic, linear, circular questions (Tomm 1987a, 1987b, 1988) will bring forth different conversations. Furthermore, therapists need to be aware of their impact on the meeting, how they may be perceived within their cultural contexts and how their positions can invite different responses from the attendees. Fredman (2007) suggests that we can position ourselves as therapists in ways that will invite respect, listening and collaboration. These should be our *preferred postures* (Fredman 2007). However, it is also contingent upon therapists to be mindful of the part they play in the system, the impact they have (Fredman 2007; Larner 2000) and to hold lightly their own views. 'We cannot escape from the reality that we are very much a part of the problem system. What we think and do can greatly influence the outcome of each [...] meeting' (Selekman 1997, p.157). Argent (2008, p.39) calls this 'grasp[ing] the nettle of subjectivity', reminding us of the complex interplay between intervening in the system, being mindful of how the system may impact upon us and influence our actions and remaining aware of how we affect and change the system by the position we take.

There are thus dilemmas and challenges inherent in facilitating Team Parenting Meetings. Argent (2008, p.49) summarises some of these predicaments succinctly, 'I have found myself gripped by the tension of paying attention to the dynamics of the group while not setting myself up as the group's therapist; trying to help the group stay on task and not being overly prescriptive.' Other challenges include how to use one's theoretical knowledge in Team Parenting Meetings to inform but not to defend against one's own anxiety and fulfil one's need to be the expert. Selekman (1997, p.157) suggests that if therapists find themselves 'parading [their] therapeutic views', it is time for them to examine their own defences. Larner (2000) highlights this predicament and cautions against leaping to premature explanations. However, he poses the question:

> how can therapists be knowing in terms of imparting a professional sense of expertise, agency, power, certainty and authority to their clients, while simultaneously adopting a not-knowing stance of open reflection, curiosity, ethical relating and collaboration in the therapeutic conversation? (Larner 2000, p.63)

There is a balance to be struck, for sharing knowledge about child development, for example, will help the parenting team decide which behaviours are normal and which belong to a chronologically younger age group, thus hinting at regressive needs being expressed by the child.

THE THERAPIST'S MULTIPLE ROLES IN TEAM PARENTING MEETINGS

In the Team Parenting model, a therapist belongs to each area team. The therapist is responsible for the mental health of all the young people placed by the team on complex and/or specialist placements. When intervening in placements, therapists make clinical decisions as to which intervention to choose. At times, therapists may be involved in facilitating Team Parenting Meetings, carrying out joint carer/ child work and/or offering consultation to foster carers and other professionals. This multitude of roles can create conflicts for the therapist. It is challenging to facilitate a Team Parenting Meeting in the ways recommended earlier and to concurrently represent the psychological intricacies of the work that is unfolding in joint sessions between a foster carer and a child. Contributing to *and* facilitating a discussion, particularly where dynamics are complex and emotions may run high, poses some very real dilemmas. In these situations, it may be helpful to bring in an external therapist to facilitate the Team Parenting Meetings. This allows for a separation of roles, where the facilitating therapist can fulfil her function in engaging the reflective function of the network in the interests of 'more coherent and less fragmented thinking' (Rocco-Briggs 2008, p.206), leaving the other therapist to contribute her own thoughts from the joint carer/child sessions. Unfortunately, such a solution is not always possible due to a scarcity of resources. In such circumstances, clinical supervision plays a pivotal role in acting as a reflective space for the therapist straddling the function of both container and participant in Team Parenting Meetings.

YOUNG PEOPLE AND TEAM PARENTING MEETINGS

Traditionally, young people do not attend Team Parenting Meetings, except when they request to do so. Usually, they attend for part of the meeting. It may be that they listen to feedback from members of the network as well as, if they wish, making a contribution themselves. However, frequently, young people may not be aware that Team Parenting Meetings are being held. The ethics of such a position needs consideration. At times it may be helpful for young people to know that their needs are being considered carefully by a concerned parenting team. However, for some young people such knowledge may feel shaming and induce a fear that they are being talked about negatively. In addition, where young people have experienced a lack of involvement regarding planning in the care system, awareness of Team Parenting Meetings may activate a fear that decisions will be made outside of their control and with no consultation.

Nevertheless, it needs to be borne in mind that young people are frequently aware that they are the subject of conversation between adults (Bird 2004; Dallos 2006). Children living at home with their birth parents will know that aspects of their care and well-being are discussed by their parents. Furthermore, young people will know that their parents or carers attend parents' evenings and talk about their progress at school with their teachers. Young people therefore grow up, developing relationships for themselves with key adults and also being aware of the key adults having relationships with each other, some of which will have them as the focus. Observing these relationships and making sense of these connections is important for internal coherence. Experiencing the relationships that key adults have with each other as collaborative and positive will contribute to security and safety. This mirrors the process that occurs in families, where 'this process of separating the roles is easier for the child if each parent clearly stays close to them and endorses the other parent's role with the child' (Dallos 2006, p.58).

Team Parenting does not offer a pro-forma or a tightly prescribed methodology. In this instance too, there is no single recommendation that can be made as to how to proceed. More, as befits any therapeutic enterprise, each situation should be considered carefully on its own merits, regarding whether to inform the young person or not about the occurrence of Team Parenting meetings. A useful overarching guiding principle is to consider what is most helpful and beneficial to the young person in the here and now.

BENEFITS OF TEAM PARENTING MEETINGS

Team Parenting Meetings create the forum for a group of professionals and carers to work together in on-going relationships with each other in the best interests of the child or young person. Whilst interagency working is a frequent aspiration for those working with children and families and is espoused by the literature and government policy (Nelson *et al.* 2011) achieving an effective, collaborative team is a challenge. However, where there is trust between professionals and clarity of roles, goals and expectation, interagency working can yield multiple benefits for its clients (Nelson *et al.* 2011). Meeting together, face-to-face around a table on a regular basis, creates the conditions for trust to form and for differentials between roles and responsibilities to be clearly defined and agreed. For looked-after children who are already disadvantaged by their traumatic early lives and consequent multiple needs, having a lack of co-ordinated services to support them is only to add to their deprivation.

For agencies to work successfully together, there needs to be agreement regarding common goals and objectives (Coulling 2000). Coulling (2000) found this particularly in respect of education where, if there weren't openly discussed and agreed goals, different professionals would be working towards conflicting objectives. Clarifying amongst the interagency group definitions of success in education helped concentrate the efforts of professionals and maximise energy towards achieving the goals. In Coulling's (2000) study, educational success was widely defined in terms of achieving potential. She found that close collaboration between foster carers and teachers greatly facilitated this. Team Parenting Meetings provide the opportunity for teachers and foster carers to meet with regularity and consistency. It is not uncommon for frustrations and disagreements to arise between schools and foster carers. When both are struggling to manage a child and young person's challenging behaviour, they can easily slide into defensive posturing and blame (Rocco-Briggs 2008). This situation can be exacerbated by the not unusual situation of a child or young person exhibiting much more problematic behaviour in one setting than another (Rocco-Briggs 2008; Sprince 2000). Managing this tension is crucial if the child or young person's needs are to remain central to those involved.

As seen above, Team Parenting Meetings can mediate where such situations arise. Not only does an understanding of each other's perspective lead to co-operative working and strategy-planning for how to manage future difficulties, children and young people report emotional benefits too. Coulling (2000) found that children and young people liked their foster carers and schools to have frequent contact with each other because they felt cared about. Moreover, it demonstrated to them that their success was important to their teachers and their foster carers. For children and young people who have experienced little positive or interested adult attention, this is important and reparative for their self-esteem. Coulling (2000) comments that the children and young people reported most benefit and liking of this when the relationships between their foster carers and school were going well. With frequent placement moves, changes of school and uncertainty about the future, the odds are stacked against these relationships flourishing naturally. Coming together in Team Parenting Meetings allows for these relationships to begin and for a rich understanding of the other's experience to be formed. This process creates the space for mutual respect. Thus, sometimes it is helpful for foster carers to know why schools struggle to manage their foster child or young person, especially when they are in desperate need of a break. Similarly, it is useful to disavow schools and teachers of any assumptions they may have of foster carers and to engender an understanding of the challenging nature of the task foster carers face:

> No longer can foster care be seen as a job which is taken on largely by the mother in the family with children of their own when there is enough space in the home for one more. The traditional stay-at-home image of the carer must change and indeed is changing. (Coulling 2000, p.33)

Interagency working can be therapeutic when it is the child or young person's perception that all those involved with her are working together in her best interests. Even when the child or young person has not met each professional, knowing that there is an interested group of adults striving to do their best for her has therapeutic potential. Sprince (2000) comments on the place she had in the mind of a child whom she had never even met, although she had worked with his professional network. Team Parenting Meetings, as well as creating the opportunity to agree common goals, provides the place to agree approaches. One of the central aims of Team Parenting is to imbue each professional and carer's interactions with the child or young person with therapeutic intent. If this can occur, then children and young people will be on the receiving end of therapeutic understanding from all those who work with them. However, not all professionals are trained in therapeutic practice or have the knowledge regarding complex trauma, attachment difficulties and the arising challenging behaviour to make this possible. Team Parenting Meetings can therefore be used as places where psycho-education can take place and possible responses to behaviours explored.

Thinking psychologically about a child/young person can come as a relief to professionals and carers, particularly when they are feeling de-skilled and inept in the face of the extremes of behaviour they encounter. Just as in consultation sessions with foster carers, it is helpful to explain the process of projective identification:

> It is powerfully known, by anybody who works with looked-after children, how they tend to express their own pain through very disturbed forms of verbal and non-verbal behaviour that may leave the adults around them with a range of feelings, including feelings of rage, rejection, abuse and shock that are difficult to acknowledge and think about. (Rocco-Briggs 2008, p.192)

Thinking together in this way and making sense collaboratively takes away any fantasy that individual therapy might cure the child or young person or take away their problems; instead, it engenders a philosophy of shared responsibility for the child or young person. Joint working also leads to less isolation, more enthusiasm and increased productivity. Fredman (2007, p.56) espouses this approach, working:

> from an assumption that we could accomplish more within a network of collaborative relationships than each on our own, I work towards co-creating a 'resource-full' community of people involved in the young person's care, facilitating our joint activity in a way that we might pool the abilities of everyone involved. Thus I pay attention to the relationships between practitioners as much as I attend to the individual or family.

Working together co-operatively not only leads to a more efficient use of resources and more co-ordinated packages of care, it also leads to hope. In the gloom of the histories of these children and young people's lives and the apparent bleakness of their futures at times, hope is much needed. As Schofield and Beek (2005b) pertinently remark, hope is a characteristic of resilience and professionals and foster carers need resilience too when working with what can seem the intractable challenges provided by the children and young people in their care.

CASE STUDY

This example of Team Parenting Meetings demonstrates the range of professionals that can be involved and the complex interplay of factors that can be addressed in this forum.

The children who were the subject of these meetings were triplets. They were 14 years old when they were placed in foster care. Two of the children suffered from a chronic physical health condition. At the time of placement, their mother was suffering with depression and was addicted to alcohol. Domestic violence was believed to be an issue in the home. The children were placed with new carers, who had two children of their own. The care plan was that the children would remain in long-term care, but the children stated regularly that they wished to go home.

The professionals involved with the children included:

- foster carers
- support worker

- Local Authority social worker
- nurse from the Children's Hospital
- staff from the hospice that had provided respite care for the children
- a teacher from the school
- psychologist linked to the Children's Hospital
- education worker
- senior supervising social worker
- consultant psychiatrist (from CAMHS)
- therapist (chairperson)
- consultants psychiatrist (from the in-patient adolescent unit)
- nursing staff (from the in-patient adolescent unit).

In the first meeting, concerns were raised about the necessity of Team Parenting Meetings, given the existence of Looked-After Child Reviews and other meetings between the health professionals. Time constraints were an issue for all involved. To address this and acknowledge busy diaries, meetings were held over lunch. Sandwiches were provided to infuse the meetings with qualities of nurturance and support. In this way, physical needs were attended to and a communication of care and consideration imparted.

One of the main objectives of the early sessions was to share information to gain a common understanding of the children's histories. Valuable contributions came from the teacher who had known the children for three years prior to their placement in foster care. She described how the children had been prior to coming into care and how improved their presentation and demeanour had been since being placed in foster care. This view helped the carers at a time when they were being challenged heavily by the children and by the birth father.

In some of the meetings, there seemed to be a 'venting of frustration' about the children's father and his combative behaviour. The therapist asked questions about what was known regarding the father's early history and parenting experience. These reflections led to increasing flickers of compassion for him to emerge. One worker asked if the father had been offered any therapeutic input. It became clear that, as a safeguarding case, the parents' own therapeutic needs had not been addressed. Action to redress this was taken by offering family therapy sessions to the parents.

During the three years in which the meetings were held, a number of challenges were held and contained by the Team Parenting Meetings. Some of these were as follows:

- A change of social worker brought a change of direction when the children were told that they might be able to return home. The general consensus of the parenting team was that this was not safe. Their existence as a well-established group meant that they could impart their views and stop this sudden change of care plan.

- One of the children became increasingly distressed and started to refuse to eat, saying she wanted to die. Having space to express concerns and worries about her, as well as agree management strategies, was important for all professionals involved.

- The father of the children throughout the time of the placement communicated with the children on Facebook and also through direct contact. He told them that they could come home when they turned 16 years old. This served to destabilise the placement. Managing this was a subject for discussion at Team Parenting Meetings.

The Team Parenting Meetings provided a forum for a range of professionals to share their thoughts, feelings and dilemmas with each other and also to share in successes and positive outcomes. Crises and events occurred that evoked powerful feelings. The Team Parenting Meetings acted as a container and thinking space for these. There was an air of respect for each other, and a sharing of different hypotheses resulted at times in a change of approach. The meetings coped with changes in personnel, including the consultant and nursing staff from the in-patient unit, which had short-term involvement. The presence of a core group of people that held these children in mind and incorporated new workers and ideas into the system assisted the care of the children to be less reactive and more reflective in its approach. The sharing of responsibility and in some cases the acceptance of the team's limitations together allowed for a reduction in responses that may have been born out of a need to 'do something' and 'rescue' rather than accept and work with what 'is'.

SUMMARY – KEY FEATURES OF TEAM PARENTING – MEETINGS

Key features of effective Team Parenting Meetings include:

- being in a situation where there are no 'up' or 'down' positions
- being part of a meeting where there is respect for each person involved
- being in a supportive environment that is non-judgemental
- being in a position for exploration of each person's thoughts and state of mind
- recognising that every person involved, including the therapist, has an impact on the outcome
- being able to recognise that whatever is happening for the young person, she is the least powerful when she is in care
- being able to recognise that the process has an impact on every individual involved
- ensuring that the relationships between different parts of the system are on the agenda and of common interest
- establishing the meetings as an interactive process which needs everyone's participation and a sharing of their knowledge and skills
- clarifying the intention as being to address the needs of the young person in placement
- ensuring that every member's perspective is accepted as being valid and meaningful
- providing a systemic overview, drawing together emerging themes and patterns
- offering therapeutic insight into the child's history, including a rich depiction of the possible structures of her inner world
- discussing ideas of how to manage specific challenging behaviours within the construct of therapeutic re-parenting
- providing knowledge on how to offer the child developmentally appropriate, attuned parenting
- keeping in mind that witnessing is helpful and therapeutic
- acknowledging and welcome difference as a resource

- creating a learning environment
- adopting a co-operative stance.

In this chapter the Team Parenting Meetings as a therapeutic intervention have been discussed. The role of the therapist in facilitating them has been explored. Chapter 6 goes on to examine joint therapy sessions with the foster carer and child or young person as a further therapeutic intervention utilised within the Team Parenting model.

THERAPEUTIC INTERVENTIONS IN TEAM PARENTING

JOINT CARER/CHILD WORK

CHAPTER CONTENTS

Working with trauma in attachment-based therapies

Therapeutic stances in joint carer/child work

The foster carer's role
  Being a therapeutic foster carer

Engaging the child or young person in therapy

Case study

Much of the therapeutic work done within Team Parenting placements is carried out via consultation with foster carers. This clinical decision is based on the recognition that for looked-after children, their primary therapeutic task is to be able to form a functional, secure attachment relationship with their foster carers. However, due to previous experiences where their trust in primary caregivers (often their birth parents) has been ruptured, they may defend against this to the best of their ability. Such defensive behaviours can shake the foundations of placement stability and induce in foster carers withdrawal and disengagement from the child or young person. This dynamic requires that foster carers understand the psychological processes at play. With enough support from therapists to manage this situation, acute episodes of behaviour can be transformed into opportunities for therapeutic encounters. Therapists working within Team Parenting therefore direct their energies into facilitating the ability of foster carers to become therapeutic parents for children or young people in placement via consultation meetings.

However, at times, it is necessary to intervene directly and undertake therapeutic work with a child or young person. This usually occurs when the placement is planned to be long term; when the child or young person seems particularly resistant to forming an attachment to their foster carer and/or when their unprocessed trauma is making it hard for them to inhabit the present, unfettered by horrific memories which pull them back to a past saturated with fear. Therapists who work within the Team Parenting model are trained in a variety of modalities. These modalities include systemic therapy, psychodynamic therapy, integrative therapy, child and adolescent psychotherapy, art therapy, drama therapy and psychology. Each therapist will draw upon her own theoretical roots and clinical experience in informing her joint work with foster carers and children and young people. It is essential that therapists are able to work jointly and collaboratively with foster carers in therapeutic sessions with children and young people, whatever their training background (Schofield and Beek 2009). Despite the range of therapists' theoretical and training backgrounds, there are some common assumptions and positions that exist in joint carer/child work within Team Parenting. In exploring the detail of joint carer/child work it is useful to delineate these central themes and concepts. These are explored below.

WORKING WITH TRAUMA IN ATTACHMENT-BASED THERAPIES

Attachment-based therapies make use of the fundamental concepts of attachment theory in order to facilitate the therapeutic process. Within the therapeutic setting this means making the assumption that exploration into psychological and emotional material can only occur when there is enough safety in the room and the therapeutic relationship (Hughes 2009; McCluskey et al. 1999). Attachment theory describes how exploration and proximity-safety-seeking behaviours co-exist, that is 'the secure base, developed in attachment theory to describe that balance between dependency and autonomy, closeness and exploration that lie behind secure attachment relationships' (Schofield and Beek 2009, p.257).

Attachment is a survival-based system – infants and toddlers stay close to their primary caregiver, who they have learnt can ensure their safety and meet their needs. However, learning is also a survival-based system and, when feeling safe, the drive to explore takes over and infants and toddlers move into exploration. At this developmental stage, exploration involves play and this play takes them further from their caregivers' side. Watch a toddler at play and it will be possible to notice her checking the presence of her caregiver. If all is well, the environment calm and settled with, and the caregiver giving reassuring glances and smiles, the toddler will return to play. However, if unsettled or frightened by an event, for example an unexpected noise, the toddler will hurry to her caregiver's side for protection. Once soothed, and insecurity and fear contained, the toddler can resume her fascination with the external world and return to play.

Attachment-based therapies make use of this thinking to inform their process. In the therapeutic environment, it is the therapist who needs to ensure enough safety to encourage the clients to be able to explore their emotional and psychological experience (McCluskey *et al.* 1999; Woodcock 2009). This requires providing attunement to the affect of the clients and making sense for her of her experience. This 'thinking and reflection to contain emotional experience' (Larner 2009, p.210) is part of the practice of psychotherapy. However, in working jointly with a foster carer and child or young person, the situation becomes more complex. It remains the therapist's responsibility to generate enough safety in the room for the therapeutic work to occur. However, the safety needs of the foster carer and the child or young person are different. For the foster carer, the goal is that she will join with the therapist to enable the child or young person to explore painful material in the session. The therapist therefore has multiple tasks: to create enough safety for the foster carer in order that they feel free enough of inhibition to work in this way; to provide regulation for the carer so that when she is becoming destabilised by the work, the therapist can intervene and slow the pace or change the direction (Hughes 1997); and to establish an environment and working alliance for the child or young person to engage therapeutically.

Given these various objectives, it is helpful for the therapist to meet with the foster carer prior to conducting any joint sessions with the foster carer and child or young person. These meetings allow the therapist to explain the theoretical thinking behind the work, the aims that the work hopes to achieve and the expectations on the foster carers of how they need to respond to the child or young person in the sessions. Clarifying therapeutic intent is particularly important as it can be the expectation of some foster carers that therapy will work to 'change' the child or young person and that the therapist, as another adult, will reinforce the behavioural expectations that she has of the child or young person. Children or young people are usually aware that most conversations in their lives about them 'privilege adult meaning-making processes' (Bird 2004, p.295). However, therapy with children or young people will attune to their experiences and prioritise their needs. Foster carers will need to set aside their task-focused requirements of therapy and instead be willing to engage in an open-ended exploration of the child or young person's inner world. If they are unable to do this, then the child or young person is likely to grasp the unspoken wish of the foster carer that the therapy will be used to change her. Implicit in this for the child or young person is the awareness that who/how she is, is not all right for the foster carer. This perception will re-engage the child or young person's defences, leading to an inability to make use of the therapeutic space.

When foster carers are able to work alongside therapists, an understanding of attachment theory and their role for the child or young person as a secure base is useful. This is particularly so because working on traumatic memories is likely to destabilise the child or young person. Understanding that their presence as a safety figure may enable the child or young person to explore difficult issues without becoming overwhelmingly distressed is imperative. It is also helpful for the foster carers to comprehend that when the child or young person does become upset, if they can move swiftly to offer soothing and containment of the child or young person's unbearable affect, then the security of the attachment between them will grow. 'The therapist directing the sessions facilitates the development of a relationship between the child and carer whereby they communicate emotionally and the child is able to experience recurring sequences of attachment, affective union, separation and reunion' (Schofield and Beek 2009, p.71). Utilising the foster carer to soothe the child or young person's feelings initiates a process where the child or young person comes to perceive overwhelming affect as manageable when the presence of a caring and interested other is available.

Working on trauma within an attachment relationship is a cyclical process (Cairns 2002a, 2002b; Hughes 2004):

> The attachment sequence of attunement, disruption, and repair occurs frequently in an attachment-based model of therapy, just as it

does in the parent-child relationship. Themes associated with terror and shame may frequently cause a disruption in the relationship. The therapist does not avoid these themes and the associated disruption, but rather provides a safe setting in which they can occur. (Hughes 2004, p.269)

Initially, there needs to be enough safety for exploration of traumatic events and memories to occur. Recalling these traumatic situations is likely to lead to emotional arousal, dysregulation and temporary disturbance. The presence of the foster carer can provide enough soothing so that the child or young person is able to engage with their thinking and make use of the interventions the therapist may use. Talking about trauma, its impact, how it affects behaviour and connecting this to the child or young person's experience, also helps her to integrate memories. Once work on this particular issue has been done, new areas of exploration will lead to a new cycle of emotional upheaval, soothing, containment, thinking, reflection and integration.

Cairns (2002b) sees early trauma as a bio-psychological-social injury which affects a child or young person's ability to regulate themselves and their feelings, make sense of the world and connect in relationship with those around them. She also advocates a cyclical process in therapeutic foster care and names three phases of recovery for the child or young person:

1. Stability incorporates the development of an attachment to one person and feeling safe in their presence.

2. Integration entails the processing of traumatic memories, locating them in the past and learning that they are survivable. This process suggests that children/young people need to move unprocessed memories locked in part of their brain to become autobiographical memories. This means that rather than memories being experienced as live and *in situ*, triggered by the smallest of events, they can be held in the past and form part of a story that is no longer being replayed in the present.

3. Become socially adaptive and connected to others in their world.

These three phases can be addressed through joint work with foster carers and children or young people, and describe the process of working with trauma in an attachment-based therapy. They can also be supported by the placement, as the foster carer's daily presence as an attachment figure in the child or young person's life will add to her sense of safety and ability to undertake work in the therapy room. As children or young people integrate their previous experiences into who they have become and how they are in the here and now, they are better able to make use of relationships. This includes making use of their relationship with the therapist to assist them in therapeutic work. Joint work additionally enhances the opportunity for improvements in relational capacity, as witnessing the relationship between the therapist and the foster carer role allows children to observe empathy and understanding at work.

THERAPEUTIC STANCES IN JOINT CARER/CHILD WORK

Hughes (2009) recommends adopting PACE as a therapeutic stance. As you may remember from Chapter 1, PACE is an acronym, standing for playfulness, acceptance, curiosity and empathy. Hughes and others also talk of intersubjectivity (Fonagy *et al.* 1991, 2011; Hughes 2009; Larner 2009; Pocock 2009; Stern 1985). Intersubjectivity is an intimate relational position where we are most open to the influence of another (Hughes 2009). For intersubjectivity to occur there needs to be acceptance, curiosity and empathy in the therapeutic relationship. With children and young people, a playful approach is an important addition if they are to become interested and engaged in the therapeutic endeavour.

Children and young people in the care system often attend therapy because of the concerns of others regarding their behaviour; they rarely elect to come of their own volition. Adults involved with them often express worries about their behaviour. It is probable that some of their more difficult behaviour arises from the emotions surrounding their unprocessed traumatic experiences which they then externalise and act out. 'Traumatic experiences can often be forgotten due to a paucity of language and a lack of conceptual maturity. The strong emotional responses that remain can gain expression in ways that are identified as problematic' (Bird 2004, p.321). Attending therapy to talk with their foster carer and a stranger about aspects of themselves that they may disown and project outward is liable to feel shameful and humiliating for children and young people. If there is to be any chance of success in engaging them in this venture, the therapist must impart to them acceptance, understanding, curiosity and empathy.

In establishing these therapeutic core conditions with looked-after children, therapists will need to be more proactive and directive than they may be used to in their other work. For children and young people who have been harmed by their primary caregivers, expressions of verbal empathy will not have the same effect as with their securely attached peers:

> Nondirective approaches are not helpful because the therapist's empathy and unconditional acceptance are coming from a way of life that the child barely knows exists. The child misinterprets the nondirective stance as permissiveness that enables the child to easily manipulate the therapist into allowing him full control of the process. (Hughes 1997, p.55)

Being in control of situations with adults is what children and young people with attachment difficulties want, but it is not what they need if they are to learn to trust and attach to their foster carer. Thus, the therapist needs to work proactively to transmit acceptance and empathy. This can be done by focusing on the here-and-now relationship of the child or young person with the therapist and with the carer. The therapist can encourage eye contact from the child or young person, inviting them to look at the therapist's face while she empathises with their affective experience. Similarly, encouraging the child or young person to maintain eye contact with their foster carer propels them into a relational position and out of isolation. When we make eye contact with another, we are forced to witness how we are impacting on them and allow them to impact on us. Observing another's facial expressions yields valuable information regarding their affective state. Too often, children and young people remain locked in solitary positions with no sharing of affect. While lack of eye contact allows original presumptions about the other to be upheld, thus creating an illusion of safety, it also keeps the child or young person entombed in self-limiting suppositions that block their need to experience being in a trusting relationship with another (Clarkson 1989; Mackewn 1997).

Empathy, as one of the core therapeutic conditions required in therapy, is often best communicated via affective attunement when working with children and young people. This is partly because children use a greater range of their senses in communication than we more verbally reliant adults do. It is also because looked-after children have not always received the type of affective attunement they required in infancy. There is therefore a developmental deficit. Communicating empathy solely by verbalisation will not impact on them in the same way as affective attunement. Affective attunement requires becoming tuned into another's affective and feeling states. We do this naturally with babies, receiving their affective communication, containing it and giving it back to them in a manageable form. Thus, when babies are hungry and distressed, we alter our facial expressions, our intonation and our body language. We impart our understanding of their need, soothe their affect and act to satiate their need. Similarly, in therapy, with a child or young person, the therapist should alter her intonation, body language and facial expression, communicating that she has been impacted upon by the child or young person's emotional state; that she can understand it and act to provide comfort and reassurance. Hughes cites the work of Schore (1994) to evidence the efficacy of this endeavour, stating that Schore 'stresses that therapy, just like the infant's early development and attachment with his mother, is fundamentally a process of the right hemisphere of the brain and of the communication between the right hemispheres of the therapist and patient' (Hughes 1997, p.62).

Affective attunement works towards conveying acceptance of the whole child or young person – that all of their emotions are acceptable and understandable, that they are respected and valued. Such a position is imperative; for the child or young person will be unlikely to be open to the influence of therapy if she believes that her self is seen as unsatisfactory by another (Hughes 2009). Feeling accepted and understood also opens the child or young person to moments of intersubjectivity. Intersubjectivity alludes to contact with another when there is shared affect, mutual focus of attention and a common goal or intention (Hughes 2009). Moments such as these are the hallmark of effective therapy. They occur within the context of a safe working relationship where an issue is being addressed, often with painful ramifications for the client. The client is moved emotionally and the therapist too is impacted upon by the client's affect. Both client and therapist are focused on the same issue and both are motivated to work towards its resolution. This relational position 'requires the therapist to be in a state of receptivity toward the other's pain and fragility, feeling it as if it were one's own' (Larner 2009, p.210).

However, the therapist maintains enough detachment to avoid being engulfed by the emotion, but at the same time remains able to transmit shared understanding of the pain and to tentatively contribute meaning-making of the feeling state for the client. This is what Fonagy *et al.* (2004) and others, in their writings on parenting, would term a 'marked' or 'contingent' response, where the emotional state of the infant is empathised with but the parent does not feel it in the same way themselves (Pocock 2009). This empathic but marked response is also a feature of intersubjectivity in therapy, where the focus can be shared, as can be the emotional state being communicated, but there is a distinction between feeling the same as each other and the experience of sharing a feeling (Sundet and Torsteinsson 2009). It is the latter which constitutes effective intersubjectivity in the therapeutic relationship and also within a caregiver and child relationship.

Moments of intersubjectivity allow us to experience ourselves through the perceptions of another. It is becoming widely accepted that infants get to know themselves partially through the impact of their self on another and the social biofeedback of this impact (Fonagy *et al.* 2011; Pocock 2009). Pocock (2009) links Winnicott's (1971) ideas of the mother giving back to the baby the baby's own self and Bion's (1962) notion of containment with the more recent ones of Fonagy *et al.* (2004). Pocock (2009, p.100) in summarising Fonagy *et al.*'s views suggests that 'through repeated interactions with an attuned parent, the child establishes a capacity to know her own emotional states of mind as well as the states of mind of another'.

This fits with the positive interaction cycle used by Fahlberg (1991). Infants/toddlers who observe their parents enjoying interactions with them come to feel efficacious in their relationships and believe that they can have a positive impact on others. This leads to the development of self-esteem and the capacity for mentalisation or reflective function. 'When a care-giver's response is appropriate, well timed, and marked, this gives the infant […] a representation of his emotional state combined with a secondary representation of the care-giver's response, which can then be internalized' (Pocock 2009, p.100).

A similar process occurs in psychotherapy, where children or young people come to know themselves through the perceptions of the therapist. The parallels between the infant/caregiver relationship in developing reflective function and that of the therapist/client relationship are best expressed by Larner (2009, p.209): 'To have a self is to be thought by the other [...] We come to know ourselves through other's knowing of us [...] In human attachment, the infant develops a sense of self by internalizing the experience of feeling known to the other.' However, this is also a reciprocal process, as we come to know ourselves via witnessing the impact of our subjective experience on the subjective experience of the other, and also by allowing their subjective experience to influence ours (Hughes 2009).

This process assists with the processing of trauma as it allows for a 'secondary representation of the original raw affect' to come into existence (Hughes 2004, p.266). So, as the child or young person affectively shares his/her experience of an event, the therapist allows herself to be impacted upon by the affect and to communicate this to the child or young person. Reflecting back a verbal representation of what has been transmitted via the child or young person's affect creates both a distancing effect, which locates the event in the past, and allows for a co-construction of new meaning. This co-construction will only have resonance for the child or young person if the therapist has adequately understood and experienced the child or young person's original affect. In giving words to the child or young person's communicated affect and experience, the therapist is facilitating his/her self-reflective capacity and the beginnings of insight into his/her inner world (Hughes 2009).

If foster carers can be present when such moments occur, it allows them a window into the child or young person's internal states and vulnerabilities. Such glimpses can be restorative if before all they have experienced are the child or young person's rigid, controlling and rejecting behaviours at home. Ultimately, the goal of joint carer/ child work is that moments of intersubjectivity occur between foster carer and child. When this happens, the child or young person can integrate their foster carer's perceptions of her and the foster carer's perceptions of the trauma experiences she has shared. This leads to a new knowing of self and a resolution of previously unprocessed, raw traumatic memories (Hughes 2009). In this way, intersubjectivity in joint carer/child work also leads to the beginnings of mentalisation for the child or young person. Therapists, working with foster carers to jointly understand the child or young person's mind and communicate to her this comprehension, facilitate the child or young person to more self-awareness of her own mind and also that of her carers (Hughes 2004).

However, while this process sounds simple on paper, it is likely to be a difficult journey, frequently disrupted and disabled by the effects of shame. Shame, as an affect, originates in the primary caretaking relationship and is a defence against the loss of this relationship (Erskine 1995). Ideally, shame experienced alongside many other affects, is felt in response to a given situation, and let go. Used appropriately, shame has a protective function which can keep a child safe in urgent situations, for example, when a toddler is about to run out into the road (Cairns 2002a). Being shouted at in this situation ruptures the relationship with the caregiver, leading the child to halt and temporarily dissolve emotionally. Rapid repair via physical comfort, soothing tones and verbal explanations restore the child and her relationship with the caregiver to a solid footing. Shame, therefore, usually has its origins in history, stemming from a break in the relationship between a significant caregiver and the young child. Shame is distinguishable from guilt because first, with guilt we are usually able to articulate what we may feel guilty about, whilst shame can leave us feeling confused and speechless. Second, guilt mostly pertains to an action we have carried out which we believe to be 'wrong' (Yontef 1993).

Shame is uncomfortable, yet disruption to the *interpersonal bridge* (Kohut 1977) between adult and child can be restored swiftly by a sensitive caregiver. It is when shame is frequent and persistent that the seeds for a more pervading internal devastation are sown. In these circumstances, overwhelming shame damages the psyche and interferes with our ability to self-regulate and be in relationship with others. This occurs when shame has been used as a generic parental control mechanism. In these circumstances, using shame as a disciplinary measure often incorporates criticism of the whole child or young person as opposed to distinguishing between him/her and his/her behaviour. In addition, children and young people who have been abused and/or neglected are likely to feel ubiquitous shame. This is because children and young people, depending for their very existence on their caregiver, cannot believe that their parent's actions towards them are fallible. Instead, they come to believe there is something wrong with them (Kaufman 1992). This leads to the development of a shame-based personality (Erskine 1995; Evans 1994) and a sense of being inherently inferior and without value.

When experiencing shame, children, young people and adults alike can feel totally isolated and alone, and while paralysed to reach out to others, the shame also hints at a secret and unaware longing for the restoration of contact and acceptance of the self. However, shame carries with it a fear that the emotional abandonment that is experienced is richly deserved.

When shame is a recurring feature of a child or young person's life, the process becomes internalised so that the child or young person feels shame before she is shamed by another. The external conflict is introjected (Perls 1951) and the battle rages internally, with the child learning to treat him or herself with the same harsh criticism used by the parent. The purpose of doing this is to relieve the actual relationship of some of its toxicity (Erskine 1995). However, the child or young person transfers this mechanism into her new relationship with her foster carers. She will be hypervigilant to experiences that will be shaming and confirm her view of self. In order to defend against repetitive shame and self-loathing, children and young people will use strategies such as rage, self-righteousness, contempt, blaming, perfectionism, withdrawal and isolation. These allow them to push the carer and their potential to shame the child or young person away and create a denial of the need for relationship.

Being in therapy, where day-to-day difficulties are likely to be recounted by the foster carer and historical, traumatic memories freshly aired, will create the conditions for shame to flourish. Therapists need to be acutely aware of this dynamic as shame will obstruct the child or young person's thinking and prevent any therapeutic work from being able to occur. Hughes (2004) suggests militating against shame by being playful and affectively attuned to the child or young person. He proposes that affective attunement creates enough safety for contentious and difficult issues to be explored. Then, whilst doing so, the child or young person can make use of the therapist's regulatory capacities to experience shame and terror and not become unregulated. 'It is an active, affectively varied, dyadic interaction that interweaves moments of interaction and reflection' (Hughes 2004, p.269).

There will be times, however, when the child or young person does become immersed in shame and/or fear. At such times, the therapist, like the caregiver with a young child, moves to initiate repair to the relationship. This is done via body language, eye contact and intonation, affectively tuning in to the child's experience. This cyclical pattern of intersubjectivity, rupture and repair are features of this style of working and mirror a sequence of interactions that many children and young people with attachment difficulties did not have enough of. 'Allan Schore (1994) indicates that developmental psychopathology has at its core a working model of poor attunement, pervasive and unregulated shame, and an inability to re-establish an emotional bond with a significant other following a shame-inducing experience' (Hughes 1997, p.67).

THE FOSTER CARER'S ROLE

Before beginning joint work with young people and their foster carers or adopters, Hughes (2007, 2011) suggests therapists undertake work with the adults. This work enables a processing of the carers' own attachment histories, and allows for the therapist to impart an understanding to the carers of their role in the joint sessions as well as assessing the ability of the carers to participate in the way that is intended. It is crucial, if the young person is not to be shamed in the sessions, that foster carers comprehend the necessity of interacting with PACE (Hughes 2007, 2011). At times, foster carers can be too embroiled in the weight of historical issues from their own early attachment relationships to be able to function in this way. When their own attachment issues are live and unresolved, they are likely to be ignited by the types of behaviours young people with attachment difficulties bring into placement. When there is insufficient insight from foster carers as to how their emotional issues may be hooked by the young person, they will be unable to bracket their emotions and concentrate on the needs of the young person. The therapist needs to assess whether some consultation sessions for the foster carer will address this issue. If not, then joint carer/child work may be inappropriate and another therapeutic intervention may need to be considered instead.

Foster carers have an important role to play in therapy sessions with a child or young person. Initially, they need to comprehend that the child or young person will probably transfer his or her internalised parent figures onto the foster carer. Transference is a psychoanalytic concept and refers, in individual psychotherapy, to the projection of an internalised historical figure onto the therapist. This is often a parent, and means that a client, for example, may imagine that her therapist will behave critically towards her in the way that her mother would have done. In dyadic work with a foster carer and child, given the carer's position as an attachment figure, the transference will often occur between the carer and child as well as with the therapist. Therapists can forewarn foster carers of the dynamics behind this powerful psychological process and support them to withstand the transference that will emerge. Hughes (1997 p.36) suggests that this transference should be facilitated in the therapy and that the child or young person be 'encouraged to transfer deeply meaningful relationship features from his past to both therapy and his life at home. Anticipated thoughts of rejection, abuse, and humiliation will emerge along with associated emotions of shame, rage, fear, and sadness'.

Being on the receiving end of a child or young person's transference can be perturbing, and a therapist can help to manage the foster carer's affect. However, the foster carer will also need to have resolved their own attachment issues if these are not to be triggered by the child or young person's transference (Becker-Wiedman and Hughes 2008; Hughes 2007). This may mean that the carer will need to have some therapeutic work themselves before they are ready to engage in the direct work with the child and therapist. It is essential that the carer is self-aware enough to contain and manage their own issues when these are triggered by the young person's behaviour towards them. This process requires them to be able to depersonalise the transference from the child or young person. If they are unable to do this, they run the risk of re-enacting the young person's history. The foster carer's task in this is similar to that of the therapist in individual therapy – the latter is trained to withstand their client's hatred in order to facilitate resolution of childhood disappointments and loss (Bland 2009). Like therapists, foster carers have to learn how to survive being hated if children and young people are to experience a different outcome and not have their history repeated.

If the therapist observes that the foster carer's responses are becoming reactive and unregulated during a session, she will need to intervene. This may mean taking a temporary break from the joint sessions in order for the therapist to spend individual time with the foster carer. The purpose of the individual time will be to allow exploration of what is happening for the foster carer, both in terms of her feelings towards the child or young person and regarding her own history. When foster carers dismiss the significance of their own emotional histories, their ability to be available for children in therapeutic work is limited (Bird 2004). Foster carers who have avoided resolving emotionally painful issues for themselves can unconsciously find themselves adopting a similar strategy with children/young people. However, the avoidance of traumatic material does not dispel its effects. 'Emotions often hang in the air unnamed while saturating every exchange. When we attempt to protect children from the knowledge of difficult or traumatic events, we forget that the emotional shadow remains, sabotaging emotional availability and connection' (Bird 2004, p.290).

It is not unusual for foster carers to become unregulated emotionally because of the behaviours they are confronted with in their homes when parenting a young person who has attachment difficulties. They may arrive for a session with their foster child, brimming with emotions from a recent event or a difficult week. When this occurs, they may feel too full of uncontained emotion to provide a reflective and empathic space for the young person. If the foster carer is still embroiled in strong feelings regarding a contemporary incident, the therapist must assess whether the joint session should go ahead (Hughes 2011). Hughes (2011) suggest that it may be that joint work should be temporarily abandoned to avoid the risk of the young person bearing witness to and being the recipient of the foster carer's uncontained affect. Instead, the therapist should spend the time working to facilitate soothing and understanding for the foster carer so she can once again attain a position of reflective function in relation to the young person. However, careful thought needs to be given as to how to explain this to the young person, who will have arrived expecting a joint session with the foster carer. In addition, a suitable place for the young person to wait for their foster carer needs to be constantly available, should such a situation occur.

It is possible that a young person may feel relieved at not having a joint session, especially if they are alert to the disquiet felt by the foster carer. Alternatively, they could feel abandoned, disappointed or even that their carer's needs are being privileged over their own. It would be wise to consider talking beforehand to each young person being seen for joint carer/child sessions to explain why this approach is taken, should this situation materialise. It is worth bearing in mind that it is helpful for young people to have awareness of not only their foster carer's relationship with them but also the relationship the carer has with other members of the parenting team. Dallos (2006) refers to how children have attachments to each parent, are aware of the relationship that each parent has with each other and also that they are the subject of the parental relationship's focus of attention at times. In Team Parenting, this concept can be extended to include not only the foster carer's relationship with his/her partner if they are in a relationship but also to the foster carer's relationships to other members of the parenting team. This can imbue young people with a sense of safety that others are working and thinking together on how best to support them. This process can also aid mentalisation. Perceiving that their foster carers have needs which can be addressed separately from their own needs and contained by another helps facilitate reflective function.

When children or young people are experiencing difficulties and their foster carers are persistently struggling to manage and understand their behaviours, they can come to feel on the edge of family life. Finding themselves on the outside of the family can threaten their sense of belonging (Bird 2004). When this is occurring, consideration should be given to including other family members in the work. Meeting all the members of the family who live in the house can be helpful, to give a flavour of the contextual circumstances and relational field that the child or young person inhabits (Bird 2004). Bird also suggests that investigating relational alliances and tensions in the foster family can help shift the focus from being located within the child or young person, who may have come to be seen as 'the problem', for the family. Naming the current tensions is important as this makes explicit knowledge that is implicitly held by the child or young person. At times, it is useful to re-orientate the discussion into an exploration and naming of the positive qualities of the child or young person. Distinguishing children and young people from the difficulties others experience with them will open a space for them to engage in therapeutic work which still addresses problem areas but in a different way. 'Identifying attributes, abilities, strengths and resources provides an essential platform from which to explore the effects of concerns/problems' (Bird 2004 p.330).

Looking after young people with attachment difficulties and participating in joint carer/child work is emotionally demanding (Hughes 1997). Hughes (1997, p.45) states that, in order to engage in it successfully, a foster carer needs to retain 'a level of maturity that allows her to engage in self-soothing and self-affirming activity'. When foster carers have these capacities, the child or young person can be enabled to explore the effect of her traumatic experiences more deeply. The foster carer's ability to be present, providing soothing and understanding, when a child or young person feels fear, anger, rage and/or sadness ensures that the connection between them is maintained. This also militates against the risk of the child or young person defending against painful feelings by withdrawing or engaging in self-protective, destructive behaviours (Hughes 1997; Schofield and Beek 2009). When foster carers can remain *psychologically present* (Hughes 2004) during episodes of the child or young person's own disintegration into unregulated emotion, there is a chance for integration and new learning to occur. The child or young person can begin to experience an *emotional richness* in their life, experiencing themselves as people who can hate and love, be rageful without this meaning that they are 'bad', and feel sad without fearing total disintegration (Hughes 1997).

This process is facilitated by adopting a curious position where the focus is on the exploration of the child or young person's perceptions, emotions and experiences. For therapy to succeed, young people need to experience the adults in the room as having enquiring, interested minds, and willing to get alongside their experience. When foster carers align themselves to what is pivotal for the child or young person and engage in a shared focus of attention, the conditions for intersubjectivity are present. If a child or young person experiences the adult's concerns dominating, they are likely to lose interest and become resistant to the therapeutic process (Hughes 2009). 'Many children/young people have substantial evidence that adult knowings and descriptions of events will always be seen as right therefore rendering their experiences and knowings as wrong' (Bird 2004, p.317).

Hughes (2009) sees this as a common mistake, where adults direct their attention to their behavioural expectations and rules without exploring the inner life of the child or young person. He recommends that foster carers should fully comprehend and immerse themselves in the child or young person's outlook before sharing their own. 'For the adult to express his perspective without fully listening to the other precludes the experience of reciprocity in the relationship and generates defensiveness and withdrawal in the adolescent' (Hughes 2009, p.132).

At times this may feel frustrating for foster carers who may have many pressing issues of their own. Again, therapists can help by explaining the thinking behind this approach. When there is shared focus of attention with the adult following the child or young person, opportunities to raise the foster carer's concerns will emerge, but more naturally. Children and young people will find it much easier to address issues of concern regarding their behaviour when assured that their foster carer is interested in them and attuned to their experience. If foster carers can be empathic with a child or young person in the midst of challenging periods, seeing their behaviours as an expression of non-verbalised emotion, children and young people will be more open to addressing areas of conflict and difficulty. Discussing identified problem areas will seem more manageable if they see their foster carers as interested in the whole of them and not solely in the problem areas of their life. Moreover, when both children or young people and foster carers are focused on the same subject, there is more possibility for the mutual influencing capacities of intersubjectivity to unfold and for each to be influenced by the other's perspective and thoughts (Hughes 2009). When children and young people observe themselves positively impacting upon their foster carers then they will find the relationship hard to resist and they will also become more amenable to having their carer positively impact upon them (Hughes 2009).

This is not to say that boundaries should not be put in place where behaviour has been unacceptable. Indeed, foster carers need to be firm with their boundaries *and* empathic to the underlying emotion in a child or young person's behaviour (Hughes 1997). This twin-track approach requires attributes of empathy and firmness from foster carers. Often foster carers find one area comes more naturally to them than another and they will need the support of the therapist to develop the area where their aptitude is weakest. If foster carers can achieve this balance, then the ground is fertile for the child or young person to perceive the distinctions between the foster carer and previous experiences of being parented. 'He is shown how discipline is not abuse, conflict is not rejection, and periodic separation is not abandonment' (Hughes 1997, p.79). Being clear about these differences removes some of the obstacles for the child or young person to begin to trust the foster carer.

BEING A THERAPEUTIC FOSTER CARER

New foster carers invariably report that despite the training and assessment process they participated in, they were unprepared for the nature of difficulties they experienced in their first placement. When applying to be a foster carer, the desire to pass the assessment period and the motivation to care for young people work to ensure that a comprehensive knowledge of the challenges they may face in their career is only dimly grasped. Where Team Parenting is well established, foster carers are recruited with an expectation that they will engage with therapeutic fostering. However, the exact nature of what this means can only ever be known via lived experience. Being a therapeutic foster carer means engaging in reflective practice that requires a process of thinking about not only the young person's mind and experiences but one's own. This can be bewildering for foster carers who may not have knowingly signed up for exploration of their own mental and emotional processes when applying to foster. Yet this is what therapeutic parenting requires – the ability to mentalise and be aware, continually and persistently, of what is happening internally for oneself as well as imagining what is happening for the young person.

This level of self-awareness requires a degree of openness and trust. Often, when placements are bemired in struggles, foster carers can feel rejected, hurt and that they are failing in some way. Defending against such painful experiences can lead them into positions of blame. They may feel that if only the young person would behave differently, and if they had the necessary support, then they would be able to succeed with this placement. Working with a therapist involves confronting what lies hidden beneath the blame. Dismantling defences entails divesting oneself of self-righteousness and sitting with uncomfortable feelings. When foster carers can do this, they are likely to be able to respond sensitively and openly to the young person's pain in placement. However, the ability to do this requires that they have engaged in a self-reflective journey, if not a therapeutic one, for themselves (Hughes 1997; Siegel and Hartzell 2004).

ENGAGING THE CHILD OR YOUNG PERSON IN THERAPY

How to engage children and young people in therapy needs careful consideration, particularly for those who are looked after. Research has highlighted that children and young people in the care system often feel stigmatised for being in care and fear further stigmatisation for seeing a therapist (Blower *et al.* 2004). Therapy therefore needs to be appealing and inviting for children and young people if they are to engage and make use of the therapeutic space. Often, this requires adopting playful and creative approaches to the work (Wilson 1998). Whilst therapists may feel comfortable relating to children and young people in this way during individual sessions, they may feel exposed working in this way in the presence of foster carers. However, this is still necessary, otherwise the child or young person is likely to experience therapy sessions as dominated by adult discourse, means of communication and knowledge. Therapy may come to seem a repetition of their school experience, where they are expected to answer questions that contain embedded expectations of the right answer (Bird 2004). To guard against this, therapists need to enter into the child or young person's world and use a forum for communication with which they are most at ease. This requires imaginative, playful ways of working, using games, art and play. It also demands of the therapist a mirroring of the child or young person's affect via affective attunement, otherwise the risk is that they will feel that the emotion that they are communicating has not been understood (Hughes 2009).

Therapists should assume a position of interested curiosity when working with children and young people. This not only facilitates curiosity in their own minds (Hughes 2004; Larner 2009) but militates against them perceiving therapy as a space for their wrongdoings to be addressed. Hughes (1997, p.64) emphasises this: 'If I am busy communicating interest, I am less likely to be communicating evaluation and criticism and the child will be more likely to feel accepted.' Therapists can share with children and young people the idea of survival strategies, which works to reframe the meaning behind some of their challenging behaviour. Communicating with children and young people that the behaviours they have come to utilise may have stood them well in the past, enabling them to endure harsh and abusive circumstances, imparts a belief in their resourcefulness and resilience. Explaining that whilst these self-protective strategies are no longer needed because they are with safe, nurturing carers and acknowledging how hard it can be to give them up, transmits empathy with the challenge inherent in changing engrained behaviour patterns.

At times it can be helpful to introduce rudimentary ideas from neuroscience, explaining how patterns of behaviour that were once useful have been learned by the brain and laid down as pathways. Encouraging the child or young person to comprehend that now they need to learn new behavioural strategies for their changed contextual circumstances and help their brains learn new pathways, takes away the blame from them when they are repeatedly drawn to using old coping mechanisms. Hughes (1997) recommends facilitating the child or young person to see incidents of undesirable behaviour as opportunities for learning. Exploring episodes of difficult behaviour with empathy and curiosity creates the space to consider what was happening for them emotionally and how they might choose to act differently next time. Instilling a belief in children and young people that they are in essence good, valued and respected human beings who can sometimes make poor choices, communicates worth in their personhood; it separates their behaviours from who they are as well as imbuing in them the concept that they have the ability to make different choices (Hughes 1997).

Externalisation is a narrative therapy technique (Epston, White and Murray 1992; Epston and White 1990; White 1995) that can further the endeavour to prevent a child or young person's identity being fused with their problems and create leverage for them to believe they have power to alter their behaviour:

> When we describe the problem as separate from the child, we are challenging the adult/child power relation through positioning the child as knowledgeable, as active, as more than the problem. We are harnessing the relational strength of the family to stand with the child in the development of change. (Bird 2004 p.302)

Externalising locates the problem outside of the child or young person. Part of the technique is to find a name for the problem that fits for the child or young person and describes how she is experiencing the difficulty. Using this name and giving the problem its own identity and a life of its own creates the space for children or young people to re-connect with their foster carers in finding ways of defeating the difficulty. For example, I worked with a young child who named his difficulty 'Alex Anger'. This enabled us to have conversations about how Alex Anger would enter his life, what made it easy for Alex Anger to do this and what made it more difficult. We looked for exceptions when he had managed to get the better of Alex Anger on his own and other times when his foster carers had helped. Such discussions enabled the therapeutic task to become a collaborative task between him, his foster carer and me, where we joined together to ensure that Alex Anger could play a more positive role in his life.

Narrative therapy techniques are also helpful in restoring to children and young people a sense of their own agency in their lives. Yuen's (2007) very useful article highlights how much of therapy with children and young people who have been abused focuses on the impact of their experiences of trauma upon them. Whilst this is important and necessary, she argues that unilaterally directing attention to this area can position children and young people as victims: 'Discourses of victimhood can obscure the cleverness, competencies, and knowledges of children. These discourses can also influence therapists. When working with children who have endured significant trauma, counsellors sometimes lose hope during the process of seeking ways forward' (Yuen 2007, p.16). Being positioned as a victim can lead to a perception of having been the passive recipient of unwanted actions by others. Yet, Yuen (2007) cites Michael White, who expounds his belief that no-one is a passive recipient of trauma (White 2006). Flaskas (2009) uses the term *transformative narratives* and maintains that such alternative stories have been shown in the literature to be important in developing resilience.

Most children and young people have been resourceful in finding ways of managing the experiences they have endured. Noticing and naming the strategies they have used points to their inherent strengths and resilience. Children and young people are more likely to become engaged in the therapeutic endeavour when conversations centre on their abilities as opposed to their wrongdoings. In her work with children and young people, Yuen (2007) explores their resilience in terms of what they have done and the skills and knowledge they have employed to survive bleak and gruelling circumstances. She proposes that such conversations lead to the development of a *second story*, where children and young people can talk about their experiences of trauma without becoming re-traumatised (Yuen 2007). When therapy focuses solely on the effects of trauma, children and young people can feel reluctant to engage in the process due to an understandable fear of raking over painful memories and the consequent emotional upheaval that follows. Instead, identifying with their resources and what they did to *get through* then and now creates for them a sense of agency, efficacy and power. 'Where previously the effects of the trauma identity story blinded the moments of exception, there was now a developing sense of personal agency' (Yuen 2007, p.9).

When foster carers are present to witness the development of this second story, they too can arrive at a different perception of their foster children or young people. Seeing them as survivors who have utilised their responses to protect themselves as much as possible creates a different image from children or young people who have been helplessly abused or are impossible to care for because of their behaviour. Having foster carers present in the therapeutic work with their foster children or young people tends to enhance their motivation in terms of understanding and providing therapeutic care (Hughes 1997). Observing the therapist work can enhance foster carers' own skills in adopting curiosity and empathy with their foster children and young people. In addition, being able to analyse and understand their foster children or young people's behaviour will lead them to respond differently to the scenarios that are played out at home (Hek *et al.* 2010). When children and young people feel understood and that their emotions can be held and contained by their foster carers, then they are liable to reduce their acting-out behaviours (Rocco-Briggs 2008). A lessening of challenging behaviours will enhance placement stability, and research has shown that sensitive, attuned caregiving on behalf of foster carers has a pivotal role to play in this (Beek and Schofield 2004).

CASE STUDY

Ben (12 years) arrived in placement after a series of placement breakdowns. In each case, after varying lengths of time, he became increasingly distressed and his carers became increasingly frustrated. Ben, always difficult for carers to reach, became ever more distant. For longer periods of time and with increasing magnitude, he screamed, cried, rocked, shouted, refused to follow instructions and turned away from support offered by his carers. His carers, feeling hopeless and exhausted, after much heartache gave up.

Ben was placed with another fostering provider, Liz, a carer well versed in the principles of carer/child work and therapeutic parenting. After several meetings between Liz, the therapist and supervising social worker to think about caring for Ben, weekly therapy sessions with Ben and Liz commenced. Each meeting was preceded by Liz and the therapist talking through Liz's thoughts and feelings as well as events of the preceding week. In Liz's view this was essential to her survival, and it also set the rhythm and tone for the proceeding work with Ben.

During the sessions Ben was much as he was at home with Liz – while being charming and polite, he disagreed without rancour with everything Liz and the therapist said. His usual answer to everything was 'no', despite any evidence to the contrary, including simple questions such as: Had he been to school? Learnt to...? Enjoyed...? Liked...? He even disagreed with the day of the week or the colour of a piece of clothing. He 'knew' whatever was talked about and didn't need help with anything because he could already do it. Ben never felt worried or anxious or sad or angry, only happy.

Liz and the therapist worked hard to understand Ben, thinking about how he may have needed to adapt to live in a hostile and critical home for six years. He couldn't trust carers and learned to protect and soothe himself as best he could. In the sessions the therapist and carer developed a playful style with lots of gentle teasing about 'disagreeing', which Ben responded to well. Conversations moved from the everyday into deeper but related subjects.

Ben loved stories and the therapist developed a story about a child who went to live alone on an island because no-one would look after him. This child met someone who helped him build a bridge back to the mainland. This became a shared metaphor for the therapy – Ben was building a bridge. Ben found it difficult to talk about himself and his experiences and feelings. Through the story he was able to think safely about himself, his past and present and to get upset on behalf of the child.

The story was revisited many times and developed nuance and meaning. After a week when Ben had managed to persuade a number of staff and pupils at school to buy him sweets or give him money, the therapist developed the story. The child, uncared for at home and hungry when he got to school, obtained both food and care from school. Ben listened, absorbed in the story, and showed signs of being upset. Reflecting on the story, he said he thought the child was upset, but he hadn't felt anything. Liz and the therapist talked quietly about how confusing it was for Ben to have such feelings he couldn't understand. With encouragement, Ben then spoke directly to the carer about feeling confused and even sometimes sad. He was able to articulate that at times he wanted to be looked after by Liz and wanted her help. This deeply emotional moment saw tears in the carer's eyes and a mutual impact of carer on child and child on carer.

Two weeks later, Ben was in trouble at school. Unable to do the work and unable to ask for help, Ben had had an angry exchange with a teacher. When Liz picked him up, Ben sat silent and Liz took the lead. She knew about the incident and how hard it was for Ben to talk about difficult things, but she wanted to help. Ben spoke hesitantly at first with his head down. He was frightened Liz wouldn't love him anymore and would send him away. Liz put her arms around him, told her she loved him and was very pleased with him for being honest. Ben told Liz how it made his tummy hurt and made him unhappy when he bottled things up. Only then, having managed Ben's attachment needs, did they talk about how he was struggling with maths and what he could do if he was finding things difficult in school, because swearing and breaking stuff was not the best choice to make.

In this chapter approaches to therapy that address trauma have been described. Joint work with the carer and child have been considered as well as therapeutic approaches that work directly with the child. Chapter 7 moves on to explore ways in which foster carers are supported within Team Parenting. Of particular importance is the role of supervising social workers and the relationships they develop with foster carers. Carer groups are also discussed as a way of providing peer support, teaching techniques, sharing theoretical knowledge and embedding reflective practice.

CHAPTER 7

SUPPORT FOR FOSTER CARERS IN TEAM PARENTING

CHAPTER CONTENTS

Social work support

Case study

Engendering the philosophy of Team Parenting in the wider team

Carer groups
ADAPT
ATTUNE groups

Case study
Conclusion

SOCIAL WORK SUPPORT

Respect for foster carers, acknowledgement of the pivotal role they play and a suggestion that they be seen as professionals in their own right proliferate in the literature (Clarke 2009; Maclay 2006; Murray *et al.* 2011; Staines *et al.* 2011; Wilson and Evetts 2006). The role of the supervisory social worker's relationship with their foster carer is seen to have a fundamental place in contributing to foster carer satisfaction and retention (Maclay, Bunce and Purves 2009; Murray *et al.* 2011). Staines *et al.* (2011) emphasise that studies have made clear the need for foster carers to have access to high-quality support and to be able to develop close working relationships with social workers. It is recognised in the literature that even low levels of stress can reduce the quality of foster care and contribute to the likelihood of placement breakdown (Whenan *et al.* 2009). Stress that foster carers experience can be mediated by good-quality social work support.

Social workers inevitably form a fundamental part of the Team Parenting approach. The role that they play is guided by legislation such as the National Minimum Standards (DfE 2011a). Within Team

Parenting, the support that social workers offer to foster carers and the quality of the relationship that develops between them is seen to be instrumental in contributing to foster carer efficacy, well-being for the fostered young person and placement success. When there are difficulties in this relationship, foster carers can feel undermined and unsupported. If this situation is allowed to go unchecked, almost invariably the child becomes lost in the ensuing conflict. Moreover, blame, criticism and splitting are likely to enter centre stage. Such factors evoke anxiety and defensiveness, reduce the capacity to think meaningfully and the ability to work co-operatively together.

In her survey Clarke (2009) finds that foster carers value feeling part of a team. Team Parenting helps to engender this by viewing social workers and foster carers as belonging to the wider parenting team. It is intended that their relationship will assist in the collaborative efforts of the overall Team Parenting approach. Whenan *et al.* (2009) recommend that foster carer satisfaction with social work support should be monitored regularly. This seems sensible advice as Clarke (2009) finds that not having enough support is a factor for some foster carers in deciding whether to continue fostering. Forty per cent of foster carers reported that they considered stopping fostering due to a lack of support (Clarke 2009).

The desirable qualities of a social worker's relationship with their foster carers are described in the literature. Clarke (2009) suggests that quick, responsive and warm support is valued. Minnis and Devine (2001, p.50) note that the qualities foster carers looked for were:

> trustworthiness, honesty, preparedness to listen, empathy, and taking them seriously. Where there was good, open, close and continuing communication between social workers and carers, they felt supported and helped in their care of the child. When this did not happen, carers were left unsupported and struggling at times.

In Minnis and Devine's (2001) study, foster carers were clear that they valued support from social workers in trying to understand the content of young people's behaviour, particularly when this seemed rejecting of the care they offered. The nature of the relationship that foster carers enjoy with young people inevitably affects foster-care well-being. Social workers' ability to offer insight into the psychological dynamics that are occurring between the foster carer and the child comes from their training. However, this is supplemented in Team Parenting by the presence of therapists who sit with social workers in their area offices. Having daily, face-to-face access to therapists for informal consultation means that social workers are able to draw upon therapeutic knowledge to assist their thinking and transfer these ideas into the conversations they have with foster carers. This process is invaluable and often results in distress in the placement being contained by the social worker, as opposed to external, specialist help being sought.

Comprehending the psychological processes that are at play and inherent in fostering traumatized young people will enable social workers to engage in empathic and reflective relationships with their foster carers. Despite the potential of the foster-carer/child relationship to offer repair from previous damaging experiences for the young person, the nature of the young person's attachment difficulties often impedes the flourishing of a warm, nurturing and caring relationship (Whenan *et al.* 2009). When experiencing repeated challenging behaviours that can be perceived as rejecting, foster carers withdraw to protect themselves. It is in these circumstances that the social worker can intervene. The support they offer is more likely to be meaningful when the relationship they have with their foster carers is a trusted and valued one. The ability of foster carers to remain neutral, contain their affect and avoid being drawn into emotional warfare will serve to support the fostering task and ultimately the young people in placement.

That foster carers wish to be able to unburden themselves of their feelings without judgment is known (Murray *et al.* 2011). How to undertake good quality supervision with foster carers needs higher priority in social work training. Supervising foster carers in a way that allows them space for their own emotions as well as a place for meaning-making and understanding requires a thorough grounding in reflective practice. Time is needed on the social work curriculum to engender the qualities necessary to become a reflective practitioner. When foster carers are supported by reflective and emotionally engaged social workers, they will be in a better position to become therapeutic carers able to work towards the resolution of young people's attachment- and trauma-related difficulties.

Minnis and Devine (2001) raise a significant point in their paper for social workers looking to support foster carers who have extensive fostering experience. Foster carers in their study who had looked after more than 30 children were more likely to experience placement breakdowns. They offer a couple of possible explanations – that experienced foster carers may have harder-to-place children placed with them or that they may be suffering from burnout and fatigue. The phenomenon of burnout is well documented in literature regarding professionals (McCann and Pearlman 1990; Walker 2004), but much less written about in connection with foster carers. Minnis and Devine (2001) point out that at least professionals have holidays and are not with their clients 24/7. In the Team Parenting approach, which encourages long-term, consistent relationships between foster-carers and social workers, a depth of knowledge and trust is generated. Social workers come to know their carers and to be able to predict situations that they may find more taxing than others. They are then able to increase support to foster carers in a timely and sensitive manner, working to buffer them against the relentlessness of caring for young people with attachment difficulties. Moreover, when a strong working alliance exists between foster carer and social worker, foster carers are more likely to turn for help more readily and feel able to confide their feelings in their social worker. In this way, social workers can offer an attuned relationship to their foster carers that meet their specific needs and facilitate carers' ability to make use of the support on offer. As Ziegenhain (2004, p.51) states: 'As a guiding principle the secure base phenomenon is extended to the relationship between the professional and the [carer] parent. A trustworthy working alliance is a central condition for an effective collaboration.'

Social workers can make valuable contributions to the fostering task in other ways too. Minnis and Devine (2001) found that foster carers reported that their ability to have clear conversations with young people in placement was significantly aided by their experience of social workers communicating clearly with them. This is an important finding and acknowledges that when foster carers are clear about plans for young people, they are able to discuss these with more clarity with the children they foster. However, sadly, due to a number of pressures and factors, coherent and explicit plans are sometimes lacking in the social care system. Supervising social workers within Team Parenting play an important role here in maintaining frequent contact with Local Authority social workers and enquiring about their planning. Discussions between supervising social workers within Team Parenting and Local Authority social workers can sometimes elucidate previous confusion and uncertainty regarding planning. Often, social workers in Team Parenting may have more daily contact and knowledge of the young person, due to the frequency of their visits to the foster carer's home, than the Local Authority social worker. The fact that they know the young person better can assist the Local Authority social worker in their planning. Resolving uncertainty regarding planning is helpful for both foster carers and young people.

CASE STUDY

The carer, Anthea, was clearly finding some of the challenges she faced with Callum difficult to cope with. This is a young person who has a complex attachment disorder and presents with aspects of being on the autistic spectrum, chewing behaviours and obsessive behaviours in relation to gaming and his desire to be a female. Although Anthea copes well on a day-to-day basis, there are many aspects of Callum's behaviour that both she and her 'new boyfriend' find challenging. Anthea has eight years' experience as a foster carer and I believe that she would have coped better with these behaviours if she had not had the additional influence of her new boyfriend, who clearly did not understand the challenges of attachment disorder and who is presently going through a Form F assessment (the assessment format used in the UK for assessing prospective foster carers and adopters).

Providing a Team Parenting approach for this particular case has provided the support needed in order for all the team involved to understand Callum in a clearer light. As well as developing a wider knowledge of complex attachment disorder via the therapist, Anthea feels supported just because she knows the team around the child are there working together in a multi-disciplinary way. I believe this allows the carer to feel that she is developing a stronger relationship with not only me as her supervising social worker, but also the rest of the Team Parenting group. Acknowledging that a placement is complex does have a positive effect on carers managing the placement better long term.

From a social worker perspective, managing such a complex case has at times been challenging. I [the supervising social worker] have found that I have had to do additional reading to help towards understanding Callum holistically. The Team Parenting approach has given me support in managing and maintaining Callum in placement through some very testing times. Knowing I can contact the therapist at any time to talk about the complexity of the case gives me a new-found confidence to take my supervision with the carer one step further. This empowers me and increases the trust that the foster carer places in me as her supervising social worker. It allows for our supervision sessions to be more in-depth in relation to analysing behaviours, as we know we both have a good knowledge base, which we continue to acquire through learning and gaining knowledge from other professionals involved through the Team Parenting Meetings.

Additionally, I believe that the Team Parenting approach in this instance has given the carer more confidence in our approach as a team and she clearly values our ideas, suggestions and management of the complex issues that Callum presents with. This, in turn, has allowed the carer to have more faith and confidence in me as her supervising social worker, which has enabled our relationship to flourish. I believe that this placement would not be able to get through those difficult times without a Team Parenting approach. This approach clearly helps all of the team to develop relationships, confidence, understanding and management of difficult issues, ultimately preventing placement breakdown. It also strengthens and provides a solid support package to manage and acknowledge the difficult issues the carer deals with in placement on a day-to-day basis.

ENGENDERING THE PHILOSOPHY OF TEAM PARENTING IN THE WIDER TEAM

As an approach, Team Parenting is rooted in and influenced by attachment and systemic theories, therapies and practice. That there is congruence and a fit between the two is now being written about (Dallos 2006). As we have seen in Chapter 1, a number of other models for working therapeutically in foster care exist both within this country and elsewhere, particularly the USA. Some of the models draw from different theoretical bases, the most common being social learning theory and behavioural theory. Given that Team Parenting is not a modularised approach and contains within it a fluidity and flexibility that befits psychotherapeutic practice, it is important to be aware of its theoretical tenets and to select most appropriate practice within these. Whilst introducing techniques and strategies from different theoretical roots may be useful at times, Team Parenting needs to retain some solid footing in its epistemological and ontological foundations if it is not to be too porous to exist as a model in its own right. Taking a meta-perspective to theory may be useful to facilitate this process. Therefore, locating for others the theoretical underpinnings of Team Parenting and identifying when an idea from another field is being utilised can be helpful. This is particularly so for newly qualified social workers, who have often been trained in a behavioural approach.

Behavioural approaches work by identifying and rewarding positive behaviours and implementing consequences for undesirable ones. Behaviour modification and structural intervention were once the hallmarks of family therapy. However, a shift has occurred from, 'behaviour and patterns of interaction to processes of meaning-making' (Dallos 2006, p.3). This position, heavily influenced by social constructionism, fits with an interest in exploring the *processes and patterns* that underlie the difficulties families experience, as opposed to diagnosing and perceiving problems as located in an individual's pathology (Dallos 2006). Team Parenting inhabits this position, where, drawing on systemic and attachment theories and therapies, it aims to explore the meaning attached to the challenges posed by caring for young people in foster care and to facilitate greater understanding on behalf of those looking after young people in placement. The central thesis is that enhanced understanding of the impact of early traumatic experiences on later functioning, together with comprehension of the interrelated nature of human existence, will alter how carers and professionals think and respond. Making sense together in itself effects change as perspectives alter, which in turn shift behaviours and actions. 'A narrative approach stresses that each telling can become an interpersonal co-construction so that in the telling the story may be modified, and we may gain new insights as we tell the story' (Dallos 2006, p.88).

When members of the parenting team employ different strategies, the result is invariably confusion and lack of a clear, coherent approach. Adhering to the theoretical roots of Team Parenting creates a foundation from which to move and incorporate other techniques when these might be useful. Viewing different approaches as domains can facilitate a conversation as to which theoretical position is being chosen. Choosing a position with intention, observing its outcome and utilising feedback to guide the next intervention is the backbone to working therapeutically. Such meta-perspectives on theory and approach allow for fidelity to the fundamental principles of Team Parenting as well as introducing other techniques when all are agreed on their fit and intended outcome.

Recruiting new members of staff to the Team Parenting approach, takes time, particularly if their training has not exposed them to systemic and attachment theories and therapies. Sharing office space with a therapist who can link practice and theory through informal case discussion supports the philosophy of Team Parenting to become embedded in everyday practice. In addition, training is provided as well as an extensive reading programme to instil in new staff the central tenets that inform Team Parenting.

However, even with these measures in place, it is not unusual for new social workers to find themselves supporting foster carers who have more expertise and knowledge regarding Team Parenting and therapeutic care than they do. This should not be viewed as a problem. Team Parenting supports the view of a group of professionals and carers working collaboratively on a shared endeavour and it values highly the expertise and contribution of all participants, whatever stage they are at. Consistent with this outlook is the positioning of foster carers as pivotal members of a professional team who can both contribute to the shared knowledge as well as gain new understanding in the same way as any other team member. Team Parenting values co-operation and mutuality over hierarchy and role status. Indeed, philosophically it would concur with Conway's (2009, p.27) aspirations:

> Foster carers need to be among the most highly valued members of our society, with appropriate remuneration, so that we also attract more people with secure attachments, high levels of self-esteem and high expectations for the children in their care.

CARER GROUPS

The importance of maintaining a satisfied cohort of foster carers in order to ensure that high-quality therapeutic foster care and placement stability can be achieved is central to Team Parenting. Ensuring that foster carers are regularly supported by their supervising social workers goes some way to meeting these goals. However, for foster carers to be able to offer therapeutic parenting they will need additional training. Such training needs to deliver a combination of increased knowledge in the form of psychological understanding and the skills to engage in reflective, therapeutic parenting. Being a therapeutic foster carer is aided by self-awareness and insight into one's own emotional and psychological processes. However, delving into one's own personal history, attachment experiences and considering their impact on one's parenting style, can be exposing and delicate work.

To address these multiple and interlinked issues, Team Parenting delivers training in therapeutic parenting and reflective practice via closed carer groups. Closed groups allow for safety and trust to be generated between group members. This is important as therapeutic theory postulates that safe working alliances allow for greater exploration and reflection (McCluskey *et al.* 1999). Thus, reflecting together in a group, surrounded by others dedicated to the same task, facilitates foster carers in exploring their own functioning and in considering how their relational styles meet and connect with what is happening in the placement and with their foster child. In addition, the group setting provides the opportunity for both peer support and learning from each other.

ADAPT

ADAPT is an acronym standing for Attachment Difficulties and Parenting Therapeutically. ADAPT groups were started in 2002 and are now run across the UK.

The rationale for ADAPT groups

Adapt groups came into existence because, through feedback from foster carers, it was realised that many carers felt confused and overwhelmed by the challenging behaviours they were experiencing with the children and young people they looked after. They lived with the common misunderstanding that if they offered children and young people love and good quality care, then the children and young people would be grateful to be away from the abuse and neglect they had previously experienced and respond well to the safety of their new environment. When this did not occur and young people behaved in ways that were rejecting of the care on offer, foster carers felt disillusioned, dismayed and despairing. Invariably, this situation compromised the quality of care on offer as foster carers withdrew to protect their own emotions. Ultimately, left unchecked and unsupported, it was observed that placement stability came to be threatened.

Maintaining placement stability was seen to be important not only to prevent the multiple losses and disruption that followed a move but also to prevent the vicious cycle that so often seemed to ensue.

Placement breakdown necessarily ruptures a child and young person's trust once more and it seemed that this disappointment would often be expressed behaviourally in their next placement, contributing in turn to greater risk for future disruption (Chamberlain *et al.* 2008a, 2008b; Everson-Hock *et al.* 2012; Price *et al.* 2008). Conversely, placement stability may ameliorate the effects of repeated disruptions, but it requires foster carer skill to manage the externalising behaviour of the children or young people for this to be achieved (Macdonald and Turner 2005).

It is acknowledged in the literature that there is a relationship between challenging behaviour and foster carer's stress, confidence and placement stability (Macdonald and Turner 2005; Morgan and Baron 2011; Price *et al.* 2008; Sellick 2006). 'Children who have difficulty giving and receiving love and affection, who constantly defy parental rules and authority and who are physically and emotionally abusive [...] place a severe strain on the foster family' (Golding 2003, p.64). When foster carers are stressed themselves and they have little hope of the situation changing, the risk of placement breakdown is high.

A link is also drawn in the literature between behavioural difficulties and parenting capacity (Chamberlain *et al.* 2008a, 2008b; Golding and Picken 2004; Morgan and Baron 2011). Chamberlain *et al.* (2008a, 2008b) identify overly harsh or excessively lenient disciplinary measures as risk factors for exacerbating unwanted behaviours, along with lack of parental involvement and unwitting reinforcement via the use of unhelpful strategies. There seems to be agreement in the literature that there is a 'close relationship between children's behaviour, parenting style and placement stability, with placements being more likely to break down when the behaviour was more challenging in the context of less sensitive parenting' (Morgan and Baron 2011, p.19).

While this situation can threaten placement stability with devastating consequences for the children and young people involved, it seems that it also has repercussions for the retention of carers. Chamberlain *et al.* (2008a, 2008b) found that difficulty in understanding and managing behaviour was a primary reason for stopping fostering. Given this situation, therapists and social workers wanted to equip foster carers with the skills to make psychological sense of the behaviour with which they were confronted in their own homes. The hope was that this understanding could be used to transform their perspective of the situation they were facing, positively influence their responses and generate greater resilience.

The literature is rife with recommendations that specialist training programmes are needed to support foster carers' resilience and to equip them with the understanding and skills to manage challenging behaviour more effectively (Everson-Hock *et al.* 2012; Golding and Picken 2004; Macdonald and Turner 2005; Price *et al.* 2008, Wilson and Evetts 2006). The social work literature is dense with acknowledgement of the specialised task foster carers undertake and their need to be imbued with sufficient expertise and skill to meet the demands of their role. 'If foster carers are to take on these increasing responsibilities, they clearly will require preparation, comprehensive support and, perhaps most importantly, the right kind of training' (Warman *et al.* 2006, p.17). The enormity of this challenge is acknowledged:

> The need for effective attachment to well-trained carers who can help promote resilience in children who need to cope with adversity and not adopt dysfunctional ways to respond to abuse or neglect is perhaps the single biggest challenge to contemporary fostering. (Pithouse *et al.* 2004, p.20)

However, a blanket approach to training has been found to be ineffective whereas tailor-made training to the specific needs of foster carers and their particular children and young people is recommended (Pithouse *et al.* 2004). Warman *et al.* (2006) highlight that on-going group training, where carers can learn new skills, go away and practise them and receive feedback from the facilitators and peers, seems to cement and integrate learning. When training is delivered via a group programme, the sessions allow for skills to be honed and new concepts embedded over time. Warman *et al.* (2006) also advocate training in groups as they found that the trust that was engendered led to a greater degree of sharing, openness and honesty as well as encouraging collaborative learning.

ADAPT was therefore designed to be a reflective, therapeutic training group which would address the needs for specific knowledge and specialised skills of foster carers. It was believed that similar results to those achieved by individual consultation sessions could be achieved utilising this forum. This supposition was being confirmed by emergent studies of foster carers receiving training in groups. Golding and Picken (2004) postulated that group work provides foster carers with both support and psycho-education. Golding (2003) reported that the groups she had run had led to new understanding for foster carers of the underlying causes behind behaviours and that this in turn created a different perspective of the relationship between them and their foster child. Furthermore, she reported that the groups were found to increase foster carers' efficacy and confidence, and enhance communication skills, and that this was believed to positively impact on the child or young person. Although using a different theoretical basis for their group, Macdonald and Turner (2005, p.1273) reported a similar finding, in that:

> many commented that this approach encouraged them to step back from a situation, examine what was going on and try to think strategically about how best to handle something. Others observed that it helped them to stay calm and in control of what had hitherto been very taxing situations.

The other factor that contributed to the rationale for introducing group work for foster carers grew out of recognition that fostering could be isolating. It was realised that the demands of looking after children and young people with traumatic early experiences and severely challenging behaviour without a support network would inevitably take its toll. Added to this were the other inherent stresses that form part of the fostering role, such as the threat of allegations being made, managing contact with birth parents and negotiating relationships with the Local Authority (Pithouse *et al.* 2004). It was perceived that foster carers needed nurture and support for themselves if they were to undertake their role effectively. ADAPT was seen as a way of providing both peer and professional support to foster carers within the same setting.

The idea of running an experiential group was born because therapists believed that foster carers would be better able to make use of the theoretical content of training and retain it if it was embedded within their own experiences. Thus, it was considered that theoretical teaching and psycho-education could best be delivered within the context of foster carers reflecting upon and talking about their own placements. This would give them the opportunity to connect theory and practice together *in situ*. This belief has been borne out by others who have run groups. Macdonald and Turner (2005) consider that one of the weaknesses of the group they ran was that there was not enough fluidity in its delivery to allow for sufficient reflection on current experiences. Moreover, they, like Warman *et al.* (2006), suggest that groups which allow foster carers to put into practice their new learning at home and then receive feedback on their experiences, allow shifts in parenting style to become more fully integrated over time.

The goals of ADAPT groups were consistent with the overall ambitions of Team Parenting. It was intended that participation in an ADAPT group would lead to: improved placement stability for children and young people in foster care; better reflective functioning for foster carers, which would enhance their capacity as therapeutic parents; minimising the number of children and young people moving into residential care; and, as an overall contribution, enhanced outcomes for children and young people.

The practice of ADAPT groups

The model for ADAPT groups was built around the following Aim and Objectives.

The aim of ADAPT is to:

- help carers gain a deeper understanding about their children's attachment difficulties, in addition to increasing carers' range of therapeutic parenting skills.

The objectives were to:

- acknowledge the difficulty of caring for a child with attachment difficulties and recognise that it is a specialised and skilled task

- enable foster carers to understand the difference between parenting birth children and parenting children who have been subject to complex trauma in their early lives

- support foster carers to offer successful, long-term placements and prevent placement breakdown

- teach therapeutic parenting strategies to foster carers

- enhance foster carers' own reflective capacities both in their parenting and in understanding their own responses to the children they have in placement

- provide a consistent time and space via a closed group for carers to share experiences, offer support and learn from each other in a safe, trusting environment

- increase foster carers' understanding of the specific situation, background, experiences and behaviour of the young person they have living with them

- increase parenting skills and decrease reactivity in responding to difficult behaviours

- reduce children's and young people's challenging behaviours.

In Team Parenting, foster carers are put forward to attend ADAPT groups by their supervising social worker. Therapists ask supervising social workers to recommend foster carers they have on their caseload who have long-term children and young people in placement with attachment difficulties and who might be interested in attending the group. Social workers know the foster carers on their caseload well and are able to identify those who might be able to make best use of the group. Foster carers who are recommended receive visits from the therapists who will facilitate the group. The purpose of these visits is to explain the closed nature of the group, its reflective/experiential style and the importance of committing to attendance each week. Usually eight to ten carers are selected.

ADAPT groups have two stages. The first stage involves meeting for ten weekly sessions. There is a break for coffee and at 1.00pm the foster carers have lunch on their own, providing important opportunities for informal interaction before coming together with the facilitating therapists at the end for a brief goodbye. The second stage involves monthly meetings over a nine-month period. This means that the total duration of the group, through both stages, is approximately a year.

STAGE ONE

The ten weeks follow a programme in terms of the content of the theoretical teaching. However, this programme is flexible and can be adjusted according to the pace and tempo of the group. The structure of all these sessions follows a format: there is a check-in, theoretical input and experiential/creative exercises before the coffee break. This structure allows enough time for discussion to make sense of the behaviours that foster carers are facing in their own homes week by week.

After the coffee break each foster carer takes it in turns to present a living sculpt of the child or young person they have in placement, using the other group members to represent key individuals in that child's life. This intervention is taken from structural family therapy (Burnham 1980).

The sculpt

The carer introduces their child and a current photograph of the child is passed around the group. The carer's introduction might include answers to: What is it like being with the child? What behaviours does the child use? What was the child's experience of living with their birth family? How are they progressing in school? What are their relationships like with their peers? What needs to change?

The carer identifies significant people in the child's life and nominates group members to play these roles, including the role of the child. After positioning the 'child' in the centre of the room, the carer directs other group members, in role, to take up positions in relation to the child to represent their life and relationships as they are now. The therapists might encourage the carer to consider people's stance and direction of gaze in relation to the child.

The therapists ask every group member, in role, to describe what it's like being in their position. Group members might consider how they feel and what they can physically see.

The therapists encourage the carer to consider how they would change the sculpt in order to represent how they ideally want it to be, reflecting too what they believe the child needs. The carer then directs group members to represent this change and feed back about how the change feels.

The group members de-role. Space might be needed to acknowledge the impact of the sculpt. Time is needed for general feedback about the experience and for thinking about possible strategies to help the placement going forward.

STAGE TWO: FOLLOW-UP AND IMPLEMENTING WHAT HAS BEEN LEARNED

Once the weekly sessions have ended, the group moves to meeting monthly. They meet on a monthly basis, nine times. The monthly meetings follow a similar format to before but the theoretical topics are chosen by the group session by session, giving the therapists time to prepare and providing the opportunity for the learning to match this particular group's on-going needs. Instead of the sculpts, the therapists facilitate group discussion, encouraging foster carers to engage in reflective practice and linking experiences within their own placements to the theory that has been taught.

This process takes its practice and principles from group clinical peer supervision. Foster carers take it in turns to describe issues they are currently experiencing in placement. The therapists and other foster carers facilitate them to think analytically and reflectively about what might be occurring for them and for their foster child. Appropriate strategies are discussed and considered with particular reference to their therapeutic impact.

Benefits of ADAPT groups

There is a paucity of robust evaluation of groups for foster carers in the literature. Warman *et al.* (2006) extemporise that while various parenting programmes have been evaluated robustly, very few fostering training programmes have received the same scrutiny. Everson-Hock *et al.* (2012, p.172) review the outcomes for a range of support groups and training for foster carers in the UK and in the USA, and comment that 'because of the overall poor methodological and reporting quality and wide variation in services, interventions and outcomes reported, the findings of this review must be interpreted with caution'.

Golding and Picken (2004) point to the lack of randomised control trials and consistent outcome measures that can be used to establish a group's effectiveness. Part of the difficulty in making comparisons is the variety of methodological and theoretical approaches used in the groups. While Macdonald and Turner (2005) conducted research into the efficacy of using cognitive behavioural techniques to improve foster carers' skills, Golding and Picken's (2004) groups relied on the teaching of attachment theory. The KEEP (see page 35) groups in the USA (e.g. Chamberlain *et al.* 2008a, 2008b; Price *et al.* 2008) have concentrated on social learning theory and the teaching of positive behaviour management skills. Moreover, not only do the approaches used vary but so do the duration of the group and the age of the children and young people being cared for by the foster carers. Everson-Hock *et al.* (2012) hypothesise that it is the latter taken together with the shorter follow-up time used in the KEEP groups that may account for their apparent greater degree of success.

In the first eight years of running ADAPT groups, a qualitative evaluation tool was used to measure satisfaction with the groups. Foster carers reported improved knowledge of attachment theory, greater insight into the child's perspective, reduced feelings of isolation, feeling supported by other foster carers and feeling recognised by the facilitators for the difficult task they undertook. The groups were described as close-knit and led to long-term friendships and mentoring arrangements. In terms of enhancing their skills, foster carers reported feeling more confident and knowing when to stay calm and not take a child's behaviour personally. Importantly, this led to a less reactive style of parenting and they described themselves becoming more reflective, spending more time watching, observing and considering how to respond. The central issue of responding to a child's developmental stage and emotional age was frequently cited as critical learning. Many foster carers also reported having more strategies at their fingertips, and knowing what practical things to do and say in moments of crisis and how to draw on positive behaviour management techniques.

A foster carer recently made the following comment following attendance of an ADAPT group in 2011:

> Initially when I was asked to attend the ADAPT training my first thought was 'more training!!' I am now halfway through the initial ten weeks of the course and I am really enjoying it. I have learned so much about who I am in relation to the child I am looking after and I am really aware of the significance of how my past, my childhood, my parenting impacts on how I view things. I have found that I am not alone, I am not the only carer who is experiencing these issues and I feel listened to and not judged in the group by other carers or the therapists. I have particularly valued doing the sculpts. These have been insightful and have provided me and other carers with a different perspective of how the work that we do affects the people in my family. Re-creating these relationships has helped me to see in a concrete way what is happening and this is very powerful. The course at times is personally very challenging and this can make me feel quite vulnerable, but I can see that it is important to be able to reflect on my life so as I can help the child that I am looking after. I would highly recommend this course to other carers.

In 2007, a social work student undertook an evaluation of ADAPT, which was fed back to the organisation but not published. The research involved individual interviews with participants who had recently completed an ADAPT group and other foster carers who had completed ADAPT groups several years previously. These foster carers attended ADAPT groups in different regions. Comparisons were made between the answers given by the foster carers, and strong convergence of opinion was found. Although the sample was small, this convergence of opinion demonstrates some consistency of experience of ADAPT within different regions, suggesting that it is the structure, content and model of the group, as opposed to individual practitioners, that contribute to its success.

The benefits of carer groups, including those that do not involve specific training, are borne out in the literature (Chamberlain *et al.* 2008a, 2008b; Golding 2003; Golding and Picken 2004; Luke and Sebba 2013; Macdonald and Turner 2005; Price *et al.* 2008). Albeit different in methodology, there seem to be common themes in design whereby groups are closed and incorporate theoretical input, space for reflection and learning of new parenting strategies. Golding and Picken (2004) found in their research that foster carers valued having space to offload and also to observe that everyone struggled at times and could make mistakes. Foster carers commented that they found this a normalising process. Like the feedback received for ADAPT, foster carers noted that understanding attachment theory helped them know where behaviours were coming from. Golding and Picken's (2004) carers, like carers who have attended ADAPT, also thought that the attachment group should be compulsory for all carers. Interestingly, a similar issue for them regarding whether partners should attend together or separately came up, with one foster carer commenting that she liked being able to discuss what she had learnt with her partner, and others identifying that the lack of their partners' presence meant they were in danger of implementing different approaches at home.

The closest in style to ADAPT are the groups that Golding and her colleagues have designed as they also utilise attachment theory (Golding 2003; Golding and Picken 2004). There are several overlaps with ADAPT, the central ones being:

- the teaching of therapeutic parenting strategies, with particular emphasis on the need to provide warmth, emotional attunement and empathy alongside clear boundaries and discipline

- the encouragement of foster carers to be less reactive, anticipate potential 'hot-spots' with their foster child/young person and deflect unnecessary confrontation

- the use of a variety of training mediums, including discussion, role-play, presentations and creative, experiential approaches

- the role of the therapist in facilitating foster carers' self-awareness regarding their own history and how this might impact on their parenting style and the interactions they have with the children and young people whom they foster

- the development of foster carers' capacities for reflective function, whereby they can interpret the possible underlying causes for a child or young person's externalising behaviours

- teaching foster carers communication skills so they can respond to children/young people's behaviours with curiosity and openness and help them make links for themselves regarding their latent feelings

- the importance of foster carers controlling *the emotional rhythm* (Golding 2003) of the house in order to facilitate a child or young person's affect-regulation

- the necessity of foster carers taking time out for themselves to nourish their own relationships and support networks

- the opportunity to directly relate the theory discussed with live examples from foster carers' daily lives with the children and young people they have in placement

- recognition of the slow and long nature of change for many children and young people, this being reflected in the duration of the group

- the importance of having the opportunity to learn new skills, practise them and then receive additional support and feedback on this experience

- the regularity of meetings and the span of the group allowing for concepts to be revisited and built upon over time.

Evaluation of ADAPT

Since 2011, in recognition of the lack of robust outcome measures for the efficacy of carer groups, therapists have started to utilise quantitative assessment tools to evaluate the impact of ADAPT. In the most recent studies, therapists have used:

- the Parenting Stress Index (PSI) (Abidin 1995) to measure changes in parental stress, parent/child interactions and the degree of difficult behaviour being exhibited by the child

- Goodman's (2001) Strengths and Difficulties Questionnaire (SDQ) to measure changes in the young people's functioning.

These tools have been used in conjunction with an evaluation questionnaire, which is qualitative in design. This questionnaire sets out to gather feedback on the changes that foster carers may have noticed in a wide range of their child or young person's functioning as a result of attending ADAPT.

Both the PSI and the SDQ are completed at the beginning of the group and at the end, allowing for comparison between pre- and post-intervention scores of both the foster carers and the young people they had placed with them.

THE PARENTAL STRESS INDEX (PSI) (ABIDIN 1997)

In order to evidence outcomes and provide some quantitative data, the Parental Stress Index short form (PSI-SF) (Abidin 1997) was used in an ADAPT group run with some foster carers in 2011, and it is now used in all ADAPT groups run within Core Assets. This questionnaire assesses the level of stress experienced in relation to the role of parenting. It is designed specifically for parents with children displaying emotional and behavioural problems. It has a total of 36 items, and the total stress score is made up of the three scales: parental distress, parent child dysfunctional interaction and child difficulty. This measure has been widely used in research studies with looked-after children and with biological families.

From the 2011 ADAPT group of ten carers, the following results were obtained:

Total stress

This scale gives an indication of the overall level of stress a parent is experiencing in relation to their parenting role. Seven out of ten carers reported reduced levels of overall parental stress at the end of the ten-week programme.

Parental distress

This subscale refers to the distress a parent is experiencing specifically within their parenting role. High scores reflect a lack of confidence in the parenting role, feelings of being restricted in life due to parenting responsibilities and a lack of social support. Six out of the ten carers reported reduced levels of parental distress after the group.

Parent–child dysfunctional interaction

This subscale measures stress related to the parent's perception of the relationship between them and the child. High scores suggest that the parent is not feeling any gratification in their role as a 'parent'. The parent may view themselves as abused or rejected by the child and may feel alienated from the child. High scores suggest that the bond between parent and child is under threat or has never been adequately established. Six out of ten carers reported reduced stress levels in the domain of parent-child dysfunctional interaction after completion of the ten-week group.

Difficult child

The difficult child subscale focuses on the carers' perception of behaviours presented by the child, and difficulty in managing them. Parents may be struggling with understanding and working with specific behaviours presented by the child. Seven out of ten carers reported lower levels of stress in relation to their perception of difficult child behaviour after ADAPT.

Extra information

The largest decrease in scores between the baseline and at completion of the groups occurred within the difficult child subscale, suggesting this is where the most improvement was seen after ten weeks.

It is important to note that this is a very small sample and that for total stress three carers' scores increased, indicating higher levels of parental stress after the ten weeks. As there are always factors in carers' lives outside of the group which are likely to affect stress levels, this must be considered when attempting to interpret the scores. However, the results do suggest a reduction in feelings of parental stress for carers. The impact of the group is likely to be different for each carer and a close look at the scores for each individual carer may be helpful in planning further support and intervention.

Strength and Difficulties Questionnaire (SDQ) (Goodman 2001)

Levels of perceived behavioural difficulties were measured using the SDQ. This is a brief behavioural screening questionnaire with 20 items. It is designed for completion by parents, and in this case was completed by carers.

Results from the SDQs suggest carers' perception of their child's behaviour is different following an ADAPT group. In the 2011 group, five carers reported lower levels of overall stress from baseline to after ten weeks. Carers reported reduced emotional difficulties and behavioural problems in four children. Of the two carers who reported 'very high' hyperactivity and attention difficulties, both reduced following the ten-week group. Perhaps most importantly, four carers reported a reduction in the impact of any difficulties on the child's life. In addition, two of the nine children predicted as 'high risk' of receiving a psychiatric diagnosis moved into the medium-risk prediction, and one moved from medium to low risk, at the end of the ten-week programme.

Overall, these scores suggest that participation in ADAPT can facilitate change and is helpful to carers and children in a number of ways. Whether or not their child's behaviour actually changes, carer's perception of change will likely enhance their resilience and prevent placement breakdown.

Qualitative evaluation of the effect of ADAPT for the foster child

We asked two groups of foster carers who had attended ADAPT in 2012 to score a series of statements to evaluate their perception of the effect of the group on their fostering experience. It must be noted that these statements evaluated foster carer's *perception* of change for their foster child. This qualitative questionnaire was designed to test the efficacy of ADAPT against the following aims of the intervention to improve outcomes for young people by:

- enhancing their capacity to have satisfactory, trusting relationships with their foster carers

- improving their functioning at school

- changing their behaviours/communication/relations with peers and foster carers

- improving placement stability

- creating greater foster-carer resilience

- changing foster-carer responses to the challenging behaviour they encountered in placement, leading to a decrease in difficult behaviour

- increasing foster-carer confidence in managing difficult behaviours

- creating greater self-awareness in the young person

- improving emotional literacy for the young person

- increasing the ability for young people to articulate and verbalise their experiences and distress, and decreased acting out unconscious feelings via behaviour.

Seventeen foster carers completed the evaluation form.

Evaluation of results

Attending ADAPT seems to have had a noticeable change for foster carers regarding the way they related to their foster child. The majority of the sample reported some change and 14 carers believed that this had led their foster child to trust them more. A greater degree of trust would indicate increased attachment security and a greater sense of safety for the child with their foster carer. This in turn would be expected to have a positive effect on their emotional well-being.

Ten foster carers reported an improved degree of relationship satisfaction with their child. It is likely that where there is improved satisfaction in the relationship for the foster carer, this will have an impact on the child's self-esteem. We know from the Positive Interaction Cycle (Fahlberg 1991) that one of the ways babies form a positive sense of self is via their relationship with their parents and their experience of how their parents relate to them. Thus, if the parents are enjoying the relationship and initiating positive interactions with their infant, the baby will respond positively too, leading to a feedback loop of a relationship characterised by warmth and affection. We would hypothesise that this pattern would occur in other relationships, including the one between the foster child and foster carer.

Thirteen carers reported an improvement in their enjoyment of themselves as a family after attending ADAPT. Greater satisfaction as a family and increased participation in family activities will lead to enhanced sense of belonging for foster children. Identity and belonging are key issues for children in care and a sense of belonging can positively affect their self-esteem.

Foster carers mostly reported that the behaviour of their foster child improved after they had attended ADAPT. Thirteen carers noticed that, after attending ADAPT, they were likely to argue less often with their foster child. This is important as most foster children, having had a background of neglect, trauma and abuse, are likely to be sensitive and hyperaroused to conflict in the environment. Hyperarousal leads to a set of reactions where we are less able to engage and relate using our orbital frontal cortex:

> In the traumatised child the loss of potentially healthy neural networks and the creation of distinct, distorted neural pathways serves to provide him with the best possibility of survival. His body will be set on 'red alert', primed for high levels of stress and his internal 'roadmaps' will be limited and rigid: hardwiring him to respond selectively to perceived threat rapidly, through 'fight, flight or freeze' stress responses. (Archer 2003, p.85)

This, in turn, has consequences for learning and cognition. Hence, a calmer relationship with less confrontation would not only support attachment security and emotional well-being but affect other areas of the child's functioning too.

The questions which asked about the children's concentration, attainment and behaviour at school revealed the least change and were often scored 'non-applicable' by foster carers. This is perhaps not surprising as it is difficult to correlate improvements in these areas directly with foster-carer attendance at an ADAPT group. Moreover, it seems that this is information that the foster carers did not have, which highlights questions regarding their participation in their child's education.

Thirteen foster carers noticed a positive improvement in their foster child's ability to relate to their peers after they had attended ADAPT. It is possible to extrapolate that where foster children are enjoying a more satisfactory relationship with their foster carers and have a greater sense of belonging in the foster family, then this will positively impact on their sense of self and their ability to enjoy relationships outside of the home.

The majority of foster carers (14) reported an improvement in placement stability as a result of attending ADAPT, with seven of these seeing this as a significant change. Closely connected to placement stability is foster-carer resilience. Where foster carers are resilient, they are more likely to be able to withstand the pressures inherent within the fostering task. Overwhelmingly, all foster carers reported an improvement in their sense of resilience. Furthermore, they also all reported an improvement in their confidence in managing the challenging behaviour of their foster child. It is likely that there is a recursive effect at play here, as greater confidence is likely to lead to an enhanced sense of resilience and therefore placement stability.

One of the aims of ADAPT is to improve the emotional literacy of foster carers and to enable them to be able to mentalise (Asen and Fonagy 2011) for their foster child. Mentalising is important for our sense of self, social interactions and personal security. Mentalising involves being able to ascribe intentions, thoughts and feelings to behaviour. It is therefore encouraging that all carers reported an improvement in their ability to understand their foster child's emotions. Understanding the foster child's emotions will enable them to help the foster child make sense of their feelings. This, in turn, will positively impact on the foster child's emotional literacy and their ability to mentalise for themselves and for others.

When foster carers learn to be curious about the behaviour of their foster child and to perceive this as in indicator for the presence of strong feeling, then their perception of their foster child tends to change. Foster carers mostly become empathic with their foster children and want to understand and support them when this shift occurs. They move from interpreting challenging behaviour negatively (e.g. the foster child is 'always naughty; deliberately nasty') to appreciating that there is a hidden, emotional communication in the child's actions. Eleven of the foster carers reported that this change in perception was significant for them and that they now mostly held this awareness in mind. All the foster carers noted that ADAPT had helped them with this understanding.

All the foster carers in the sample believed that an improvement in their understanding of their foster child's emotions and their ability to communicate this to their child, had improved their foster child's self-awareness. Enhanced self-awareness will affect a child's ability to relate to others as well as positively impact their emotional well-being. In addition, all the foster carers reported feeling more skilled at being able to talk to their foster child about their feelings as a result of attending ADAPT, with the majority (11) seeing this as a significant change.

All the foster carers in the sample believed that attending ADAPT had had a positive impact on their foster child. A majority of the foster carers (ten) indicated a strong positive response and a perception that their learning and experience on ADAPT had benefited the well-being of their foster child.

Conclusion

The perspectives of this very small sample suggest that ADAPT groups are achieving ADAPT's aims, impacting positively on foster children's relationships with their foster carers, placement stability, foster-carer resilience and foster children's levels of self-awareness and emotional literacy. Most significantly, foster carers report on a change in their confidence, skills, perceptions, understanding and ability to manage challenging behaviour. They identify that these changes in themselves led to altered relationships with their foster children, enabling them to achieve greater satisfaction in these relationships and to offer an improved level of therapeutic parenting – that is, mentalising for their foster child and helping them to understand their feelings. Improved relationships for the foster child and enhanced placement stability may be expected in the longer term to translate into positive changes in terms of educational attainment. Stability, security and emotional literacy are known to affect cognitive ability, suggesting that over a longer time-frame the children in this sample may demonstrate improved outcomes at school.

These findings provide small-scale qualitative evidence that working with foster carers in groups positively benefits foster children. In their role as attachment figures and through their daily presence in foster children's lives, foster carers are best placed to positively affect change for children and young people. Up-skilling foster carers to become therapeutic parents enables them to support children and young people to resolve some of the trauma of their past, form secure relationships with their foster carers and achieve their potential relationally, socially, emotionally and academically.

ADAPT groups have been accredited by the Centre for Excellence and Outcomes in Children and Young People's Services[1] as being an area of promising practice.

ATTUNE GROUPS

As a result of the success of ADAPT groups, Core Assets introduced a new carer group, known as ATTUNE groups. ATTUNE is an acronym for Thinking Therapeutically and Understanding New Experiences. ATTUNE groups are for newly approved carers. The idea of a group for recently approved carers was a response to the rapidly growing carer and placement numbers and the subsequent high number of referrals for carer consultations. The hope was to provide additional support for carers and to help them develop their understanding and practice of therapeutic care through regular meetings with a social worker and therapist. ATTUNE groups are different from ADAPT groups in that they are shorter in length and they are facilitated by a social worker and a therapist, instead of by two therapists.

The practice of ATTUNE groups

The twin aims of ATTUNE were to:

- provide additional support (peer and professional) to carers

- help them develop a reflective approach to their practice early in their career.

The objectives were within a friendly and supportive environment to:

- help carers develop a thoughtful and reflective approach to their practice

- introduce theoretical ideas, where deemed appropriate

- develop practical skills

- help carers develop supportive networks.

GROUP STRUCTURE AND PREPARATION

The group involves up to eight carers who have been approved in the past year. A discussion in a team meeting with supervising social

---

1   www.c4eo.org.uk

workers identifies carers who fit the criteria for the group, who are then invited to join. A therapist and a social worker facilitate the group. Eight two-hour weekly sessions are involved and no further participants can join.

PRINCIPLES OF THE GROUP

The therapist provides structure and focus to the sessions and facilitates carers to think, talk about, and reflect on themselves, their children and their role as foster carers. The group is theoretically underpinned by ideas from attachment theory. The link between parental capacity for self-reflection and the attachment orientation of children is emphasised (Hughes 2009; Siegel and Hartzell 2004). It is suggested that carers' capacity to reflect upon their own experience, as well as their capacity to reflect upon the mind of the child, will be critical to children's development and burgeoning awareness of themselves, others and their environment.

Theoretical ideas, reflections and strategies are introduced as more or less useful and not as factual or concrete approaches for intervention. The group aims to provide a safe environment where ideas, thoughts, feelings, perspectives and suggestions are shared and discussed. The hope is that group members develop an approach to thinking about 'problems' in a multi-dimensional way which offers benefits rather than seeking to arrive at specific, global 'solutions' or cures.

SESSION CONTENT

ATTUNE does not have a manual or a programme, as is the case with ADAPT. The structure of the groups tends to be informal and there is no agenda for sessions other than sessions 1 and 2, which have a specific focus. A decision is made by the members of the group and the facilitators on what to cover in each session and which approach will be used. The approaches that are used within ATTUNE can be split into two broad categories:

- reflection on practice
- activity-based ideas.

Session 1

The first session introduces carers to attachment theory, principles of therapeutic parenting, reflective practice and 'mind-mindedness' (Fonagy *et al.* 1991).

Key themes covered in the session may include:

- nurturing and dependable relationships as the building blocks of healthy childhood development

- human beings as being hardwired to connect

- how attachment relationships change the brain

- child development as an interplay between nature and nurture

- self-regulation as essential for childhood development and lifelong health

- the process of change for children and young people

- risk and protective factors for child development

- features of secure and insecure attachment styles

- Maslow's Hierarchy of Needs (Maslow 1943).

Session 2

This session involves more detailed introductions of the foster carers and the children and young people they have in placement. Methods used include invitations to talk about self and invitations to talk about the child or young person. The facilitators may ask questions such as:

- What led you to become a foster carer?

- How does it match with current experience?

- What might you like from the group?

- How might the group be useful to you, given your experiences so far?

Further sessions

In later sessions the group facilitators start either with a 'check-in' which may lead to topics for further discussion in the session, or with an idea for discussion often developed from dialogue in the previous session. Topics covered have included anger, loss and conflict, and might involve a brief exercise or conversation around carers' experiences. Sessions focus on promoting foster carers' reflective abilities.

The facilitators invite foster carers to bring current situations for discussion in the group. The group then thinks about what might be happening for the child. Questions which are frequently asked of foster carers are:

- What might have triggered the difficulty?

- What might be the child's thoughts, feelings or beliefs?

- What might be happening for the carer?

- Where might their beliefs about the child's behaviour come from?

- How might their beliefs determine their actions?

- How might their actions determine the possible outcome of the situation?

From these suggestions it is possible to think about new responses to situations.

The following is a structured reflection exercise that can be used to explore a situation in detail. In ATTUNE, one carer is asked to volunteer to explore with the group a situation that is occurring in their placement. The questions below are used to gather information and stimulate discussion.

1. Nature of experience:

   a) Background to the experience.

   b) Key events as the situation unfolded.

   c) Cause and effect.

   d) Final outcomes – immediate and delayed.

2. Personal (or organisational) involvement:

   a) What was my (our) involvement: reactions, actions and decisions?

   b) What was I trying to achieve or gain?

   c) Why did I act as I did?

   d) How did my actions affect:

      - My goals?

      - Me personally?

- Other people?

- Other people's goals?

e) What did I think and feel at the time of events?

3. Factors which created the result:

a) What factors influenced my actions, decisions, judgements?

4. Alternative actions:

a) What other choices were open to me?

b) What might have been their consequences?

c) What would I do if the situation recurred?

5. Learning and growing:

a) How do I feel about the situation now?

b) What have I learnt?

c) How have I changed?

d) If unclear, what advice, feedback, information or procedure might help?

Activity-based ideas

As well as using the group as a forum for the discussion of reflective practice, facilitators may choose to engage the group in activities together. This can be useful if there is a tendency for one or more foster carers to dominate the space. Group activities give opportunities for more reticent foster carers to become engaged. Suggestions for group activities are as follows:

- 'Check-in'.

- Drawing and discussing each child's chronology.

- Sculpts and role-plays.

- What your child is like – making a visual picture.

- What you are like as a carer for this child – making a visual picture.

- To think about the child, draw around a person on sheets of flip-chart paper stuck together. Use post-its to stick onto the figure what you think every child needs to have as she's growing up. Use a different coloured set of post-its to stick on what you feel your child hasn't had – or had enough of – as they've grown up so far.

FEEDBACK

The groups run have been extremely well attended and the feedback from carers has been very positive, both in what they say and through their enthusiasm for the group and their work together. They especially appreciate the chance to talk about their work and to develop and try out new ideas, which they have continued to use beyond the end of the group. They say they understand the child's behaviour better and now 'stop and think' before acting.

There have been many comments on how useful it is to meet regularly, share how ideas have worked in practice and get support. The groups have usually continued to offer informal links to their members without becoming cliquish. Many carers seem to find the group an accessible form of therapeutic support and continue to make good use of therapy thereafter.

CASE STUDY

In a recent meeting a carer brought concerns about a child who 'never gave her a moment's peace', following her round the house and asking the carer to watch her or do things with her. This was particularly irksome when the carer wanted to watch a TV programme which the child did not enjoy. We focused on this event. The questions 'What might be happening for the child?', 'How might they be feeling?' and 'What might they be thinking?' were considered.

This discussion led to many suggestions, such as, the child was attention seeking, controlling, anxious, lonely, and angry. We then took some of these ideas forward for further scrutiny, asking more questions (e.g. Where did the carer's ideas come from? Did they explain the events described?). Other questions and conversations focused more on the child's situation: 'Why might the child be angry?' 'What might the child believe when their carer ignores them?' In the process the carer remembered some aspects of the child's early experiences which fit with their current response and helped to explain some of their actions.

We then took some of those ideas forward again to look for practical ways to respond to the behaviour. Again, we generated as many ideas as possible. If we believe the child was anxious when the carer watched TV, then what might help? If we assume the child is anxious, does ignoring help? How does explaining what we want the child to do help the child feel less anxious? At this point the carer was asked to listen only and to imagine how the child might respond to each suggestion. The carer shared her view of listening and what ideas she felt might work.

The group then developed a very concrete strategy based on an appreciation of the child's behaviour as anxious. The child is frightened when the carer watches TV and thinks the carer no longer knows she exists. Strategies that help her feel less anxious by letting her know she is in the carer's mind (my words) were forthcoming. These included: inviting the child to sit alongside the carer and play on a handheld game console while the programme was on, occasionally touching her or stroking her feet, especially if she seemed agitated, talking in the break, looking at the child to let her know she is seen.

During this discussion the carer addressed some of her own anxieties about being controlled by the child, and her frustration about not having any time to herself. She was able to put this strategy in place and bring back the results to the group. The strategies proved highly successful and the whole group was able to share in this success.

CONCLUSION

There is agreement in the literature that the training of foster carers is essential. Particular emphasis is given to a focus on attachment theory:

> Foster parents' understanding of the attachment cycle and the subsequent development of disordered attachment are imperative if the foster family is going to welcome a challenging child into their home. (Craven and Lee 2006, p.291)

While it is also acknowledged that the training support of foster carers is no guarantee of improved outcomes for children and young people and increased placement stability, the lack of an adequate programme equipping foster carers in their task can only serve to undermine placement success (Pithouse et al. 2004). Given the recent work on self-efficacy and its relationship to fostering, it seems likely that the existence of ADAPT, ATTUNE and a comprehensive training programme will go a long way to achieving one of Team Parenting's central aims – placement stability. Morgan and Baron (2011, p.19) propose that:

> parents who feel efficacious are less likely to feel overwhelmed by parenting tasks and may also be more warm, nurturing and less punitive in their behaviour management.

Considering the importance of sensitive, attuned caregiving within a well regulated environment for foster children and young people, actions that can enhance the self-efficacy of foster carers are likely to increase their capacity to be resilient, therapeutic carers. There is, of course, a feedback loop, as foster carers who are more sensitive and resilient to challenging behaviour are likely to experience greater success, which will further enhance their efficacy. Where carer efficacy is low, this may lead to less capable and more punitive parenting, which is liable to exacerbate behavioural difficulties and further undermine the foster carer's confidence (Morgan and Baron 2011). Therefore, as Morgan and Baron (2011, p.29) conclude:

> Interventions that help foster carers to understand the challenging behaviour of looked after young people, provide strategies for working with it, and enhance feelings of parenting efficacy, confidence and ability to cope with the stress of their task, may have a significant effect on carer psychological well-being and improve placement stability for looked after young people.

This is what Warman *et al.* (2006, p.21) found:

> They discover that when they are able to respond in ways that are clear, warm, responsive, consistent and encouraging, they are often rewarded by positive changes in the child's behaviour and in their experience of the relationship with them.

This is what ADAPT and ATTUNE aim to achieve.

In this chapter the crucial role of the supervising social worker in supporting foster carers within Team Parenting has been discussed. In addition, carer groups as a mechanism for furthering the support delivered to foster carers, providing the opportunity for training, the development of theoretical knowledge, learning new strategies and practising being reflective practitioners have been explored. Chapter 8 discusses the role of education officers and support workers in contributing to the Team Parenting approach.

THE CONTRIBUTION OF EDUCATION AND MENTORING IN TEAM PARENTING

CHAPTER CONTENTS

THE EDUCATION SERVICE

Looked-after children are vulnerable to poor outcomes in education (Ferguson and Wolkow 2012; Harker, Dobel-ober and Berridge 2004; Hayden 2005; Liabo, Gray and Mulchay 2012; O'Sullivan and Westerman 2007). The reasons for this are many and include a poor start in education in their early lives, mental health issues, frequent placement moves meaning changes in school, learning and behavioural difficulties, educational needs not being prioritised by foster carers or social workers, low expectations, lack of access to learning materials and poor collaborative planning between agencies (Berridge 2012; Cocker and Scott 2006; Ferguson and Wolkow 2012; Fernandez 2008; Harker *et al.* 2004; Hayden 2005; Vacca 2008; Weyts 2004; Zetlin, Weinberg and Shea 2006). Zetlin *et al.* (2006) highlight a common dynamic whereby the importance of removing young people from abusive home experiences, working to stabilise them in foster care and address their trauma means that their education is frequently not seen as a priority. Hayden (2005) makes a similar point, stressing that social workers are often so preoccupied with finding placements or focused on placement stability that they do not concentrate on education. This contrasts strongly with children living in middle-class families where success at school is invariably a key focus. Ferguson and Wolkow (2012) echo this, highlighting that it is often the emotional and behavioural difficulties that young people exhibit in school that are the focus of professional attention to the neglect of their academic achievement. Liabo *et al.* (2013, p.10) postulate: 'Education may be seen as primarily a middle-class value and professionals may see attitude and motivation as more achievable than changes in attainment'.

The vulnerabilities with which looked-after children enter the education system can quickly deteriorate into a vicious cycle where behavioural difficulties, school moves and problems with learning result in young people disengaging from education. Looked-after children are more likely to have higher rates of absenteeism and be subject to disciplinary measures including exclusions, and consequently they achieve less well than their peers (Vacca 2008). Looked-after children receive more frequent exclusions and disciplinary measures than their peers and their education and attainment are inevitably affected. Scherr (2007) hypothesises that looked-after children are *unfairly targeted by unprepared systems*. She argues that looked-after children are three times more likely to have faced disciplinary measures and that there are 31 per cent in special education as compared to 13 per cent of the general population. Ferguson and Wolkow (2012, p.1143) concur:

> In general, young people in care are marginalized at school. Though most are in need of specialized support, their educational needs are often neglected or at best given minimal attention by the individuals and agencies in charge of their care.

Whatever the factors contributing to looked-after children's struggles in the education system, the outcomes are plain to see: 'Looked-after children are four times more likely to be unemployed and sixty times more likely to be sent to prison' (Cocker and Scott 2006, p.18); also, in 2012, only 14 per cent gained five A*–C GCSEs (including Maths and English) compared to 58 per cent of all children, five A–C grades being the perceived threshold for employability (Staines *et al.* 2011).

These and similar statistics are echoed by Fernandez (2008), O'Sullivan and Westerman (2007) and Vacca (2008) in their papers. Ferguson and Wolkow (2012, p.1145) cite a recent study which depressingly revealed that 'one-third of foster care alumni lived at or below the poverty level (three times the national poverty rate), one-third had no health insurance, and more than 20 per cent experienced some degree of homelessness since leaving care'. Meltzer *et al.* (2003) found that 60 per cent of all looked-after children had difficulties with reading, spelling or maths. These young people were also found not to socialise with their peers and Meltzer *et al.* (2003) point to a correlation between relational and emotional difficulties. This theme is supported by Cocker and Scott (2006) who draw links between behavioural problems and negative experiences in education. These experiences are mirrored around the globe, suggesting that the problem is not purely a systemic one limited to the UK (Liabo *et al.* 2013; Weyts 2004).

One of the difficulties seems to be the paucity of genuine, collaborative working (Ferguson and Wolkow 2012; Harker *et al.* 2004). 'Key departments involved in looking after children are not always successful in adopting a corporate parenting approach' (Harker *et al.* 2004, p.179). It seems that a rift exists between the social care and education sectors. Ferguson and Wolkow (2012, p.1146) state that they found 'adversarial relationships, suspicion and disapproval' between the social care and education sectors. The consequence of this was that interagency co-operation floundered. Cocker and Scott (2006, p.19) elucidate that 'schools are generally the least well integrated in partnerships working for looked-after children'. Again, this finding reverberates throughout the literature (Fernandez 2008; Hayden 2005; Vacca 2008; Zetlin *et al.* 2006). Vacca (2008) points to the lack of co-ordination and information sharing that frequently accompanies school moves, which means that individualised, specific understanding of a child's needs in their new school is delayed or lost. Ferguson and Wolkow (2012) extemporise that a school's wish for more information regarding the background of the child is often frustrated by social workers' reluctance to divulge certain details. Whilst this can be framed as different understandings regarding confidentiality, Ferguson and Wolkow (2012) and Harker *et al.* (2004) emphasise the opportunity for hostility and resentment between the agencies to be generated as a result.

Yet, this notwithstanding, Harker *et al.* (2004) believe that the aspirations for effective interagency working exists at senior management level. However, these good intentions are often not easily translated into practice in the field – not due to any disagreement with the philosophy behind them, but more due to other practical factors. They highlight the fact that social workers' busy caseloads are often dominated by more pressing crises, which means that the educational needs of young people in foster care are not prioritised. Furthermore, frequent staff changes, whilst not undermining the belief in interagency working, can create a *moratorium* while the new staff member becomes inducted into the team and the knowledge regarding this particular child is shared (Harker *et al.* 2004). Hayden (2005, p.346) has a corresponding view: 'There is something of a reality gap in care planning in social work, between theory, guidance and practice'.

This fragmentation within a multi-agency team can have detrimental consequences. For instance, a hiatus or breakdown in interagency working can result in delays in school places being found once a young person has moved to a new placement. Despite government initiatives in England (Section 52 of the 2004 Children's Act) which have sought to address this problem by stipulating that a school place must be established before a foster placement is made, the situation remains relatively unchanged (O'Sullivan and Westerman 2007).

These difficulties in interagency working and co-operation create obstacles to looked-after children having an optimal experience in education. This situation is exacerbated by the fact that many young people in care lack an advocate who will work to ensure their educational needs are met in school and who will positively promote their attainment by focusing on learning at home (Cocker and Scott 2006; Coulling 2000; Vacca 2008; Zetlin *et al.* 2006). Looked-after children rarely have the presence of a consistent, interested adult in their lives who can integrate knowledge of their previous educational experiences and translate this into meaningful information for teachers in their new school. The absence of such an adult means that young people do not have access to the support of another who can think with them about the upheaval that accompanies a school move (e.g. new teachers, rules, friends, building, expectations) and support them through the transition (Vacca 2008):

> Initial entry into care was described as a traumatic experience which negatively affected some children's ability to concentrate in school. Placement changes were also described as unsettling and disruptive to school. Many reported a lack of supportive and caring adults who took an interest in their education or encouraged them to do well. (Ferguson and Wolkow 2012, p.1146)

This lack of continuity in relationships is emphasised by O'Sullivan and Westerman (2007, p.15): 'Losing touch with friends and supportive teachers who know them also reduces the young people's chances of success.' They are at pains to elucidate the stress that adults experience when they move house or get divorced. They illuminate that for young people in care, moving placement entails moving to a new place and the loss of relationships. Added to this, they suggest that the young person may feel guilty and responsible for the breakdown, rejected by their current foster carers and that these wounding emotional experiences are likely to be compounded by early life histories barren of acceptance, warmth and care. O'Sullivan and Westerman (2007) note that even if it is not the young person who is moving, foster homes often have more than one foster child and that witnessing others come and go will also be a destabilising and unsettling experience. Necessarily, this will impact on a young person's sense of safety and impede their ability to unreservedly focus on school work. Furthermore, both O'Sullivan and Westerman (2007) and Ferguson and Wolkow (2012) discuss the timing of moves which, if occurring at particular points in a young person's school career, can be particularly damaging. O'Sullivan and Westerman (2007, p.17) provide some startling statistics to support this point:

> Placement moves are inevitably disruptive to children and in this study, of those who were moved more than ten times during their time in care, 60 per cent did not sit any GCSE examinations and 34 per cent sat their examinations but achieved no A*–C grades. In fact, of all the children who were moved more than ten times, only six per cent achieved any GCSE passes at grade A*–C and none achieved five passes at grade A*–C.

It is this situation that the role of the education officer in Team Parenting is intended to address. Jackson (2004) argues that Local Authorities and social workers should focus on and prioritise the education of children in their care in the same way as well-intentioned parents. To that end, Team Parenting fully integrates school and other education support workers to determine how the short- and long-term educational needs of young people can be accommodated.

THE ROLE OF THE EDUCATION OFFICER
IN TEAM PARENTING
Supporting interagency working

Acknowledging the paucity of positive educational outcomes for looked-after children and being aware of the vast discrepancy in this arena for this population as compared to their peers, Team Parenting aims to redress these issues. A central feature of Team Parenting is the role of the education officer. As soon as it is known that a young person is moving into a new placement, the education officer becomes involved, negotiating a school place for them and ensuring information is shared between the old school and the new school. Team Parenting Meetings can facilitate this process where a move has been planned. Staff members from the old school and the planned new school are invited to attend the same Team Parenting Meetings. This enables a visceral sharing of knowledge about the child from one teacher to another as well as facilitating detailed planning to ensure the young person is supported in their school move in a way that will best suit their individual requirements. For the new school, having a fuller knowledge of the context and background of the young person's life as well as meeting others involved with her and being part of that team, is likely to promote her engagement, understanding and interest. This ensures that the young person will be thought about and supported in transitioning to the new school.

Education officers are vital in supporting effective interagency working, which is a fundamental value enshrined in the Team Parenting approach. The fact that they are qualified teachers themselves and have previous experience in the classroom means that they are able to engage with schools with confidence, knowledge and comprehension of the education system. Harker *et al.* (2004) suggest that *effective working relationships* depend on understanding each other's roles both as individuals and as different agencies. This process is greatly facilitated by the presence of education officers who communicate regularly with schools and are more readily accepted by schools as being key players by virtue of their prior experience in education. Furthermore, education officers can liaise between schools and foster carers, supervising social workers and Local Authority social workers. Being part of a social work team ensures that their knowledge base straddles both social work and education sectors. Thus, frustrations regarding information sharing or the lack of it can be negotiated by them. This works to enhance understanding on all sides of the positions that different agencies take. Improved understanding militates against blame between agencies and defensive posturing, where accountability for lack of progress is passed around and acknowledgement of the *corporate responsibility* for the education of looked-after children is lost (Harker *et al.* 2004).

Education officers are often instrumental in encouraging teachers and schools to attend Team Parenting Meetings. Team Parenting recognises the difficulties for teachers of taking time out from their classrooms to attend meetings. Whilst many meetings are consequently held in schools to support teachers to attend, having the value of the meetings imparted by an education officer can be more convincing than from a social worker or therapist. Once representatives from schools do start to attend Team Parenting Meetings, the teachers invariably find them invaluable, in terms of gathering background knowledge regarding the child's history and learning how he/she functions on a daily basis in the foster placement. Chapter 5 explored the role of the therapist in facilitating Team Parenting Meetings. It is worth noting that Harker *et al.* found that in Local Authorities where a lead officer had the specific role and therefore capacity in their diary to promote interagency working, this appeared to cement its practice. 'Lead Officers were praised for their inter-personal skills and enthusiasm, and their ability to convince personnel of the importance of inter-professional cooperation' (Harker *et al.* 2004, p.189). This is the role that therapists carry out within Team Parenting Meetings, and they are supported in this outside of the meetings with schools by education officers.

It is a resounding theme throughout the literature that greater interagency collaboration and co-operation will benefit looked-after children educationally. 'The most universally expressed recommendation is to facilitate co-operation and coordination between the various agencies and individuals in charge of the educational needs of children in care' (Ferguson and Wolkow 2012, p.1147). It is also acknowledged that, at least initially, interagency working can seem to entail a greater use of resources, create additional demands on time and be besieged by difficulties. In particular, high staff turnover can mean a sense of shared knowledge and teamworking never really gets off the ground (Harker *et al.* 2004). However, it seems that teachers do value the opportunity to discuss individual pupils (Hayden 2005) and meet the other important people in their lives. Often, once professionals experience the benefits of interagency working via Team Parenting Meetings, commitment to it grows and practice becomes embedded over a period of time. 'Nonetheless, there was a perception that over time joint working practice became a matter of course and the level of effort and input required lessened' (Harker *et al.* 2004, p.190).

Interagency working does require *on-going commitment* (Liabo *et al.* 2013). Where professionals have been meeting regularly via Team Parenting over a period of time, commitment becomes self-generating. Relationships become cemented and professionals appreciate the chance to work together, both receiving support from each other, collaborating on a shared endeavour, garnering valuable information and perceiving that their contributions are valuable too.

The role of education officers in Team Parenting is similar to the Education Initiative project described by Zetlin *et al.* (2006). She comments on the challenges:

> Problems included inability to obtain a child's school records, refusal by a school district to enrol a child in school, inappropriate denial of special education eligibility, failure to provide required special education services, inappropriate school placement, and inappropriate suspension or expulsion of a child. (Zetlin *et al.* 2006, p.269)

In the project she is describing, education officers concentrated on training social workers to focus on educational needs, whereas education officers within Team Parenting have a wider remit, working closely with foster carers and with education authorities. The presence of education officers as part of area teams means that no referral system is needed and they can work speedily on finding a school place for a young person, thus minimising delay when there has been a change of foster placement.

Advocating for looked-after children

Education officers also have an important role to play in schools once a young person starts to attend. Elliott (2002) argues that teachers often expect looked-after children to do less well academically and that this can become a recursive loop. In effect, the low achievement of looked-after children generates low expectations from teachers, which in turn impact upon performance. As with any feedback system, it is difficult to pinpoint where the cycle begins. Elliott cites the renowned study by Rosenthal and Jacobson (1968) whereby, 'preconceived ideas about how people should perform can create a self-fulfilling prophecy' (Elliott 2002, p.58).

In Elliott's study, teachers did expect looked-after children to hand in homework less frequently and predicted that they would be bullied more often. Elliott (2002) suggests that these may be *well-intentioned assumptions* of teachers, formulated out of the reality of the landscape of the lives of many looked-after children. Although this study has not been successfully replicated to the same degree, it is important that teachers examine their own expectations and assumptions regarding looked-after children. Education officers play a valuable role here in empowering foster carers to have the confidence to challenge low expectations and advocate for foster children's educational needs to be met and prioritised.

Education officers also play a crucial part in educating teachers and schools about what it means to be looked after (Weyts 2004). Frequently, schools and teachers have little or no understanding of the global impact of complex trauma and disrupted early attachment relationships on a young person's functioning. Education officers run workshops within schools and consultation sessions for those involved with young people in foster placements. Enabling teaching staff to understand that attachment difficulties affect young people's cognitive abilities, emotional functioning, behaviour, mental health, relational skills, psychology and socialisation can be hugely enlightening. Coulling (2000) argues that input to teaching staff is essential so that they can understand the specific requirements of each child, the kinds of difficulties their histories can generate and how to work in an interagency setting. Training and advice for teachers about what it means to be looked after will not only enhance their psychological understanding but facilitate greater collaboration between agencies (Weyts 2004). Such increased knowledge of teachers together with a commitment to interagency working can support young people in foster carer to reach their educational potential.

The necessity of promoting the educational chances for young people in care has been enshrined in government policy since the beginning of this century. Legislation such as Quality Protects, the Children Leaving Care Act 2000 and Care Standards Act 2000 all pay attention to looked-after children's educational needs (Weyts 2004). In 2000 the Department for Education and Employment and the Department of Health, stipulated that every looked-after child should have a Personal Education Plan or PEP (DfEE/DoH 2000). These were intended to facilitate shared and joint-care planning and interagency working (Weyts 2004). However, a number of practical difficulties have impeded their optimal operation (Harker *et al.* 2004; Hayden 2005). These obstacles have typically included misunderstanding about whose responsibility it is to initiate them, Local Authority social workers being too busy and distracted by other more pressing crises to prioritise them and a lack of confidence for social workers in navigating school systems and communicating within educational settings (Harker *et al.* 2004; Hayden 2005). Hayden (2005) quotes one social worker, who, with 100 children on her caseload, doubted that she could manage the first PEP, never mind the reviews. This leads Hayden (2005) to doubt the meaningfulness of PEPs and whether they have the power to introduce change. She hypothesises that they may merely reflect what is already working but are not practical enough in a school setting to really redress difficulties. In contrast, Ofsted (2012) suggests that PEPs are key to effective outcomes, noting that the quality of PEPs (in particular targets) was variable. The best had sharp focus on educational attainment, taking into account behavioural, social and emotional needs.

Education officers have a key role to play here in ensuring that PEPs remain a priority and are undertaken by social workers and schools. It is understandable that they easily become submerged by the demands of a social worker's busy caseload or the pressing needs of a teacher's classroom of pupils. By initiating meetings to undertake them, education officers champion the educational requirements of young people in care and ensure that their needs remain at the forefront of the minds of all professionals involved with them. Furthermore, being qualified teachers themselves, education officers do not experience the low confidence or lack of knowledge issues that can make PEPs seem daunting to some social workers.

Their qualified teacher status provides an additional advantage in that schools feel more assured that the pressures they face are known and understood. It is interesting to note that Hayden (2005) finds, for all her questions regarding the efficacy of PEPs, that they do highlight education as an issue and make it an agenda item for looked-after children. That education officers are in a position to ensure that they are completed and are supporting this process is vital in working towards improving the educational experiences for looked-after children.

Promoting foster-carer involvement

Having positive experiences of education affects not only academic achievement but also self-esteem, mental health, resilience, behaviour and placement stability. Staines *et al.* (2011) argue that the active participation in the professional network by educational professionals can reduce the risk of placement disruption. They propose that an integrated assessment of need and identification of how all facets of the young person's life can be addressed together rather than in isolation 'can help the young person to develop in a secure and stable environment' (Staines *et al.* 2011, p.319). Education officers facilitate this process in a number of ways. One of their primary roles is consulting foster carers regarding their role in the young person's education, the particular educational needs of the young person they have in placement and how they can be part of meeting them. Coulling (2000) found that many foster carers did not appreciate the pivotal part they could play in determining a young person's educational success. Education officers can help foster carers to understand this and to be engaged in their foster child's education in the way that Coulling (2000, p.33) recommends:

> Foster carers should be actively involved in the foster child's schooling, attending open days and meetings, helping with homework and supporting the educational experience in conveying high but realistic expectations. They should be aware of the foster child's needs socially and encourage extracurricular activities and the fostering of good peer relationships.

Gilligan (2008) moots a similar point, postulating that foster carers can play a significant role in helping young people make up for lost ground, particularly in maths and literacy.

In Coulling's (2000) study she found that where young people perceived the relationships between their foster carer(s) and school to be good, then they felt supported, more motivated and tended to achieve better results. Young people want adults to take an interest in their school work and to expect them to achieve (Fernandez 2008). The role of the education officer is to facilitate this burgeoning relationship, particularly where there are disagreements between schools and foster carers. Unfortunately, these disagreements are commonplace when both are struggling with the complex behaviours of a young person and looking for more support from each other or looking to blame each other.

Education officers can also offer additional, individual tuition time to young people, particularly when they are struggling with a subject or approaching exams. Tutoring in a one-to-one friendly environment facilitates young people in forming a trusting relationship with the education officer and promotes their confidence in themselves and their abilities. The involvement of an adult, who knows them, encourages and pushes them to achieve, is beneficial for young people (Vacca 2008).

Education officers have an important role to play with foster carers, specifically bearing in mind the educational backgrounds of many foster carers. Berridge (2012) critiques what he considers to be too narrow an interpretation of the research evidence about looked-after children's poor educational achievement, which is often attributed to the care system. Instead, he points to contextual factors and the young people's early experiences of poverty and social class as being poor introductions to optimal success in education. He argues that we need to consider a young person's starting point in education and evaluate their progress over time, otherwise statistics are 'static, simplistic and misleading' (Berridge 2012, p.1172). He highlights that it is more likely to be the detrimental factors that led a young person coming into care than their actual entry into care that has the greatest negative impact on their education. To illustrate this he points to a statistic stating that by six years old low-ability children of higher social status are doing better than high-ability children of low social status. Harker *et al.* (2004, p.179) dispute this, postulating that 'pre-care experiences and the characteristics of looked-after children' cannot fully explain their lack of progress educationally.

Nevertheless, Berridge's (2012) position is an important one as it calls into question the emphasis that foster carers place on education within their homes. Berridge (2012) asks the uncomfortable question of whether we need to recruit better-educated foster carers. Currently, foster carers on average have slightly lower levels of education and income than the general population (McDermid *et al.* 2012). Berridge (2012) broadly links poorer households and social class, although he qualifies this by saying that poverty affects attainment in education regardless of social class (Berridge 2007). Other writers have alluded to the middle-class values that accompany a focus on and prioritising of education (Hayden 2005; Liabo *et al.* 2013).

Berridge (2007, 2012) points to the many factors that encourage education in middle-class households, specifically: the resources available in the home (e.g. access to computers, the internet, books); the tendency of middle-class families to plan their holidays around school breaks; the role-model effect of observing parents benefit from educational achievement via their own careers; the expectations parents have of their own children; the time parents set aside to support homework activities; parental influence on friendships, meaning that young people are more likely to mix with like-minded friends, thus militating against young people forming inappropriate peer relationships. He recommends (2012, p.1175) that foster care should replicate these actions, postulating, for example, that placement moves should be planned around school holidays, exclusions should be avoided and that 'carers and others need to work hard at creating a positive culture of expectation concerning educational achievement and its continuation'.

The values that Berridge (2007) identifies with middle-class families – belief in the importance of a good education, positive attitudes towards learning, valuing discipline and prioritising hard work – are ones that education officers can discuss with foster carers. This is a potentially sensitive area, bridging class divides, value bases and socio-cultural issues. However, the role of education officers in imparting to foster carers the significant role they can play in their foster child's education, both with their involvement at home and at school, can be pivotal in a young person's life. As Berridge (2012, p.1175) says, it is not as if a good education can solve all difficulties, but it 'can make some difference and that difference is worth having'. This is especially so when the decline of industry means that there are fewer unskilled jobs available than ever before (Bynner *et al.* 2002). Without a satisfactory education, looked-after children are increasingly likely to struggle to find employment. Education can influence the *social trajectory* for young people, both in terms of income and employment (Berridge 2007).

Foster carers may also need support from education officers in playing a more prominent role in their foster child's education. Education officers are all qualified teachers who have at one time been teaching staff themselves and who understand the education system. This knowledge is invaluable in advocating for young people's educational needs to be prioritised. Vacca (2008) postulates that foster carers often feel disempowered and unable to advocate, especially when there have been multiple moves and rapid changes of educational placement. Vacca (2008, p.1083) also makes the following criticism: 'There is no single person or agency that is ultimately held accountable for the foster children's academic results. The important people involved in the foster children's education have a fragmented relationship with one other'.

The presence of the education officer in Team Parenting militates against this. Education officers work to secure optimal school places in a timely fashion for children in new placements and ensure that information is accessed and shared as soon as possible. This process supports the foster carers in their management of the placement, contributes to placement stability and facilitates foster carers being informed and thus feeling involved in the child's education from the outset.

Expansion of the education officer role

There is room for expansion of the education officer role in Team Parenting. Ferguson and Wolkow (2012) suggest that more monitoring of educational outcomes for children in care could inform service development. Education officers do collect statistics of the educational performance of looked-after children, monitoring those with a school place or in alternative educational provision, attendance, fixed-term exclusions, permanent exclusions, special needs status, PEPs, Key Stage 2 National Curriculum test results and GSCE results. However, collation of statistics could be tighter, more analytical and used to identify need. Whilst education officers provide individual tutoring for pupils in Year 11 taking their GSCEs, young people who need this support should be identified earlier. This supposition could easily be tested against outcomes.

Education officers could also play a stronger role in arguing for placement moves to occur outside of key transition times in a young person's education. There are times when placements break down irredeemably and little can be done to persuade foster carers to continue. However, at other times decisions to end placements are made by Local Authorities due to their own priorities. When these decisions are made at a strategic level due to fiscal or service pressures, the individual requirements of young people are often lost. Education officers can spearhead or support schools in insisting that these decisions take greater consideration of where young people are at in the trajectory of their school careers.

EDUCATION AND RESILIENCE

There is increasing interest in the literature in the concept of resilience. Resilience, according to Rutter (1999, p.119), 'refers to the phenomenon of overcoming stress or adversity'. Resilience is closely linked to mental health (Cocker and Scott 2006). As a concept it is distinct from self-esteem or social competence (Rutter 1999). Resilience does not describe or define fixed characteristics, nor is it a predictive phenomenon. It encompasses an individual's coping abilities in response to a particular set of challenging or adverse circumstances. The exact interplay between which experiences will threaten resilience and what personality traits will enable a young person to recover from traumatic situations is not known. However, what does seem clear is that factors can cluster together to contribute to or reduce a young person's capacity for resilience. The affect is therefore cumulative (Cocker and Scott 2006). Furthermore, it is often not a single factor itself that has an impact, but the context surrounding that factor. Rutter (1999) distinguishes between risk indicators and risk mechanisms. Thus, divorce may be a risk indicator but it is not predictive of reduced resilience in itself for young people. More often than not it is the mechanisms surrounding divorce that are more influential, for example the levels of parental discord preceding the divorce, the upheaval afterwards and the loss of being held in mind by two people who care about each other (Rutter 1999).

Resilience therefore involves a complex relationship between risk and protective factors that are not static or fixed (Rutter 1999). If cultivating resilience is a cumulative process, then facilitating individual factors that contribute to overall resilience at any given point is important (Hek *et al.* 2010). Achieving in education is known to further resilience (Fernandez 2008; Gilligan 2001; Masten, Best and Garmezy 1999). Performing well academically is likely to lead to enhanced confidence, a sense of competence and an experience of mastery and achievement. Most young people who come into care have not had a good start in education or the opportunities to discover their interests, talents and abilities. When adults take an interest in their education and believe in their potential, the chance for a different experience is initiated. This is fundamental as 'it is evident that, in order to break the vicious circle, new experiences which provide a break from the past and open up new opportunities are likely to be important' (Rutter 1999, p.132).

Such a change can represent a *turning point* (Rutter 1999) for a young person, where they come to experience themselves differently and comprehend that interested adults may hold perceptions of them that are contrary to what has been communicated to them hitherto (Fernandez 2008). This situation can set in motion a sequence of *positive chain reactions* (Rutter 1999) which includes opportunities for young people to defuse their self-concept and identity from being inextricably linked to their social-care status (Gilligan 2001). However, for this to occur, thought and planning needs to be optimised and it is the role of the education officer to drive this process with foster carers and schools. Team Parenting Meetings can cement this, facilitating 'good carer and teacher relationships [that] can provide important buffers in helping children cope with changes and adversities they encounter' (Fernandez 2008, p.10).

Having a positive experience in education is thus a protective factor for young people. There is agreement in the literature that education should be prioritised. Cocker and Scott (2006) argue for it to be given the same focus as placement stability, and Fernandez (2008) suggests that it is an intervention in its own right. The fundamental role that teachers can play in looked-after children's lives should be recognised by professionals together with clear understanding of the positive difference foster carers can make via their involvement and contribution in education. It seems likely that there is a cyclical relationship between placement stability and education, with stable placements supporting young people to remain engaged in school and their active participation in learning contributing to foster carer satisfaction and commitment to the placement. However, even when placements fail, schools can provide some sense of stability and familiarity if attendance at the same school can be maintained (Northwest Institute for Children and Families 2007).

CASE STUDY 1

Background

Katie hadn't been attending education provision consistently for the past two years. Different strategies had been used previously to encourage Katie to attend school. She had been offered different education provision and had been supported by the Education Team for looked-after children in her Local Authority, who, as well as attending meetings with Katie, had transported her to school.

From September 2008 to June 2009 Katie's school attendance was 8 per cent. From November 2008 to May 2009 Katie only attended 3.5 days of school.

Education support given by the education officer

The education officer attended the placement planning meeting. She then organised individual education sessions to be held with a mentor whilst a school place was established. Some mainstream national qualification units were completed. The sessions with the mentor continued over the summer holidays to work on Katie's self-esteem. The education officer liaised regularly with the Local Authority social worker, the education team for looked-after children and the behaviour support team.

A school place was established at the local secondary school. With support from the education officer, Katie attended an introductory meeting. This was the first education meeting she had managed to remain in for a year. The education officer advocated that Katie should go on roll at the school, whilst she was also referred for a place at a hospital school where it was believed her needs could best be met. The education officer collated a report for the special needs panel and liaised with the principal educational psychologist. In October 2009 Katie was given a place at this school.

Initially, Katie worked on a one-to-one ratio with staff from the hospital school at home, then gradually her time in school increased. Katie then attended every morning until lunchtime and hasn't missed a session since she started at the school.

The education officer co-ordinated and attended PEP meetings.

Outcomes

- 100 per cent attendance (based on part-timetable).
- All staff feedback was positive. Comments on Katie's school report from the head-teacher: 'I have been impressed by Katie's attitude and concentration in school. She has worked hard and made excellent progress'.
- The foster carer engaged in supporting and encouraging Katie to achieve educationally – Katie gained two passes in the national tests at 16 years old in Adult Numeracy and Literacy Level 3.
- Katie had a place at college to study for a Business and Technology Education Council (BTEC) First Diploma in Child Care in September 2010. The education officer liaised with the looked-after children's mentor at her college to ensure she had the necessary support when she commenced the course.

CASE STUDY 2

This case study has been written to evidence the value of having experienced teachers (education officers) to support young people in care with school issues. In brief, the study shows how the teacher, through her years of experience of working with children with emotional and behavioural issues and her knowledge of invigilating exams, was able to ensure a young person sat his GCSEs at a time when he was refusing to do so due to his emotional instability.

Year 7

Sam joined Giresh High school in Year 7 (at 11 years old).

Years 8, 9 and 10

When Sam entered Year 8, the inclusion co-ordinator at the school wrote to the local CAMHS requesting therapeutic support for Sam. The inclusion co-ordinator mentioned several very violent outbursts at school, which may have been strategies for coping with extreme anxiety. She also mentioned how, when Sam talked about girls, he referred to sexual acts in an inappropriate way. When reproduction was studied in Science, Sam refused to go to the lessons and became very agitated.

During school Years 8, 9 and 10, Team Parenting Meetings were held regularly at the school to ensure relevant members of staff could always attend and all agencies could work as a team in dealing with Sam's inappropriate behaviours. Sam attended some therapeutic sessions with CAMHS. The education officer sent Sam certificates whenever he had achieved good behaviour and results at school to provide him with as many positive experiences as possible.

Year 11

During Year 11, Sam's behaviour again became very difficult, both at school and in his foster placement. On one occasion Sam took a sharp knife from the Design and Technology room and ran down the corridor with it and then out into the community. He was arrested for having a dangerous weapon in public. The governors met in due course and agreed to exclude Sam permanently. However, in recognition of the fact that he was soon to sit his GCSEs, they decided to put him on a 30-day exclusion with the offer of Sam being able to sit his GCSE exams, providing they were sat away from all other Year 11s and invigilated by the education officer. This would involve the education officer collecting Sam from his home to ensure he arrived at school in time for the morning or afternoon exam. Sam received some tuition in the home from the education officer during the 30-day exclusion to prepare him for his exams.

Unfortunately, Sam's foster placement broke down just a week before his first exam and the nearest alternative available carers lived almost an hour by car from the school. Sam was very distressed by the breakdown and told his Local Authority social worker (LASW) that he didn't want to sit his exams.

The first GCSE exam

On the day of Sam's first exam the education officer arrived at his home at 11.30am to chat with him and to take him to school. Sam kept his head down, not wanting to make eye contact. He said he did not want to sit his exams, but eventually with gentle encouragement, Sam made the journey to school. The front car park was full and it was necessary to park in the rear car park in front of a classroom. Sam was keen to see his Design Technology teacher about his woodwork project and discuss how to get it home. The education officer took him into the storage area and discussed with staff how they would transport it to the foster home. Sam returned to the car park and spotted his girlfriend in the adjoining classroom eating her packed lunch. Having just had a positive response from his teachers he went in to say hello. Sam was challenged by the teacher in that room, who reminded him that he was excluded and should not go into any areas other than the Sixth Form block to do his exam. Sam took exception to this challenge and ran off and hid. Staff could not find Sam but the education officer thought he would want to go home and found him hiding behind her car.

At this stage Sam was refusing go into school at all to do his exam. Attempts to persuade Sam to take his exam by his teachers failed. The education officer decided to suggest to Sam that they should go home but she had in mind stopping the car a mile or so from the school and talking to him. Sam was keen to go home. A mile from school the car was stopped in a side street and the education officer said that she felt both she and Sam were spoken to in a very unhelpful way by staff at the school and she would like to return to discuss this with the Head. In addition, she said she didn't want the school to have 'won' by Sam missing his exams and this spoiling his future career by not taking his GCSEs. Having invigilated exams in the past, she knew it was crucial to get Sam back to start his exam within 30 minutes or he would not be allowed to sit it. She also knew to take a detour to the Sixth Form block to avoid seeing the staff that had angered Sam, in case the sight of them enflamed the situation again. All this was achieved and Sam sat his first exam. He went on to sit all his other exams too.

August
Sam received his results: he passed nine of the national tests that 16-year-olds sit in England.

THE CHILDREN AND YOUNG PEOPLE'S SUPPORT SERVICE

Children and Young People's Support workers (or Chyps workers as they are known), play a mentoring role in supporting placements within the Team Parenting approach. I refer to them in this section as mentors as this describes their role within the Team Parenting approach and is more universally recognisable than Chyps workers. The theoretical importance of their role is explored in more detail below. It is important to note, though, that mentors potentially spend the greatest amount of time with young people in foster care (apart from foster carers). Their role involves them spending individual time with young people and their remit will differ with each young person as the service they offer is designed to fit the young person's own particular needs. Mentors (Chyps workers) therefore engage in a whole range of activities with young people. These can include:

- leisure activities (e.g. going to the cinema, bowling)

- sporting activities

- activities which facilitate a young person's social needs (e.g. attending youth clubs with them)

- teaching new skills (e.g. cooking)

- activities that will assist with independent living (e.g. budgeting)

- identifying and acquiring new hobbies and interests (e.g. arts and crafts)

- outdoor activities (e.g. camping, adventure, climbing).

As Staines *et al.* (2011, p.328) identify, Core Assets:

> believes that activities provided for the young people such as creative workshops (music, art, drama, story-telling) and physical activities (swimming, walking, football) are likely to be of therapeutic benefit. This kind of informal support to children is important in building their resilience (Gilligan 2008), can widen and strengthen relationships in their social networks and, in turn, may lead to increased educational attainment and achievement (Davey and Pithouse 2008; Gilligan 2007; Mahoney, Cairns and Farmer 2003) and contribute to placement stability.

The benefits of the mentors are closely linked to the concept of resilience. Resilience has been explored in the section in connection with the Education Service. To recap, resilience represents the concept of an individual managing better in life than might have been predicted due to their experiences of previous *serious adversity* (Gilligan 2008). Key to resilience is the theory that it is not one static trait that contributes to its existence but a variety of factors – some internal and some external. Furthermore, resilience is believed to be variable across contexts and situations. Therefore, one person may be resilient in terms of education but lack resilience with regards to social competence (Gilligan 1997). This multi-faceted nature of resilience means that there are multiple opportunities to add to young people's coping abilities across several different *domains* of their lives

– for example, school, home, community, faith settings, clubs, social networks (Gilligan 2008). It also means that interventions can be targeted at areas where their functioning is at its weakest and this can positively impact on the unfolding trajectory of young people's development (Gilligan 2008). As Gilligan (2008, p.38) states: 'As a modifiable process, resilience may operate, under certain conditions, for certain periods, and in different ways, in one or more facets of a young person's life and circumstances.'

Resilience is closely linked to the concepts of self-esteem and self-efficacy, as are feelings of *competence and confidence* (Schofield and Beek 2009). A young person's self-esteem can be thought about as a lens through which they view themselves and the rest of the world (Schofield 2001). Self-efficacy refers to a belief in one's capacity to manage new situations. This includes confidence in one's ability to ask for support and help in facilitating this process where necessary. Children, who have endured on-going experiences where their needs have not been privileged by those who look after them and have lived in the kind of high-criticism low-warmth households which typically feature in neglect and abuse, often have decimated and punctured self-esteems. In addition, growing up with carers who not only are unavailable to offer help and assistance but may respond punitively to vulnerability and the need for support will have serious consequences for a young child's developing and emerging sense of self-efficacy.

Resilience is also conceptually connected to self-agency and the idea that young people are active participants in their lives (Pinkerton and Dolan 2007). It is to be hoped that young people can act with wishful intention, choosing their friendships, hobbies, interests and so on. However, the degree to which young people are able to be agents of their own lives is affected by their life experiences. Young people in care are at greater risk of having a diminished sense of agency and can become trapped by a limiting self-identity as a looked-after child. Invariably, being 'looked after' entails a range of other professionals making decisions and plans about young people's lives and this can contribute to a growing sense of powerlessness and lack of self-agency.

The damaging effects of the looked-after experience on resilience is likely to have begun before young people enter the care system. They are likely to face more risk factors than protective factors, purely due to the circumstances which led to them becoming looked after in the first place, together with the invariably connected paucity of good early experience in education (Cocker and Scott 2006). Targeted interventions can help here, as Gilligan (1997, p.14) so persuasively argues: 'The challenge for those who seek to influence the child's well-being is to try to cultivate, carefully, as many protective factors as possible and to minimise risk factors so that resilience may manifest itself.'

The research on resilience is helpful in guiding avenues for intervention. It suggests that variable characteristics, mechanisms, factors and processes all have a part to play in contributing either to risk factors or protective mechanisms for resilience. This knowledge increases the scope and breadth of available sources of intervention in supporting a young person's burgeoning resilience. In Team Parenting, the mentors play a fundamental role in bolstering the protective factors that are known to enhance resilience.

It is important to bear in mind that resilience is not something that people are born with, although certain internal characteristics do seem to contribute to its existence. Schofield (2001, p.9) cites Sroufe (1997, p.256):

> Resilience is not something some children 'have a lot of'. It develops. A capacity to rebound following periods of maladaptation (or to do well in the face of stress) evolves over time within the total context of developmental influences.

Knowing that we can assist in developing protective factors that will aid a young person's capacity for resilience is important in considering service design. Gilligan (1997) warns against the historical tendency in foster care to concentrate on permanence as an ultimate goal. His thesis is that doing so may lead to the neglect of other factors that can contribute to a young person's resilience. Mentors work to ameliorate this by identifying resources and additional relationships that are available to a young person. This is particularly important where their placements at home or at school are strained.

The involvement of mentors in the lives of young people is therefore a crucial part in the Team Parenting approach. The activities that mentors undertake with young people contribute to a young person's resilience in a number of ways which are explored below. These factors in and of themselves are likely to contribute to placement stability, due to more confident, engaged and active young people exhibiting less externalising behaviours at home. However, mentors, whilst primarily providing an additional relationship and support for the young person, also act as a buffer for foster carers.

RESILIENCE AND MENTORING

A one-to-one relationship with an adult

Having a variety of supportive adults in a young person's life playing different roles contributes towards protective factors that facilitate resilience (Gilligan 2008). As Gilligan (1997, p.13) states: 'The research evidence suggests that relations with caring adults other than parents may be an important source of support, and indeed attachment.' Young people have a 'hierarchy of attachment figures' (Gilligan 1997, p.13). Even in normative circumstances, a young person's development is nurtured by relationships outside of her nuclear family. These relationships cover a broad range of contexts and can be found within extended family, community, school and social networks. Often, due to the circumstances which brought them into care, the opportunities for young people in foster placements to develop relationships with their extended family are limited. Moreover, a history of multiple moves and new placements can diminish other opportunities to form consistent, continuing relationships with adults in other settings. Becoming involved with a mentor provides young people with the chance to establish a positive relationship with a supportive adult away from their home setting.

Good interpersonal relationships are strongly associated with resilience, and spending time with a mentor provides opportunities for these to occur (Rutter 2007). Pinkerton and Dolan (2007) noted in their study of youth projects in Ireland that young people valued learning new skills alongside an adult. Specifically, they cited enjoying the presence of an adult spending time with them and appreciating having someone to listen when they wanted to talk. This finding is echoed by Gilligan (2008) who cites Jackson and Martin's (1998) study. They found that care leavers who did well identified one person in their lives who had made time to talk and listen to them whilst they were growing up. For young people, having a sense of a range of adults who care about them militates against behavioural problems and mental ill-health (Gilligan 1997). Schofield (2001) highlights that it is not the longevity of the relationship or the legal status that is important, but the availability of the adult and the concern and caregiving shown.

Mentors provide for young people a relationship that is not embedded with the expectations that imbue their other relationships at home and at school. Focusing on an activity whilst talking can free up a young person to talk in a way that may feel less inhibiting than when there is no other distraction. Engaging together in activities can break down the barriers that block more informal relating for young people in care with other professionals (e.g. social workers). Experiencing an enjoyable, relaxed relationship with an adult who observes, praises and encourages the learning of new endeavours will further facilitate the success of this relationship. Such experiences invariably contribute to the emerging self-esteem, self-efficacy and confidence of young people in care. These assets are important as they are all internal protective factors for resilience and will aid young people to navigate future stress as well as potentially overcome some of the impact of their past adverse experiences.

Mastery and achievement

Mentors engage young people in a range of activities. These can be one-to-one activities, (e.g. cooking, craft), group activities or sporting activities. Participating in extra-curricular activities like this may lead to a sense of mastery and achievement for young people. Learning new skills, undertaking fresh challenges, becoming competent at different ventures and observing one's own progress and development are all likely to impact positively on emotional well-being, self-confidence and resilience. These experiences are liable to have an itinerant effect whereby, once a task has been mastered, young people become motivated to set themselves further goals. Goal setting contributes to the capacity for planning (Mahoney et al. 2003). This is an important skill both in education and the workplace. Which activity is chosen is not necessarily important according to Mahoney et al. (2003). Rather, they argue that three characteristics are necessary for optimal positive benefits to be reaped. These are that the young person should enjoy it, that there should be structure in terms of it being led by an adult and being held in a consistent place with agreed rules at a certain time, and that it should incorporate a degree of challenge.

Education

Education, as identified in the section above, is often problematic for young people in the care system. Staines et al. (2011) found that over a third of foster carers said that they had disagreements with their young person about school and nearly a third believed that their young person had little (21 per cent) or no confidence (8 per cent) in their schoolwork. Foster carers also identified problems with socialising and a lack of confidence for young people in their ability to make friends. Extra-curricular activities have been associated with improved performance at school (Gilligan 2007; Mahoney *et al.* 2003). Mahoney *et al.* (2003) argue that extra-curricular activities lead to enhanced interpersonal skills and an increase in initiative which contribute to educational success. It is easy to see how, for young people in foster care, undertaking extra-curricular activities with a committed and interested adult who provides structure, challenge, support and encouragement will improve their ability to relate to adults as well as boost their confidence.

Learning new skills is also likely to stimulate an interest in learning elsewhere, for example in schools. Acquiring competence in different areas may contribute to a young person's confidence that they do have the ability to learn successfully and that this asset can be transferred into the school environment. Mentors facilitate this thinking by observing for young people their achievements and linking these to their capacity to manage well within school. Furthermore, developing new abilities with mentors gives rise to opportunities for young people to learn to trust others to support them in their learning and to ask for help when needed (Schofield 2001). When young people utilise the relationship with a mentor to assist in the development of their relational capacities, this also can have an impact on their education. Mahoney *et al.* (2003) suggest that while a lack of interpersonal competence seems to lead to disengagement from education, improved interrelating skills leads to re-engagement in learning, not only in schools but later in further education and the workplace. The totality of these experiences allows young people to learn different behavioural strategies that are helpful in the school environment.

Social support

It is perhaps not surprising, given the disruption to their early attachment relationships, a history of abuse and neglect, and an unsettled and transitory home life, that young people in care often struggle to form satisfactory relationships with their peers. However, the ability to form and enjoy friendships is an important barometer for emotional health (Gilligan 1997). This view can be found elsewhere in the literature, for example: 'It is well established that social support assists resiliency, has a buffering effect in dealing with stress and aids positive mental health' (Pinkerton and Dolan 2007, p.220).

Pinkerton and Dolan (2007) and Gilligan (2008) draw a distinction between informal support and formal support. Informal support refers to the support that friendships and social networks in the community and at school provide, whereas formal support alludes to the input that is available from professional systems. Social capital was defined by Bourdieu (1986) as the potential resources linked to a person's social network and recognition. It reflects the combination of support that includes school, social settings, recreational groups and professional relationships. Pinkerton and Dolan (2007) suggest that where young people have good social capital, then their resilience will be increased.

However, both Pinkerton and Dolan (2007) and Gilligan (2008) suggest that formal support tends to be utilised either when informal support does not have the expertise or resources to manage the situation (e.g. emergency health care), or when the informal support available is weak and insufficient to meet the presenting need. For looked-after children, the latter is often the case. Disruptions to informal support occur both via the move into care and by moves within the care system. Informal support networks are lost, and, due to difficulties in forming relationships, young people may struggle to form new support networks in their new communities and schools. Pinkerton and Dolan (2007, p.222) suggest that some young people will need assistance in building informal support: 'For some young people, realizing this personal potential will require additional formal family support interventions aimed at bolstering the type and quality of social support available to them.'

Mentors can play a useful role in this arena as they straddle formal and informal support. In one sense, being part of an organisation and becoming involved with young people as part of their work duties, locates them in formal support. However, their lack of professional status and their role in facilitating extra-curricular activities places them some way along the spectrum to informal support. Moreover, mentors can assist young people move further along the polarity from formal support to informal support by enabling young people to engage in activities which require mixing with their peer group. This can be by accompanying young people to youth clubs or other social settings. Mentors will support young people with their developing social skills by attending such clubs with the young person when necessary. As the young person becomes more confident, the mentors may reduce their support, taking the young person to the club and collecting them afterwards. Talking to the young person about difficulties they have socialising and in the relationships with their peers provides an outlet for the young person and a source of support. Mentors can also help advocate for the young person with club leaders, explaining the particular needs of the young person and why they may have difficulties forming relationships, and negotiating problems as they arise.

Frequently, mentors assist young people in identifying areas of interest for themselves (e.g. drama, dance, music etc.). Attending new activities with the support of an interested, engaged adult enhances young people's confidence. It also leads to chances to mix with a new group of peers. This has the dual advantage of giving opportunity for enhancing social competence but also for ensuring that young people associate with appropriate peers who are motivated and engaged in their own lives (Gilligan 2007). Rutter (1999) suggests that monitoring the desirability of a young person's peer group and providing attractive alternatives, plays a role in resilience. This is an area where mentors can support the Team Parenting endeavour as young people may be more likely to confide in them difficulties and conflicts they experience than confide in their foster carers or social worker. Often, too, mentors can entice young people to try new social settings whereas others have just met with resistance.

Identity

Young people in care are at risk of fusing their identity with their looked-after status (Gilligan 2008). They can feel stigmatised by others and painfully aware of their difference from the majority of their peers who live at home with birth parents. Engaging in extra-curricular activities provides opportunities for them to broaden their identity across different domains. Mentors can assist in this by taking young people to different activities. Engaging in social activities gives young people the opportunity to form positive relationships with peers and adults outside of the classroom. This can assist with furthering the scope of their social identity (Mahoney et al. 2003).

Attending both regular activities such as clubs, and one-off leisure activities such as bowling, enjoying them, having fun and talking about them all help normalise life for young people living in care and add breadth to their self-concept.

CONCLUSION

In working to promote resilience in young people, both Gilligan (1997) and Schofield (2001) suggest that a lifespan perspective is necessary. At times, progress with young people in care, who have been damaged and hurt by their early experiences, can seem painfully slow. In addition, it is not unusual for young people to appear to be making gains in their lives only to seemingly revert to previous destructive behaviours and undo the progress they have made. Hope can be gleaned from research into care-leavers' perspectives (Gilligan 2008). Young people who do well when they leave care report that the availability of an adult who listened and talked to them was important. However, these relationships are not quantified by the longevity or role but by their availability. Mentors can be available to fulfil this function. This can only add to lifetime goals of imbuing young people with the qualities needed to grow up to become good partners, parents, workers and members of society (Gilligan 1997; Schofield 2001).

It is perhaps reassuring too, that changes in direction for young people or *turning points* as Rutter (1999) terms them, can occur late (Schofield 2001). Working with resilience as a theory means accepting that this is an asset that occurs across the lifespan, is variable, contextual and can be mediated at different points via various domains. We can never predict what will make the difference, but using mentors to intervene more informally with young people in settings outside of school and social work creates additional opportunities for *turning points* to occur.

> Yet across various turning points a term used in the resilience literature (Rutter 1999) […] such as being sent away to school or being in trouble with the police, it was possible to see how downward spirals could be halted and transformed into upward spirals by the presence of supportive relationships. (Schofield 2001, p.7)

We can seek to make the ground fertile for such downward spirals to be reversed and positive chain reactions to be formed by incorporating ideas of how to foster resilience in care planning. Planning how to best use mentors to meet the specific needs of individual young people can turn vicious cycles into *virtuous* ones (Gilligan 1997, p.14).

CASE STUDY

Hassan was referred as an unaccompanied minor. He was 13 years old and had travelled on his own to England, having fled from Pakistan where he had been severely beaten. He had gone to Iran and stayed there with his uncle who then paid for his passage to England. Hassan is of Muslim faith. When he arrived in the UK, he spoke Farsi and no English.

Hassan was found by police at the side of a motorway. At that time he was extremely frightened. He received input from the Children and Young People's Support Service over a period of four years. The support plan was developed in consultation with Hassan, the support staff, his Local Authority social worker, the supervising social worker and his foster carers. The support package consisted of direct support for education and befriending and activities with a clear focus on promoting his social inclusion.

The education support worker started working with Hassan on an outreach basis, twice a week providing one-to-one sessions of education. Regular visits to different educational settings, libraries, museums and so on, supported Hassan and allowed him the chance to learn about English culture. This was at Hassan's request.

During the sessions within the office he learnt enough English to enable him to fit in when a school placement was found. He also took homework to complete in his own time. The foster carers were also very supportive in his learning and enrolled him at a local library.

Hassan was offered a place within a large local comprehensive school, where he is still attending the Sixth Form. The education support worker was able to continue to support Hassan within school twice a week for two terms, to allow him to be confident with the routines and settle into his new environment. Hassan continued at school and gained the equivalent of 11 GCSEs. He is currently studying for his A Levels. Hassan recently had support from the education support worker with filling in application forms for apprenticeship schemes and jobs. The senior education officer has attended all PEP Meetings and any other related school meetings that were necessary.

Hassan is very keen on football, so, when he first arrived, he also had support from the Children and Young People Support

Services team, who offered outreach sessions twice a week for six months, gradually reducing, as he made friendships and his confidence grew, to once a week. The session aims were to help Hassan build up relationships with people and to occupy his time in social activities. Hassan has continued with his love for football and attends football practice on a weekly basis. Hassan has also represented the region at the fostering provider's national football tournaments, giving him the opportunity to meet other young people in the same circumstances as himself and form friendships as a result of this.

Hassan was supported in accessing and attending mosque and supported by his carers and support worker in celebrations and identifying specific activities and clubs associated with his religion and beliefs.

Recently, Hassan was part of a group of children and young people involved in the arranging of the fostering provider's regional achievement awards. He stood on stage with another young person in front of over 300 people and delivered a motivational speech to other children and young people and presented awards. Hassan celebrated his own achievements with the audience and shared his experience and gratitude for the support he had received from the individuals he had worked with over the four years. He paid tribute to his carers and the support service for their commitment, consistency and friendship, saying that 'you are my family, you have accepted me and I feel like I belong, thank you'.

Hassan has been able to help with the mentoring of other young people who have arrived as unaccompanied young people seeking sanctuary. He has been involved in the consultation and planning of events and holidays for other young people and carers within the organisation. This has also included him acting as an interpreter within school and being able to communicate with other young people. Hassan has also been heavily involved in his role as a care leaver, also providing workshops for staff, carers and young people at the annual conferences.

In this chapter the contributions of the Education Service and the Support or Mentoring Service to young people in foster carer within Team Parenting are delineated. It is argued that both can significantly aid the development of young people's resilience and self-esteem. Furthermore, the critical role of education being involved in the overall interagency ethos, which is at the heart of Team Parenting, has been emphasised. Chapter 9 moves on to examine other developments within the Team Parenting approach. These include the use of Key Development Assets as a strengths-based recording tool for foster carers, the introduction to Team Parenting within fostering in other cultures and countries and the utilisation of Team Parenting with families and young people outside fostering. The vision for the future of Team Parenting is that it is a way of working that can be implemented with children and young people as they move along the continuum of care.

CHAPTER 9

FURTHER DEVELOPMENTS IN TEAM PARENTING

CHAPTER CONTENTS

KEY DEVELOPMENTAL ASSETS (KDA)™

DEFINING ASSETS

The skills, abilities, characteristics and qualities that a person has, develops, builds and utilises to survive, adapt, grow and, one hopes, to flourish can be referred to as 'assets' (Diehl, Howse and Trivette 2011). We develop assets during our entire lifespan as our brains retain the ability to learn and adapt throughout our lives. This neural ability is referred to as 'plasticity' (Zolli and Healy 2012). Some assets are genetically influenced, such as our height and facial features, and are thus developed and nurtured *in utero*. Others require repetition and environmental conditions in order to appear and strengthen. The assets we develop come from a complex web of life experiences, genetics and physiology that can be impacted upon at any stage in our development (Huffman 2012; Ryff, Singer and Dienberg-Love 2004).

It is possible to think of these assets as tools in a tool belt that each person carries with them in their daily lives. Being able to use these assets as adaptive tools to manage a situation successfully, interact with others, solve problems and make decisions, contributes to a person's sense of self-efficacy and personal well-being (Duckworth, Steen and Seligman 2005). When we do not have the assets we need to negotiate the life circumstances we experience, stress and trauma result. These are a consequence of our coping strategies not being effectively proportionate to the challenges we face (Varela and Vernberg 2003). Furthermore, if we draw upon our assets and misapply them in situations, the outcome can also be problematic. This inappropriate use of assets can be referred to as maladaptive (Krenke, Aunola and Nurmi 2009).

The functionality of an asset is determined by the context in which it is applied. We operate in a multitude of contexts daily. The relationships we have, the people we interact with in our home, school and neighbourhoods, and the culture and norms of our country and community are all part an interconnected web of external factors within which we all live. In addition to this are a myriad set of internal factors such as our physical state, emotional functioning, past experiences of trauma, abuse, neglect and even success. Knowing which 'asset' to use in any given situation and applying the asset adaptively are essential to optimal function. The acquisition of such knowledge is therefore a fundamental task of human development.

It seems reasonable to hypothesise that the more assets a person has that can be adaptively applied, the greater the likelihood that he/she will enjoy success and well-being. This premise is supported by research within the genres of positive youth development, positive psychology, integrative coaching and wellness (Henderson 2003; Kobau *et al.* 2010). There are many ways a person can acquire and learn to implement new assets. For learning to flourish, direct experience, observation, support, feedback, encouragement and opportunities to practise are required. As social beings, we learn within the contexts of relationships. Our brains are hardwired to facilitate our social development. This promotes our chances of survival and ensures that we receive the optimal care we need during infancy and childhood. This situation influences all other developmental pathways (Allen,

Bruss and Damasio 2005). When we do not have access to the asset we need at the right time, we need to be encouraged to accept and think through our maladaptive uses of assets. This occurs best within a social and attachment relationship where we can garner the support to learn, unhindered by scorn, shame and guilt. For children and young people this is the essence of developmental care – the process of creating the supportive and positive environment for them to gain assets and to learn to apply them adaptively and appropriately.

As identified in the previous chapter, Team Parenting is a strengths- and resilience-based approach to working with children and young people in foster care. Strengths-based practice involves facilitating the adaptive use of assets. Combining developmental care with a strengths-based approach focuses on building assets *and* influencing the contextual use of assets. The KDA™[1] focuses on 20 Assets relevant for children and young people who have experienced early life adversities. These Assets represent competencies which can be identified and developed to positively advance human potential.

The 20 KDA™ were originally selected from the Search Institute's 40 Developmental Assets[2] which were shown to influence young people's future life chances as they transitioned through adolescence to young adulthood. Achieving on 20 or more Assets was found to lead to greater outcomes in later life. Building from empirical research with more than three million children and young people, the 40 Developmental Assets identified by North America's Search Institute[3] are described as 'concrete, common sense, positive experiences and qualities essential for raising successful young people'. Their research shows that the more Assets young people have, the less likely they are to engage in risky behaviours. Research has shown that these assets promote academic success, divert young people from risky behaviours, increase community engagement/ citizenship and give young people the strengths they need to make positive choices in life.

The KDA™ were born out of a desire to change the way people within helping professions worked with, and recorded the life and development of, others. This involved a paradigm shift of practice and the development of conscious competence in using everyday

---

1   www.keydevelopmentalassets.com
2   www.search-institute.org/content/40-developmental-assets-adolescents-ages-12-18
3   www.search-institute.org/research/developmental-assets

experiences to record the developmental progress of children and young people and identify their on-going needs. The KDA™ model focuses on describing and nurturing the positive experiences, relationships, opportunities, and personal qualities that young people need to grow into healthy, caring and responsible adults. The KDA™ framework is grounded in research on child and adolescent development, risk prevention and resilience. Asset building is about fostering relationships which can help a young person succeed. By encouraging foster carers to notice, observe and develop individual children and young people's assets, KDA™ enhance the strengths- and resources-based approach to foster care employed by Team Parenting.

Within the Team Parenting model, foster carers are trained in KDA™. It is their task to create the opportunities for children and young people to positively build on the assets they already have as well as learn new ones. Knowing how to do this is facilitated by the requirement that foster carers observe and record progress against the 20 KDA™. Becoming familiar with these, paying attention to them and noticing their expression and presence in daily life enhances foster carers' skills in asset growth, learning and development for children and young people. By using the KDA™ model, the aim is to improve the quality of care, practice, recording and reporting standards in relation to young people in placements. The model can enable reflective and responsive care recording and planning.

Core Assets has further utilised KDA™ to develop an online recording tool, which is completed weekly by foster carers. This system uses an online web-portal called KDA™ Online. Recording from the perspective of the day-to-day life space and context of the children and young people helps document, track, monitor and support asset development and use. This system allows foster carers to enter weekly recordings, which are immediately sent electronically to the supervising social worker. The 20 Assets foster carers record against (with suggestions for what to notice and observe) are listed below. The Assets are divided into external and internal ones.

External Assets

Safety: Give an example from home, school or the community where an adult has said something or taken action to ensure the child/young person's health and safety.

Positive carer/child communication: Give an example of any positive communication, in words or gestures, with the child/young person.

Family and other adult relationships: Give an example of the child/young person accepting any support from an appropriate adult outside your home.

Childcare/school or college environment: Give an example of how teachers, tutors, carers, workers or peers have used a consistent/supportive approach to the child/young person's learning and development, taking account of their level of ability, language and learning style.

Carer involvement in childcare or education: Give an example which illustrates your level of involvement or contact which encourages the child/young person in a childcare, education or work setting.

Carer family support: Give an example where you have provided the child/young person with emotional or physical care, or given personal attention to their needs, worries or achievements.

Service to others: Give an example where the child/young person has carried out a simple but significant and helpful task for you or others.

Play/social activity: Give an example of the organised activities the child/young person attended this week which have involved interaction with others.

Carer family boundaries: Give an example which demonstrates the setting of understandable and appropriate boundaries or ground rules for the child/young person.

Childcare, school or work experience boundaries: Give an example of childcare workers, teachers or supervisors setting understandable and appropriate boundaries for the child/young person.

Adult role models: Give an example which demonstrates how you or another adult provided a positive role-model for this child/young person.

High expectations: Give an example of where you or another adult expected and supported the child/young person to do their best and where their achievements were acknowledged.

Internal Assets

Planning and decision-making: Give an example of where the child/young person has told you about or demonstrated his/her capacity to plan ahead or make a decision appropriate to his/her age and stage of development.

Engaging in learning activities – at home/school/community: Give an example to illustrate the level at which the child/young person has actively taken part in a learning activity.

Motivation to achieve: Give an example of how the child/young person demonstrates a willingness (outside school) to improve their skills, try out or master new things.

Learning opportunities and homework: Give an example linked to an educational or formal setting which illustrates the level of support the child/young person has sought or the extent to which they have been encouraged in their learning.

Personal power: Give an example of the extent to which the child/young person is making some sense of their own views and feelings and those of others, and is at least starting to voice an opinion and take action relating to their lives.

Responsibility: Give an example, however small, which illustrates the child/young person's ability to take responsibility for their own actions or their personal care.

Peaceful conflict resolution: Give an example which demonstrates the extent to which the child/young person has managed their own emotions and behaviour in a difficult situation.

Positive view of personal future: Give an example which demonstrates how the child/young person views themselves, others or their future, taking account of their own cultural identity, a growing awareness of difference and the diverse world around them.

The Assets are also plotted onto a diagram as below for quick and easy reference:

Figure 9.1: KDA™ diagram

Source: KDA™ information is included by permission of
Key Developmental Assets™

THE RECORDING TOOL

The recordings generated by a foster carer are an integral part of understanding and reflecting on a young person's life throughout the time span that they are in care. They also provide them with a journal of their life story for them to access when they reach adulthood. Children and young people often move placements and the verbal narrative about their journey through life can become lost. At times this can lead to misunderstandings about a young person's abilities and difficulties. The KDA™ recording tool enables the young person's narrative to be kept alive throughout their childhood and their journey of developmental milestones to be mapped out for them ready to be referred back to in later life, should they wish. This narrative also provides the professionals who are supporting the young people with valuable information about their strengths and the concerns they experience and face. Focusing the KDA™ recording on key assets enables foster carers to capture a true picture of the young people's progression, likes, dislikes and characters, giving the supporting professionals a much fuller picture to reflect on.

FOSTER CARERS

The KDA™ recording tool encourages foster carers to record in a strengths-based way. It encourages them to take time to think reflectively about the young person and focus on key areas where the young person has achieved, as well as on aspects of life with which he/she might be struggling. Considering achievements alongside areas of difficulty encourages as balanced a perspective as possible of the young person's world. It is known that enabling foster carers to work reflectively with young people can promote modification of problematic behaviours and encourage belonging and stability (Warman *et al.* 2006). The recording tool showcases the foster carers' professional skills and knowledge, can provide a snapshot of the young person's ability to form a strong attachment and can also show evidence of the growing reciprocal relationship between young person and foster carer. This process itself promotes the foster carers' efficacy as they can start to see differences and reflect on the work that they are undertaking on a day-to-day basis with the young people and celebrate their development. Efficacy is a vital component of maintaining a foster carer's confidence and ability to care effectively, particularly for young people with complex difficulties (Morgan and Baron 2011). Within the recording system is a supportive guide of helpful hints and tips for foster carers to use and take ideas from. This provides examples about activities to do with young people to help them develop skills, which can be useful as a first point of call to help foster carers who are beginning to feel that they have used all the ideas that they had to support their young people.

THE FOSTER CARER AND YOUNG PERSON RELATIONSHIP

The attachment relationship between the foster carer and the young person can be influenced directly through using the recording tool together. Young people are welcome to take part in the weekly recording, giving them an opportunity to 'say it their way'. This provides a medium for both the foster carers and young people to communicate openly regarding the week they have had. In addition, a forum is created whereby foster carers and young people can consider together on a regular basis the strengths and resilience of the young person, together with any worries each may have. Such a process enables both parties to gain insight into each other's perspectives, which in turn facilitates mutual understanding and the building of their relationship. Of course, it is the foster carer's responsibility to be more proactive in this, working hard to mentalise for the young person and engender in them a curiosity and reflectiveness regarding their assets and characteristics.

When there are concerns, being able to think about these in a strengths-based way can reassure the young person that the foster carer is trying to understand situations and is able to listen, rather than criticise and judge. Knowing that foster carers are noticing achievements and celebrating these builds on young people's efficacy, sense of competence and self-esteem. KDA™ recording provides the vehicle for this process to occur as it requires carers to observe and record specific attributes and assets which they notice that the young person is developing. As foster carers engage in this methodology and become more adept in their own strengths-based practice, children and young people will be on the receiving end of a style of foster care which is motivated by a desire to support and understand them, to help them develop and achieve new things. The KDA™ recording evidences for young people that this process is occurring.

An additional benefit to recording in this way is the transparency that underlies it. This obviates the need for young people to ruminate negatively about how other people see them and works towards dispelling any concerns they may have regarding what their foster carers and other professionals write about them. For young people returning as adults, the KDA™ recording and achievement profile will provide a fuller, more positive narrative of their life story in foster care from childhood to adulthood, detailing how they developed, concerns along the way, the skills/attributes/assets they achieved and when they achieved them.

"You managed your emotions and actions in potential conflict situations by..."

listening to my reasons for grounding you for a day and understanding that you had pushed the boundaries too far. I know that you hated being kept in but you understood that it had been your choice to come in late the night before and I had clearly warned you that this would happen if you came in late once more. I was impressed at how well you accepted this consequence.

Score: Achieving

"You have demonstrated personal responsibility this week by..."

accepting the reasons for being grounded without a big argument. I heard you tell one of the friends who came to the door that you were grounded because 'I came in really late last night so I have to stay in'.
You said this without rancour and his told me that you understood the reasons for this consequence.

Score: Mostly Achieving

"Another adult has helped you this week by..."

telling you that he was really worried when you didn't show up at his house to play with his nephew as arranged. He understood that you met up with some other friends on the way, who were playing football and you got distracted but he took the time to explain to you that he really cared about your safety and that you must never worry him like that again. You understood and were genuinely apologetic (and told me later that you thought it was nice that he cared about you so much).

Score: Achieving

"You have helped somebody this week by..."

You have taken our neighbours dog for lots of walks (and played football with her) after they left her with us for four days while they went away.

Score: Achieving

"You have made a strong decision or voiced your opinion by..."

telling me that you would only attend the street party for an hour because you wanted to play football with your friends. I thought this was an excellent compromise.

Score: Achieving

PHYSICAL DEVELOPMENT
"Your physical growth and development, including health and dental care this week..."

He is fit and healthy and has now grown to a height on a par with others his age. Saw the dentist on the 1st - no issues. He was sick for a day with a headache and vomiting but bounced back to health the following day. Bed wetting is sporadic but has decreased and does not appear to be linked to any anxiety.

Score: Achieving

Figure 9.2: KDA™ excerpt from recording for a young person
Source: KDA™ information is included by permission
of Key Developmental Assets™

THE CARER JOURNAL

The carer journal provides a summary of a four-week period and is a tool for supervising social workers (SSW) and foster carers to use to review recordings as a part of their monthly supervision. The journal contains:

- all the foster carer's notes that are securely sent between themselves and their SSW

- the SSW's comments they interject at the bottom of recordings

- the recordings under the outcome measures chosen, including the graphs to consider alongside the narrative.

The fact that supervising social workers regularly review carers' journals means that identifiable issues in the placement are addressed quickly and trends/patterns that are emerging can be highlighted and analysed. The journal provides the forum for foster carers and SSWs to consider together the specific skills the foster carer needs to care optimally for this particular young person. From this discussion additional training, group work or therapeutic support can be put in place where necessary to support the foster carer and develop their competency as a strengths-based carer.

ACHIEVEMENT PROFILES

The KDA™ Online system allows social workers/practitioners to automatically create a report which highlights trends and patterns in the individual's personal development over time, using up to 12 periods of recordings entered by the foster-care providers. These reports are called achievement profiles. Achievement profiles are the 'end product' of the information that our foster carers input into their weekly recordings, and they:

- are an amalgamation of up to 12 'periods' of carer recording

- provide a graphical summary of carers' 'scoring' in charts

- have a narrative explaining the graphs and giving the story of the period

- allow identification of trends and patterns

- allow an evidence-based evaluation of interventions employed

- form a detailed planning tool to inform future interventions and care planning

- can be used to report against national agendas.

As mentioned above, the achievement profile is generated every three months. This working tool can be used to provide a summarised overview for professional meetings; including Team Parenting Meetings, looked-after children reviews, strategy meetings, disruption meetings and so on. The achievement profile consists of ribbon graphs, which form a visual cue for a quick indication of how the young person's 12 week period has been in terms of their development. The graph must be considered alongside the narrative provided by the foster carer in their recording, the supervision notes from the SSW, any phone calls, reports from professionals, court reports and so on. This information is considered and written into a summary, explaining the young person's 12- week period. From this profile it is easy to obtain information regarding the young person's difficulties and strengths over that period of time.

Using the achievement profile during Team Parenting Meetings can:

- enable foster carers to recall the events from the three-month period clearly

- provide the ability to look more deeply and with greater clarity regarding unfolding trends and patterns

- facilitate the ability to predict and avoid potential difficulties for the young people from the information that is currently held

- assist the mechanism to hypothesise about potential reasons for difficulties, trends and patterns and think about whether the young person may have any transferrable skills from other areas where they are achieving consistently that can be used to support them in these areas

- aids the parenting team to consider together strategies that foster carers, teachers, social workers and others who are involved with them can use with the young person to promote their on-going optimal development.

External agencies which attend Team Parenting Meetings find that the achievement profiles provide an invaluable review of a period of time in the young person's life. The profiles are visual and the significant events, progress and difficulties for the young people are depicted clearly.

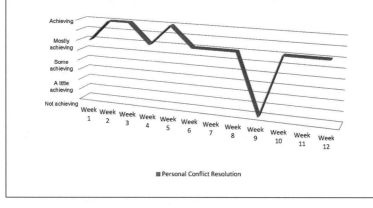

Peaceful conflict resolution – summary

The young person has struggled with conflict at times. He tends to react immediately, but after a period of time, and talking it through with his foster carer, he seems to be able to consider his actions and apologise where necessary. However, at times he still needs some encouragement to apologise. Playing in a football team has given him the opportunity to learn how to manage team dynamics and be considerate of others. He now tends to remove himself from a conflict situation rather than react to it inappropriately. He has also learned to manage social relationships and people making jokes with him. During this period he has also been better at accepting sanctions and taking responsibility for his actions and not adhering to boundaries put in place. This was tested during Week 9 when he struggled to accept the boundaries put in place by the carer during his first holiday abroad.

Figure 9.3: KDA™ excerpt from a young person's achievement profile
Source: KDA™ information is included by permission of Key Developmental Assets

OTHER USES

KDA™ and achievement profiles are versatile and can be used in other ways. They can be employed in the following ways:

- As a screening tool identifying areas where a young person may be struggling and require additional support. By providing evidence of patterns and difficulties, complex needs can be identified and additional support accessed quickly and appropriately (e.g. referral to a CAMHS team).

- Court proceedings – the data entered into the recording system can be tracked to the time and date of every input and can be formed into a supporting report enabling the foster carers recordings to be considered as a reliable piece of evidence in a court of law.

- As an outcome measure as progress can be tracked throughout the lifespan of a placement. Furthermore, the model operates as a screening tool.

CASE STUDY

Matthew, aged 11, was a vibrant and energetic young person, keen to please everyone around him. He was hardworking at school and had been awarded responsibilities of supporting younger students. This helped to build his self-esteem. However, it became noticeable that every month or so Matthew's school work and energy levels dropped and he would struggle to do the tasks that he was allocated for a day or two. Then he would readjust and be back to his usual self. This behaviour had been a mystery to his foster carers and school. Following the first 12 weeks of recording on the KDA™ system an achievement profile was generated. During the next Team Parenting Meeting the professionals and foster carers examined together the data provided for the 12-week period the achievement profile was reporting on. It became clear that following contact with his grandparents, which occurred monthly, Matthew would struggle briefly before returning to normal. Following this discovery, some work with Matthew and his grandparents was initiated. This revealed that Matthew felt upset each time he said goodbye to his grandparents and was so distressed by considering the long interval before he could see them again that he was temporarily disorientated emotionally and battled to maintain his usual degree of functioning. It was therefore agreed by the Local Authority that contact with his grandparents would be increased and that they would be able to be more involved in Matthew's schooling. School also agreed that on the days following contact he would not have too many responsibilities and he could access the sanctuary at school if he was feeling sad.

On this occasion KDA™ revealed the pattern that provoked a turning point for this young person, the school's understanding and that of the foster carer. The achievement profile enabled the professionals surrounding Matthew to gain more insight into his development and difficulties. This information could be used to find a better arrangement for Matthew to enable him to continue developing and feeling safe, secure and supported.

KDA™ are used in the context of Team Parenting within Core Assets fostering provision in other countries and it is this provision to which the chapter now turns.

CULTURAL RELEVANCE

Team Parenting in the UK has evolved and changed since its original inception in 2002. As Core Assets has extended its reach, developing fostering services in Ireland, Finland, Sweden, Germany, USA, Canada, New Zealand and Australia, Team Parenting has been introduced in these countries. Core Assets started to become involved in fostering internationally in 2005. In most of these countries this was instigated by an individual seeking to raise the quality of foster care in their jurisdiction. In many places the concept of fostering as an altruistic occupation with minimal support and training prevailed, with the result that carer numbers were in decline while the numbers and complexity of needs for children coming into the care system was increasing. Central to Team Parenting is recognition of the foster carer as the primary agent of change for the child, operating within a network of professionals. This has been difficult to implement in some Commonwealth countries and parts of Europe.

The development of the Team Parenting model in new global developments is work in progress, adapting as in the UK to the local culture and context, but informed by its foundation and practice in the UK. As with any initiative, a balance is needed between capacity building and upholding the principles of Team Parenting. It would be unsustainable economically to employ a full-time education worker and therapist in a new team which has only five children placed. However the principles underpinning the model and the emphasis on collaborative working around the child in the placement are a given, regardless of the composition of the team. Recruiting sessional or contract staff from the desired disciplines addresses this issue, and enables permanent positions to be appointed when resources permit.

In Western Australia, a fostering team was established in 2007–8. The prevalence and specific issues for Aboriginal children in the care system were clear to be seen. The history of colonisation as well as historic governmental practices of assimilation, removal of Aboriginal children from their families and segregation of Aboriginal people on designated reserves has taken its toll on individuals and communities. Aboriginal children continue to be over-represented in the childcare system across all States. As of 30 June 2010, Aboriginal and Torres Strait Islander children comprised 4.6 per cent of all children aged 0–17 years in Australia (AIHW 2011) yet in 2009–10 they constituted 32 per cent of those children placed in out-of-home care.

Checking that the Team Parenting model had cultural relevance for the Aboriginal children and communities was a key challenge for the development of services in Western Australia. The University of Curtin in Perth, WA, was commissioned to undertake a series of focus groups with Aboriginal women, to discuss the Team Parenting model with them and how it might be adapted. Aboriginal people have a strong spiritual, historical and psychological connection to their land, and felt that a model which reflected the colours of the rock, the natural world and the sun would be more appropriate. They were also bemused that community was not a feature, and so it was inserted into the Team Parenting diagram as an inner circle, as was the inclusion of a cultural consultant to inform staff and foster carers and to support carers in meeting the cultural needs of the child in placement. Though they could relate to the concept of all working together for the good of the child, they were sceptical about how this would play out, given historical factors (Bornhorst 2012).

Subsequent developments in Northern Ontario in a primarily Aboriginal (Cree) community confirmed that the Cree community were also more comfortable with this revised version. However, more complex than this initial exercise has been the on-going learning in adapting Team Parenting to fit diverse contexts and cultures. Maintaining relevance for contexts in which there are variations in the nature and causes of children coming into foster care, distinctive local customs and practice, divergent styles of parenting and family life, other languages, world views which are different to those in the West and challenges of geography and location are but a few of the factors that have needed to be taken into account in introducing Team Parenting abroad. The commitment to employing people from the countries and communities where fostering services were being developed, rather than relocating workers from the UK, has been fundamental as this has enabled practice developments to be informed by local knowledge. Examples of this amelioration and adaptation of fostering practice and the Team Parenting approach are described below.

In New Zealand, children from the Maori group of people are over-represented in childcare. The tribal affiliation (*pepeha*) of the child is important in order to ensure continuity and connection for the child – to provide them with 'turangawaewae', a place in which they can assuredly stand. Working to meet the child's cultural needs in partnership with the extended family (*whanau*) as part of Team Parenting is essential, along with a recognition that often there will be family members beyond birth parents who have a primary and significant role in the child's upbringing.

Children in Finland, a country with a small population (5.4 million), are given a greater degree of independence and autonomy than their British counterparts – for example, coming home alone from school at an earlier age and being less subject to adult supervision as they play in the woods and lakes around their homes. UK concepts of safety and safe care for foster children are constantly questioned and a compromise has been reached which has avoided imposing on carers the 'risk averse' requirements which have been a feature of recent UK childcare practice (Milligan 2011).

Core Assets has needed to enhance its own learning in relation to 'Social Pedagogy', a concept of education of the child in a broader holistic sense, which is better understood and developed in neighbouring European countries than in the UK. It has also been necessary for Core Assets to understand the perspectives of professionals in other places on child development and medical care. For example, in Bulgaria the medical model of disability stemming from Soviet occupation has drawn huge numbers of children into institutional care. In the USA and Canada the use of psychotropic medication for children with emotional and behavioural issues is widely accepted (Khan 2013). In such instances it is important that there is dialogue with medical practitioners and that they are included in Team Parenting Meetings.

In its international endeavours, Core Assets has had to develop more flexibility in its expectations of family life in working with foster carers. Some of the norms within UK foster care, such as the foster child having their own bedroom, are seen as bizarre and potentially isolating in other cultures. For example, in Japan, the concept of having a bedroom in itself is alien, as most families sleep together in their living space. It would be inappropriate for Core Assets to impose this as a standard in communities where housing stock is limited in space, or where the cultural norm is for children to share.

In the UK the majority of children enter the care system for reasons of abuse and neglect, and the commitment to permanency plans for children, generally supported by legal interventions, enables the local authorities to share parental responsibility and decision making with parents. However, in Finland, Sweden and Germany, legal intervention by the State is much less common and parents retain more control over their children's lives. There is therefore an expectation that professionals in social care establish closer working with birth families than is the norm in the UK. This needs to be taken into account in Team Parenting alongside understanding the impact on the child of the greater involvement with the birth family. In Finland, for example, most of the respite entitlement for foster carers is provided by the child returning to the birth family. It is therefore more likely that it would be appropriate to include birth parents in Team Parenting Meetings and in Team Parenting interventions.

Children in care in Bulgaria have not, like their counterparts in the UK, generally had traumatic or difficult experiences of family life. In fact, most have no concept of family life at all, having started out as newborn in large and impersonal institutions. Work in Bulgaria must take into account children who may never have had a secure attachment to anyone – whose opportunity to experience life outside of an institution may have been limited to a series of short expeditions, and therefore transition to living with a family can be a terrifying and incomprehensible experience.

In Northern Ontario it is important to understand the long-term intergenerational impact of severed attachments. Historically, generations of Native children from the age of seven were forcibly removed from their family and placed in residential school in the interests of 'assimilation'. The legacy of the trauma that families and communities experienced needs to be understood by the system working around the child. Similarly, developing an understanding of ethical conduct in this and other indigenous communities, where emotions may not be openly expressed in the interests of maintaining community harmony, is important. For example, the concept of shame, understood in attachment theory as a protective developmental factor for the child, may be something to avoid at all costs in other cultures. Some of the practices which have gained recognition in the UK context as attachment promoting, such as eye contact between a younger person and an adult, can be seen as disrespectful in other societies – for example, Australian indigenous cultures, and some Eastern cultures. Proximity of contact between people of different sexes within the foster home also requires careful and respectful handling in some families – for example, within Muslim and some indigenous communities.

In conclusion, Team Parenting has been found to have wide applicability in other countries and cultures although it has needed to adapt to fit local contexts and communities. The underpinning expectations of child- and carer-centred practice, close collaboration between all involved with the child and a commitment to work together creatively to meet the child's needs are valued by professionals and service providers in other countries and are already evidencing positive results for children and their foster families. By listening and learning, taking on board cultural values and ethics, diverse world views, different parenting practices and understanding the historical and political context within which the working model is applied, the aim is not only to develop models of practice which are best suited to individual children wherever they live, but to bring back the learning of these rich encounters and developments to inform the evolution of the Team Parenting model in its UK context.

WHAT TEAM PARENTING MIGHT LOOK LIKE IN THE CONTEXT OF OTHER SERVICES

The Team Parenting approach has been extended beyond fostering and taken out into the wider world of social care, specifically with Youth Offending Teams working with cases of sexually problematic and harmful behaviours.

SEXUALLY PROBLEMATIC BEHAVIOURS (SPB) – THE PROFESSIONAL EVOLUTION

Children and young people with identified sexually problematic behaviours are subject to social care, health and youth offending interventions. They may be taken into care as a result of their behaviour within their family, they may be in foster or residential care already because of other issues in their history or they may be living with their own family but be subject to youth offending preventative interventions or referral orders following conviction of an offence.

Recent developments in practice and research in this area have drawn from work within the fields of psychology, neuroscience, resilience and trauma. The 'good life' (Ward and Stewart 2003) model is a practice-based approach that utilises this new knowledge to deepen current understanding of childhood, adolescent and adult problematic sexual behaviours. As practice and interventions in this area have evolved, the imperative of working with developmental dynamics and the social environment of the child have come to be seen as crucial aspects of the work. Team Parenting, as a systemic and attachment-based model, well acquainted with delivering therapeutic interventions within a context of professionals, parents, carers and young people, is well placed to deliver this approach.

Practice in this field has evolved in other ways too. The evidence-based and supported risk factors behind sexual re-offending in adolescents can be found in the literature (Calder 2002; Cavanagh Johnson 2004; Hackett 2004). They include incomplete treatment, social isolation and emotional loneliness, a history of abuse, having witnessed domestic violence, attitudes and beliefs that support sexual offending, problematic parent-offender relationships/parental rejection and a lack of intimate peer relationships. Recently the traditional interventions based on the above list of *risks and deficits* has been joined with an approach based on the growing research into the significance and influence of *strengths and resilience* factors in determining a child's response to adverse circumstance, and, in this area, in preventing recidivism. SPB-specific resilience factors include: willingness to engage, acknowledgement and regret of offence, talents or interests, problem-solving skills, communication skills, the involvement of a positive adult who is emotionally, physically and socially healthy and who has good coping strategies, positive relationships with professionals and teachers. Again, this emphasis on resilience and a strengths-based approach fits neatly with Team Parenting, which encompasses these theoretical and practical tenets within its philosophical assumptions and its delivery.

Interventions which are systemic and integrated demand a clear focus on building positive relationships between the individual, their family and the professional network. These facets are the hallmarks of current recommended practice. Whilst Team Parenting is optimally placed to work in this way, it is necessary for practitioners to keep abreast of emerging thinking in the field too. For example, there are interesting findings in the literature which postulate that some traditional beliefs about risk factors around this behaviour are not supported by research with young people, including denial (Kahn and Chambers 1991; Worling and Curwen 2000), lack of victim empathy (Langstrom and Grann 2000), non-sexual crimes (Worling and Curwen 2000) and a personal history of sexual abuse (Worling and Curwen 2000). Key factors from research (Cavanagh Johnson 2004; Hackett 2001, 2004, 2006) in providing safe and therapeutic care for young people with sexual behaviour problems are delineated in the literature and include: avoiding exposure to sexual violence and determining the triggers, teaching privacy and healthy boundaries, teaching safety and self-protection, teaching sex education and appropriate sexual expression, encouraging open and honest communication, interrupting and redirecting misuses of power and distorted thinking, talking to others in the family, using positive parenting techniques. Cavanagh Johnson (2004) advocates the parent discussing the behaviour openly with the child and creating a plan together. She suggests that this plan may not work if the child is living in an unstable environment, the caregivers do not follow the plan through or shame the child, the child does not understand or agree with the plan, the child or parent is too overwhelmed with feelings, previous trauma or other issues, there is unexpressed resentment and anger between the child, parent and professionals. These approaches invite professionals to share responsibility with the young person and their family. They also suggest that it is fundamental to create interventions which motivate and sustain meaningful engagement so the young person and the family can gain from them.

TEAM PARENTING TAKES TO THE FIELD

A Team Parenting informed intervention reflects current evidence, providing an integrated, strengths-based service and making the best possible use of the resources in the professionals, families and young people. The approach sees the children and young people as individuals separate from their behaviour and works with them to overcome behaviours that are a problem for themselves and others. These children and young people are all vulnerable and many have severe emotional and/or learning difficulties. Helping them understand and overcome harmful sexual behaviours with the best possible treatment and support is vital, both for their own well-being, and for that of potential victims.

Within Team Parenting, sexually harmful behaviour is seen as connected to other issues in the child's life and the aim is to help everyone involved make sense of the past behaviour and to ensure that the behaviour doesn't make sense in the future. If the behaviour met an emotional need, maybe for control, affection or attention, then how to meet that need individually or in relationships is worked upon. If the behaviour re-enacted a trauma, then a way is found to process this trauma without replaying it. If the rules about sex and relationships were not clear, then they are made clear. Drawing on the strengths within the child, family, community and professional, the aim is to restore safety, promote protection and support positive outcomes for everyone involved.

Experience and psychodynamic theory suggest that the individuals within the caring and professional network will be personally and professionally affected by their work in this area. Carers and workers can experience secondary trauma and specifically experience aspects of the traumagenic dynamics of sexual abuse including betrayal, stigmatisation, powerlessness and traumatic sexualisation (Finklehor and Brown 1986). These dynamics can emerge in their professional and personal lives and in particular within the dynamics of the parenting team around these children. Team Parenting is designed to identify and re-address these dynamics – aiming to inject reparative processes of trustworthiness, positivity, effectiveness and empowerment into the lives of the children and carers and into the practices of professionals.

THE PROGRAMME – STRUCTURED TEAM PARENTING

To meet the needs of the professionals commissioning services, discrete therapeutic programmes which are clearly defined in time and intention, have been created. The programme includes processes drawn from Team Parenting interventions within fostering, and evidence and research interventions from the field of sexually harmful behaviours. Within this setting the Team Parenting approach always has two therapists working on each case. In this way it differs from

Team Parenting in fostering. One therapist is responsible for the systemic work and facilitating the Team Parenting Meetings, whilst another undertakes the direct work with the young person.

The first task is to create the team and *weave the collaborative network* (Fredman 2011). The first network meeting is based on a Team Parenting Meeting with the addition of the young person. It invites everyone with an investment in the emotional well-being and sexual safety of the young person. The aim is to *warm the context* (Burnham 2005) around the way the work with the family is going to take place and garner support and motivation for the endeavour.

Individual work with the young person and their parent(s) brings together all that is known about engagement, facilitating motivation, insight and transformation. It draws from fields of psycho-education, resolution of trauma, attachment (Gerhardt 2004; Schore 1994) and cognitive behavioural therapy[4] (Stallard 2002). The purpose of the work is to respond to and influence the emerging ways in which the young person and their family have come to think, act and respond to the problematic behaviour.

Liaison between the two therapists and between the therapists and other professionals and the family throughout the period of work challenges commonly held assumptions around confidentiality within therapeutic work. However, this is framed within a strengths-based narrative model as *spreading the news* (Freedman and Combs 1996). This practice positively encourages the young person to consider with whom to share news of their progress. These chosen people can then function as *outside witnesses* (White 1995), adding strength to this new narrative, and cementing success made through observation, noticing, celebration and encouragement. Therapeutic availability and feedback to the family and professional network is reassuring to professionals involved in risk management and to families who are challenging their own thinking and preconceived ideas as well as engaging in a significant change process themselves alongside their child.

A review network meeting, an encouraging letter to the young person and family and a final family session are all designed to hand over the task of restoring and maintaining safety and respect to the young person, their family and, if necessary, their professional network. There is a commitment to making maximum impact over the

---

4   Cognitive Behaviour Therapy rests on the premise that our feelings, thoughts and behaviour are interconnected and impact on each other. Change is believed possible by either altering cognition (thoughts), which will lead to shifts in behaviour and feeling, or by introducing behavioural change, which will then affect cognitions and feelings.

given timeframe, but on-going therapy of some nature is sometimes recommended to support parents with emerging issues, to encourage restorative processes or to maintain fragile progress.

CHALLENGES FOR THE FUTURE

The timescales for this work are often very tight, defined by orders and finances. Such timescales present the challenge of joining with parents and professionals who are not previously known to the therapists. Trusted, working alliances need to be established quickly in order for the intervention to be meaningful and effective.

Utilising Team Parenting in the context of sexually problematic behaviour work is an evolving and recursive process, where learning and development occurs with each intervention. Learning occurs from the professionals who talk about their work, from the families who share their stories and from the young people who teach the professionals how sexual behaviours can make sense, what hurts and what helps.

Interest is turning to the prospect of delivering longer-term interventions and therapeutic interventions for young people in custody for sexual offences – enabling a sustained therapeutic relationship with young people and their families through this very challenging period in their lives. Team Parenting would need then to include the prison staff and instil in them an understanding of their task in nurturing the strengths and resources within young people in these settings. Young people can then use these strengths and resiliencies to draw upon when they have returned to their families and communities.

This chapter has looked at how Team Parenting has extended its reach and moved into new areas. Specifically, the use of KDA™ as a strengths-based recording tool within Team Parenting, the introduction of Team Parenting into other countries and cultures, and the utilisation of the Team Parenting approach in social care fields beyond fostering are discussed. It is believed that Team Parenting as an approach can be used with children and young people along the whole continuum of need and is not to be exclusively implemented within fostering. The next and final chapter (Chapter 10) looks to the future and explores implications for the future practice and research of Team Parenting.

CONCLUSION

WHERE NEXT?

CHAPTER CONTENTS

Implications for future research

Implications for the provision of services

Implications for future training of professionals

IMPLICATIONS FOR FUTURE RESEARCH

The practice of Team Parenting is influenced by emergent thought and research. In recent years, neuroscience and its confirmation and validation of psychotherapeutic practice (Cozolino 2010) and attachment theory, has played an important role in informing the continued evolution of Team Parenting. The knowledge, now embedded in science, that the structure of our brains evolve and take shape within the context of the nature of our early care experiences, has profound implications not only for understanding the difficulties with which children in care present but in clarifying how therapeutic foster care may effect change:

> the integration of these two scientific streams is demonstrated in the now established tenet that the maturation of the infant's brain is experience-dependent and that the critical experiences that facilitate the brain growth spurt (Dobbing and Sands 1973) in the first year of human life are embedded in the affect transacting relationship co-constructed by the infant and primary caregiver. (Schore 2001, p.2)

Utilising knowledge from research to inform practice is essential to ensure that interventions are efficacious. Whilst Team Parenting has usefully integrated cutting-edge thinking from research into its practice, there has been a lack of studies to measure its effectiveness.

Team Parenting is not unusual in this respect – the paucity of outcome studies in relation to fostering, attachment interventions and multi-agency working is commented on in the literature (Dozier *et al.* 2002; Kelly *et al.* 2003; Leve *et al.* 2012; Sellick and Howell 2004). Canavan *et al.* (2009, p.385) pertinently state that:

> a general weakness of the wider literature in the children's services arena is the absence of strong empirical evidence demonstrating that an outcomes approach within policy leads to aggregate improvements in children's well-being. A similar argument can be made in relation to integrated working – can we say that as a consequence of a wider policy commitment to integrated working, children's lives are better?

Even the use of attachment theory to inform therapeutic interventions remains under-researched – 'their empirical significance is mostly by implication only' (Ziegenhain 2004, p.46). Going forwards, a systematic evaluation together with a comprehensive research programme to measure the impact of the Team Parenting approach is sorely needed. This is particularly so in the current climate of economic stringency. It is not enough to rest on the laurels of individual case studies and feedback regarding the success of Team Parenting.

However, producing an evidence base is fraught with methodological challenges, given the wide-ranging experiences and multi-dimensional factors looked-after children bring with them. Conducting randomised control trials (the gold standard of evidence-based practice) seems daunting, given the nearby impossibility of finding a statistically matched, control group with children with such idiosyncratic characteristics. That notwithstanding, the need remains for Team Parenting to utilise clear outcome measures in order that the quantitative evidence base can be extended. Ample qualitative evidence exists via case studies, and these, sitting alongside quantitative evidence, would provide a rich and textured description of how Team Parenting can work. It is the quantitative evidence that is lacking and in the world of Improving Access to Psychological Therapies (IAPT) and the government's mental health strategy (No Health without Mental Health) emphasising goal planning, data collection, recording recovery rates and personalised care, Team Parenting needs to systematically evaluate its interventions if it is not to become an expensive add-on that few Local Authorities can afford. Quantitative research employing comparison groups and rigorous outcome measures is required to establish the efficacy of the approach across all its provinces and aims.

IMPLICATIONS FOR FUTURE PRACTICE

In line with the lack of research identified above, National Institute for Clinical Excellence (NICE) and Social Care Institute for Excellence (SCIE) published guidance (NICE and SCIE 2010) for working with looked-after children that also refers to this deficit. It states unequivocally that there have been insufficient rigorous studies or clinical trials that elucidate which intervention works best for whom and what offers optimal monetary value. Bearing these limitations in mind, the guidance that is published is helpful in considering service design. Many of the recommendations corroborate the goals and aims of Team Parenting. Below is an extract of some of the key guidance from the NICE *Public Health Guidance for Looked After Children and Young People PH 28* (NICE and SCIE 2010) that can be embedded in future practice by following a Team Parenting approach. *Comments in italics point to Team Parenting's potential to address the recommendations.*

Recommendation 1: Prioritise the needs of looked-after children and young people. This:

- focuses on effective partnership and multi-agency working

- addresses the health and educational inequalities for looked-after children and young people

- stresses the importance of providing access to extra-curricular activities

- urges an improvement in the stability of placements and education.

Team Parenting is a multi-agency approach that aims to holistically address young people's needs via a range of professionals on the team. Therapists, education officers and support workers collaborate to achieve the recommendations listed above.

Recommendation 2: Commission services for looked-after children and young people. This states that services for looked-after children should be integrated, preferably on the same site, and have expert resources to address physical and emotional health needs.

Having a therapist, education officer, social worker and support worker situated in area teams and working from the same office base ensures this recommendation is met.

Recommendation 6: Professional collaboration is needed in order for the 'team around the child' to function optimally. Only with professional collaboration will sensitive and relevant information be shared in a timely manner. Working non-defensively together on multi-agency teams contributes to the effective management of complex and challenging cases.

Team Parenting Meetings provide the forum for effective, non-defensive professional collaboration to occur.

Recommendation 8: Evidence suggests that early intervention to promote mental health and well-being can prevent the escalation of challenging behaviours and reduce the risk of placement breakdown.

Having a therapist working alongside supervising social workers and sharing office space, ensures that early concerns regarding a young person's mental health can be identified quickly. The lack of a referral system and the team approach of Team Parenting guarantees speedy intervention.

Recommendation 37: The recommendation here is to:

- help social workers to have reflective conversations with foster carers that include emotional support and parenting guidance
- ensure foster carers are included in the 'team around the child'.

Social workers are enabled to have reflective discussions with their carers by consulting regularly with the therapist in their office. These conversations can serve as a form of clinical consultation whereby social workers can incorporate therapeutic ideas into their practice. Foster carers are always part of the parenting team, and regular respite carers are included too.

- to improve education for looked-after children and young people:

Education that encourages high aspirations, individual achievement and minimum disruption is central to improving immediate and long-term outcomes for looked-after children and young people. Evidence indicates that looked-after children do not generally do as well at school as their peers, which reduces their opportunity to move to further education, and affects their employment or training opportunities. It is important that education professionals are equipped with the necessary skills, knowledge and understanding to help looked-after children and young people get the most out of their time in education and to successfully negotiate their educational careers. (NICE 2013, p.3)

The education officer works to support carers in order to achieve this goal.

Recommendation 41: Ensure all teacher training programmes have a core training module that looks at the needs of looked-after children and young people. This should include an understanding of:

- the impact of stable care and education on children and young people and how to help them have a stable education

- the impact of loss, separation and trauma on child development, attachment and cognitive functioning

- the value of engaging in activities outside the school curriculum and in the community.

Education officers and therapists consult with teachers and schools to ensure that this knowledge is embedded where looked-after children are being educated. Support workers support the pursuit of extra-curricular activities.

Recommendation 42: There should be designated teachers who are responsible for PEPs, individual education plans and a pastoral support plan. These teachers should engage with the Local Authority social workers to make every effort to ensure educational placement stability.

There are designated teachers in every school and the role of virtual heads in leading the virtual school service in each Local Authority became statutory in 2013. Education officers in Team Parenting carry out this role and ensure that all young people on their caseload have an up-to-date PEP.

Recommendation 44: Young people should be supported to find routes into further and higher education. Help with the application process should be provided as well as ensuring they have accommodation during the holidays. Return to foster carers during vacations should be considered. Young people should also receive support once they leave higher education.

Education officers are instrumental in this process and provide additional tuition for young people to achieve their educational aspirations.

Recommendation 46: Young people should be provided with support in transitioning to independence, particularly with reference to necessary skills, such as cooking and budgeting.

This is provided by the support or mentoring service which works alongside foster carers to ensure that young people are equipped with the skills needed to leave foster care and live in the community.

IMPLICATIONS FOR THE FUTURE TRAINING OF PROFESSIONALS

Multi-agency working has been enshrined in government policy since 1945 and the death of 13-year-old Dennis O'Neill, who was beaten to death by his foster father. The blame was reported to be partly poor communication between the staff and agencies responsible for his care (Conway 2009). More effective communication between professionals is regarded as increasing the safety of children living at home, contributing to placement stability when placed out of home and enhancing educational achievement for the looked-after population. However, despite legislative backing, multi-agency working often fails to produce the expected and longed-for results. Conway (2009) theorises that one of the reasons for this is the powerful psychological dynamics that are propelled into the professional system when a child has been abused, neglected and/or traumatised at the hands of his/her caregivers. She delineates clearly the psychoanalytic concepts of 'splitting' and 'projection', describing how these two defences can swiftly collapse a professional network, resulting in a culture mired in blame, hopelessness and despair:

> in the system around the child there are two powerful dynamics at play: splitting, which divides the world and the people in it into separate, often hostile groups or states of mind; and projection,

which fills people up with very powerful communications and feelings that can feel unbearable. (Conway 2009, p.23)

Conway (2009) perceives the damaging rifts that can occur in professional systems where blame abounds, and the overwhelming affect that can paralyse the ability to think coherently as emanating from the child's broken early attachment relationships. She describes both of these defences as forms of communication from the child, being utilised because verbal communication is inaccessible. Lobatto (2013, p.136–7) extemporises that there may be other systemic explanations for professional divisions and debilitating affect: 'We can debate to what extent it is the children who project their experiences of failed parents back into the adults around them, or to what extent this is a mirroring function of different layers of the system.'

However, whatever the causes, both authors recommend that awareness and acknowledgement of these powerful psychological processes is necessary if multi-agency working is to have a chance, since 'clearly these dynamics can militate against partnership working and are helpful to note in order to mitigate their worst effects' (Lobatto 2013, p.137).

Team Parenting acknowledges these dynamics and works with them both in Team Parenting Meetings and in consultations. However, it would aid multi-agency working further if such concepts were taught as part of training for social workers and, to a lesser extent, teachers. This is not to say that the intricacies of psychological understanding should be given as much space for these students as for trainee psychotherapists or psychologists. Yet, they should also not be the province of mental health professionals alone (Conway 2009). In order to work successfully with young people whose emerging brain structure, *endocrine system* and psychology have been profoundly affected by their early experiences (Conway 2009), a degree of psychological awareness and reflective function is required. Reflective function is an important part of the mix because an objective understanding of these dynamics is not enough. Anyone who has worked with looked-after children for long enough will know the extent of the emotions that can be evoked in one's self. Making sense of these unbidden feelings will need technical knowledge together with an ability to attend with awareness to one's own emotions, thoughts and behaviour and that of others.

References

Abidin, R.R. (1995) *Parenting Stress Index: Professional Manual* (3rd ed.). Odessa, Florida: Psychological Assessment Resources, Inc.

Abidin, R.R. (1997) 'Parenting Stress Index: A Measure of the Parent Child System.' In C.P. Zalaquelt, R.J. Wood and M.D. Lanham *Evaluating Stress: A Book of Resources*. Lanham, M.D.: Scarecrow Education.

Adoption Act (1976) London: HMSO.

Adoption and Children Act (2002) London: HMSO.

Ainsworth, M.D.S., Blehar, M., Waters, E. and Wall. S. (1978) *Patterns of Attachment: A Psychological Study of the Strange Situation*. Hillside, New Jersey: Lawrence Erlbaum Associates.

Alexander, J.F., Barton, C., Gordon, D., Grotpeter, J. Hannson, K. and Harrison, R. *et al.* (1998) *Blueprints for Violence Prevention: Functional Family Therapy*. Boulder, CO: Venture.

Alexander, J.F. and Parsons, B.V. (1982) *Functional Family Therapy: Principles and Procedures*. Carmel, CA: Brooks/Cole.

Allen, B. (2011) 'The Use and Abuse of Attachment Theory in Clinical Practice With Maltreated Children, Part II: Treatment.' *Trauma, Violence and Abuse 12*, 1, 13–22.

Allen, J.S., Bruss, J. and Damasio, H. (2005) 'The Aging Brain: The Cognitive Reserve Hypothesis and Hominid Evolution.' *American Journal of Human Biology 17*, 673–689.

American Psychiatric Association (1994) *DSM-IV-TR: Diagnostic and Statistical Manual of Mental Disorders*. Arlington, VA: American Psychiatric Publishing.

Archer, C. (2003) 'Weft and Warp. Developmental Impact of Trauma and Implications for Healing.' In C. Archer and A. Burnell (eds) *Trauma, Attachment and Family Permanence: Fear Can Stop You Loving*. London and Philadephia: Jessica Kingsley Publishers.

Argent, K. (2008) 'What's happening? Some thoughts on the experience of being in a work discussion group.' In M. Rustin and J. Bradley (eds) *Work Discussion: Learning from Reflective Practice in Work with Children and Families*. London: Karnac–Tavistock Clinic Series.

Asen, E. and Fonagy, P. (2011) 'MBt-F: Mentalization Based Family Therapy.' In A.W. Bateman and P. Fonagy (eds) *Handbook of Mentalizing in Mental Health Practice*. Washington, DC: American Psychiatric Publishing.

Australian Institute of Health and Welfare (2011) *Young Australians: Their health and well-being 2011*. Canberra: Australian Institute of Health and Welfare.

Baldwin, S.A., Christian, S., Berkeljon, A., Shadish, W.R. with Bean, R. (2012) 'The Effects of Family Therapies For Adolescent Delinquency and Substance Abuse: A Meta-Analysis.' *Journal of Marital and Family Therapy 38*, 1, 281–304.

Barber, J.G. and Delfabbro, P.H. (2003) 'Placement Stability and the Psychosocial Well-being of Children in Foster Care.' *Research on Social Work Practice, 13*, 4, 415–431.

Barth, R.P., Crea, T., John, K., Thoburn, J. and Quinton, D. (2005) 'Beyond attachment theory and therapy: Towards sensitive and evidence-based interventions with foster and adoptive families in distress.' *Child and Family Social Work 10*, 257–268.

Barton, C., Alexander, J.F., Waldron, H., Turner, C. W. and Warburton, J. (1985) 'Generalizing treatment effects of functional family therapy: Three replications.' *American Journal of Family Therapy 13*, 16–26.

Bateson, G. (1972) *Steps to an Ecology of Mind*. San Francisco, CA: Chandler.

Becker-Weidman, A. (2006a) 'Treatment for children with trauma-attachment disorders: Dyadic Developmental Psycho-therapy.' *Child and Adolescent Social Work Journal 23*, 147–171.

Becker-Weidman, A. (2006b) 'Dyadic Developmental Psycho-therapy: a multi-year follow-up.' In S.M., Sturt (ed.) *New Developments in Child Abuse Research.* New York: Nova Science Publishers.

Becker-Weidman, A. (2006c) 'The Report of the APSAC Task Force on Attachment Therapy, Reactive Attachment Disorder, and Attachment Problems.' *Child Maltreatment 11*, 4, 379–80.

Becker-Weidman, A. and Hughes, D. (2008) 'Dyadic Developmental Psychotherapy: an evidence-based treatment for children with complex trauma and disorders of attachment.' *Child and Family Social Work 13*, 3, 329–337.

Becker-Weidman, A. and Hughes, D. (2010) 'Dyadic Developmental Psychotherapy: an effective and evidence-based treatment – comments in response to Mercer and Pignotti.' *Child and Family Social Work 15*, 1, 6–11.

Becvar, D.S. and Becvar, R.J. (2009) *Family Therapy* (7th ed.). Oxford: Pearson.

Beek, M. and Schofield, G. (2004) *Providing a Secure Base in Long-term Foster Care.* London: BAAF.

Berridge, D. (2007) 'Theory and explanation in child welfare: education and looked-after children.' *Child and Family Social Work, 12*, 1, 1–10.

Berridge, D. (2012) 'Educating Young People in Care: What Have We Learned?' *Children and Youth Services Review, 34*, 6, 1171–1175.

Biehal, N., Ellison, S. and Sinclair, I. (2012) 'Intensive Fostering: An Independent Evaluation of MTFC in an English Setting.' *Adoption and Fostering 36*, 1, 13–26.

Bion, W. (1962) *Learning from Experience.* London: Heinemann.

Bion, W.R. (1971) *Attention and Interpretation.* London: Tavistock Publications.

Bird, J. (2004) *Talk That Sings: Therapy in a New Linguistic Key.* Auckland, New Zealand: Edge Press.

Blair, T. (1998) *The Third Way: New Politics for the New Century.* Fabian Pamphlet 588. London: The Fabian Society.

Bland, J. (2009) 'Working With Unconscious Processes: Psychoanalysis and Systemic Family Therapy.' In C. Flaskas and D. Pocock (eds) *Systems and Psychoanalysis, Contemporary Integrations in Family Therapy.* London: Karnac.

Blower, A., Addo, A., Hodgson, J., Lamington, L. and Towlson, K. (2004) 'Mental Health of "Looked after" Children: A Needs Assessment.' *Clinical Child Psychology and Psychiatry 9*, 1, 117–129.

Bohart, A.C. and Greenberg, L. S. (eds) (1997) *Empathy Reconsidered: New Directions in Psychotherapy.* Washington, DC: American Psychological Association.

Borduin, C. M., Henggeler, S. W., Blaske, D. M. and Stein, R. (1990) 'Multisystemic Treatment of Adolescent Sexual Offenders.' *International Journal of Offender Therapy and Comparative Criminology, 35*, 105–114.

Borduin, C.M., Mann, B.J., Cone, L.T., Henggeler, S.W., Fucci, B.R. and Blaske, D.M. (1995) 'Multisystemic Treatment of Serious Juvenile Offenders: Long-term Prevention of Criminality and Violence.' *Journal of Consulting and Clinical Psychology 63*, 569–578.

Bornhorst, M. (2012) *Some Truths about Aussie Culture! Patterns of cultural difference between Anglo-Australian culture and other cultures in communicating politeness, courtesy, and respect.* Available at: www.mbcross-cultural.com.au [accessed 18 May 2013].

Bourdieu, P. (1986) 'The Forms of Capital.' In J. Richardson (ed.) *Handbook of Theory and Research for the Sociology of Education.* New York: Greenwood.

Bowlby, J. (1969) *Attachment and Loss Vol. 1.* London: Hogarth Press.

Bowlby, J. (1973) *Attachment and Loss Vol. 2; Separation, Anxiety and Anger.* London: Hogarth Press.

Bowlby, J. (1979) *The Making and Breaking of Affectional Bonds.* London: Tavistock Publications.

Bowlby, J. (1988) *A Secure Base: Parent–Child Attachment and Healthy Human Development.* New York, NY: Basic Books.

Bowlby, R. (2010) Educational Videos on Attachment Theory. Unpublished material available from Richard Bowlby, London.

Briskman, J., Castle, J., Blackeby, K., Bengo, C. *et al.* (2012) *Randomised Controlled Trial of the Fostering Changes Programme* (DfE Research Report 233). London: DfE [online]. Available at: www.education.gov.uk/publications/eOrderingDownload/DFE-RR237.pdf [accessed 16 May 2013].

Brunk, M., Henggeler, S.W. and Whelan, J.P. (1987) 'A Comparison of Multisystemic Therapy and Parent Training in the Brief Treatment of Child Abuse and Neglect.' *Journal of Consulting and Clinical Psychology 55*, 311–318.

Bucci, W. (1997) 'Symptoms and symbols: A multiple code theory of somatization.' *Psychoanalytic Inquiry 17*, 151–172.

Burnham, J. (1980) *Family Therapy.* London: Routledge.

Burnham, J. (2005) 'Relational Reflexivity: A Tool For Socially Constructing Therapeutic Relationships.' In C. Flaskas, B. Mason and A. Perlerz (eds) *The Space Between.* London: Karnac Publications UK.

Bynner, J., Elias, P., McKnight, A., Pan, H. and Gaelle, P. (2002) *Young People's Changing Routes to Independence.* York: Joseph Rowntree Foundation.

Cairns, K. (2002a) 'Making Sense. The Use of Theory and Research to Support Foster Care.' *Adoption and Fostering 26*, 2, 6–13.

Cairns, K. (2002b) *Attachment, Trauma and Resilience.* London: BAAF.

Cairns, K. (2012) 'Transitions, Trauma and Resilience: Helping Children To Survive and Thrive.' Kate Cairns Associates training materials, Personal Communication.

Calder, M. (2002) *Working With Young People Who Sexually Abuse – Building the Evidence Base of Your Practice.* Lyme Regis: Russell House Publishing.

Cameron, R.J. and Maginn, C. (2008) 'The Authentic Warmth Dimension of Professional Childcare.' *British Journal of Social Work 38*, 6, 1151–1172.

Canavan, J., Coen, L., Dolan, P. and Whyte, L. (2009) 'Privileging Practice: Facing the Challenge of Integrated Working for Outcomes for Children.' *Children and Society 23*, 5, 377–388.

Care Standards Act (2000). London: The Stationery Office

Carr, A. (1991) 'Milan systemic family therapy.' *Journal of Family Therapy 13*, 3, 237–263.

Carr, A. (2006) *Family Therapy.* Chichester: Wiley and Sons.

Carstens, C., Panzano P.C., Massatti, R. and Roth, D. (2009) 'A Naturalistic Study of MST Dissemination in 13 Ohio Communities.' *The Journal of Behavioral Health Services and Research 36*, 3, 344–60.

Cashdan, P. (1988) *Object Relations Therapy: Using the Relationship.* New York and London: W.W. Norton and Co.

Cavanagh Johnson, T. (2004*) Helping children with sexual behaviour problems: A guidebook for professionals and caregivers.* California, U.S.A: FVSAI publishers.

Cecchin, G. (1987) 'Hypothesising, Circularity and Neutrality Revisited: An Invitation to Curiosity.' *Family Process 26*, 4, 405–413.

Chaffin, M., Hanson, R. and Saunders (2006) 'Reply to Letters.' *Child Maltreatment 11*, 4, 381–386.

Chamberlain P. (2003) 'The Oregon multidimensional treatment foster care model: features, outcomes, and progress in dissemination.' *Cognitive and Behavioral Practice 10*, 4, 303–12.

Chamberlain, P., Price, J., Leve, L.D., Laurent, H., Landsverk, J.A. and Reid, J.B. (2008a) 'Prevention of Behavior Problems for Children in Foster Care: Outcomes and Mediation Effects.' *Prevention Science 9*, 1, 17–27. .

Chamberlain, P., Price, J., Reid, J. and Landsverk, J. (2008b) 'Cascading Implementation of a Foster and Kinship Parent Intervention.' *Child Welfare 87*, 5, 27–48.

Chamberlain, P. and Reid, J. B. (1987) 'Parent observation and report of child symptoms.' *Behavioral Assessment 9*, 97–109.

Childrens Act (1989) London: The Stationery Office.

Childrens Act (2004) London: The Stationery Office.

Children and Young Persons Act (2008) London: The Stationery Office.

Children (Leaving Care) Act (2000) London: The Stationery Office.

Children's Workforce Development Council (CWDC) (2011) *Training, Support and Development Standards for Foster Care.* Leeds: CWDC.

Chimera, C. (2010) 'An interview with Pat Crittenden.' *Context.* Available at: http://content. yudu.com/Library/A1or6v/ContextAugust2010/resources/14.htm [accessed 16 May 2013].

Ciccheti, D. (1989) 'How Research On Child Maltreatment Has Informed the Study of Child Development: Perspectives From Developmental Psychopathology.' In D. Ciccheti and V. Carolson (eds) *Child Maltreatment.* New York: Cambridge University Press.

Clarke, H. (2009) 'Getting the Support They Need: Findings of A Survey of Foster Carers in the UK.' London: The Fostering Network. Available at: www.fostering.net/sites/www. fostering.net/files/public/resources/reports/support_survey_240909.pdf [accessed 18 May 2013].

Clarkson, P. (1989) *Gestalt Counselling in Action.* London: Sage.

Clausen, J.M., Landsverk, J., Ganger, W., Chadwick, D. and Litrownik, A. (1998) 'Mental health problems of children in foster care.' *Journal of Child and Family Studies 7*, 283–296.

Cocker, C. and Scott, S. (2006) 'Improving the mental and emotional well-being of looked after children: connecting research, policy and practice.' *The Journal of the Royal Society for the Promotion of Health 126*, 1, 18–23.

Conway, P. (2009) 'Falling between minds. The effects of unbearable experiences on multi-agency communication in the care system.' *Adoption and Fostering 33*, 1, 18–29.

Coulling, N. (2000) 'Definitions of Successful Education for the "Looked After" Child: a Multi-agency Perspective.' *Support for Learning 15*, 1, 30–35.

Cozolino, L. (2010) *The Neuroscience of Psychotherapy.* London and New York: W.W.Norton and Company.

Craven, P.A. and Lee, R.E. (2006) 'Therapeutic Interventions for Foster Children: A Systematic Research Synthesis.' *Research on Social Work Practice 16*, 3, 287–304.

Dallos, R. (2006) *Attachment Narrative Therapy. Integrating Narrative, Systemic and Attachment Therapies.* Maidenhead: Open University Press.

Davey, D. and Pithouse, A. (2008) 'Schooling and looked after children: Exploring contexts and outcomes in Standard Attainment Tests.' *Adoption and Fostering 32*, 3, 60–72.

Delaney, R. (1991) *Fostering Changes: Treating Attachment Disordered Foster Children.* Oklahoma City: Wood 'N' Barnes Publishing and Distribution.

Delaney, R. (2006) *Fostering Changes – Myth, Meaning and Magic Bullets in Attachment Theory* (3rd ed.). Oklahoma City: Wood 'N' Barnes Publishing and Distribution.

Dent, H. with Brown, S. (2006) 'The Zoo of Human Consciousness: Adversity, Brain Development and Health.' In K.S Golding, H.R. Dent, R. Nissim and L. Stott (eds) *Thinking Psychologically About Children Who Are Looked After and Adopted. Space for Reflection.* Chichester: John Wiley and Sons Ltd.

Department for Education (DfE) (2010) *The Care Leavers (England) Regulations.* London: The Stationery Office.

Department for Education (DfE) (2011a) *Fostering Services: National Minimum Standards.* London. Available at: www.gov.uk/government/publications/fostering-services-national-minimum-standards [accessed 30 June 2013].

Department for Education (DfE) (2011b) *The Munro Review of Child Protection, Final Report: A Child-Centred System.* London: The Stationery Office.

Department for Education (DfE) (2012) *Children Looked After by Local Authorities in England (including adoption and care leavers)* – year ending 31 March 2012. Available at: www.education.gov.uk/rsgateway/DB/SFR/s001084/index.shtml [accessed 30 June 2013].

Department for Education and Employment/Department of Health (DfEE/DoH) (2000) Guidance on the Education of Children and Young People in Public Care. London: DfEE Publications.

Department for Education/National Statistics (2012) *Statistical First Release: Outcomes for Children Looked After by Local Authorities in England.* London: DfE.

Department for Education and Skills (DfES) (2003a) *Keeping Children Safe.* London: The Stationery Office.

Department for Education and Skills (2003b) *Every Child Matters.* (Green Paper). London: The Stationery Office.

Department for Education and Skills (DfES) (2004) *Every Child Matters: Next Steps.* Nottingham: DfES Publications.

Department for Education and Skills (DfES) (2006) *Care Matters: Transforming the Lives of Children and Young People in Care after Lives of Children.* London: The Stationery Office.

Department for Education and Skills (DfES) (2007) *Care Matters: Time for Change.* London: The Stationery Office.

Department of Health (DoH) (1998a) *Modernising Social Services: Promoting Independence, Improving Protection, Raising Standards.* London: The Stationery Office.

Department of Health (DoH) (1998b) *The Quality Protects Programme: Transforming Children's Services* (LAC 98(28)). London: HMSO.

Department of Health (DoH) (2002) *Fostering for the Future SSI Report on the Inspection of Foster Care Services.* London: HMSO.

Department of Health and Social Security (DHSS) (1976) *Fit for the Future: Court Committee Report on Child Health Services.* London: HMSO.

Diehl, D.C., Howse, R.B. and Trivette, C.M. (2011) 'Youth in Foster Care: Developmental Assets and Attitudes Towards Adoption and Mentoring.' *Child and Family Social Work 16*, 81–92.

Dobbing, J. and Sands, J. (1973) 'Quantitative Growth and Development of Human Brain.' *Archives of Diseases of Childhood 48*, 757–767.

Dozier, M. (2003) 'Attachment-based Treatment for Vulnerable Children'. *Attachment and Human Development 5*, 3, 253–7.

Dozier, M., Albus, K., Fisher, P.A. and Sepulveda, S. (2002) 'Interventions for Foster Parents: Implications for Developmental Theory.' *Development and Psychopathology 14*, 4, 843–860.

Dozier, M., Stovall, K.C., Albus, K. and Bates, B. (2001) 'Attachment For Infants in Foster Care: The Role of Caregiver State of Mind.' *Child Development 72*, 1467–1477.

Duckworth, A.L., Steen, T.A. and Seligman, M.E.P. (2005) 'Positive Psychology in Clinical Practice.' *Annual Review of Clinical Psychology 1*, 629–51.

Elliott, A. (2002) 'The Educational Expectation of Looked After Children.' *Adoption and Fostering 26*, 3, 58–68.

Epston, D. and White, M. (1990) *Narrative Means to Therapeutic End.* New York: WW Norton and Co.

Epston, D., White, M. and Murray, K. (1992) 'A Proposal for a Re-authoring Therapy: Rose's Revisioning of her Life and a Commentary.' In S. McNamee and K.J. Gergen (eds) *Therapy as Social Construction.* London: Sage.

Erskine, R.G. (1995) 'A Gestalt Approach to Shame and Self-righteousness: Theory and Methods.' *The British Gestalt Journal 4*, 2, 108–117.

Evans, K.R. (1994) 'Healing Shame: A Gestalt Perspective.' *Transactional Analysis Journal, 24*, 2, 103–108.

Everson-Hock, E.S., Jones, R., Guillaume, L., Clapton, J., *et al.* (2012) 'The Effectiveness of Training and Support for Carers and Other Professionals on the Physical and Emotional Health and Well-being of Looked-after Children and Young People: A Systematic Review.' *Child: Care, Health and Development 38*, 2, 162–74.

Fahlberg, V.I. (1991) *A Child's Journey Through Placement.* Indianapolis: Perspectives Press.

Fairtlough, A. (2003) 'Attachment, Trauma and Resilience by Kate Cairns.' *Journal of Child and Family Social Work 8*, 1, 82–83.

Ferguson, H.B. and Wolkow, K. (2012) 'Educating Children and Youth in Care: A Review of Barriers to School Progress and Strategies for Change.' *Children and Youth Services Review 34*, 6, 1143–1149.

Fernandez, E. (2008) 'Unravelling Emotional, Behavioural and Educational Outcomes in a Longitudinal Study of Children in Foster-care.' *British Journal of Social Work 38*, 7, 1283–1301.

Finklehor, D. and Brown, A. (1986) 'Initial and Long Term Effects: A Conceptual Framework.' In D. Finklehor (ed.) *A Sourcebook on Child Sexual Abuse.* Beverley Hills, CA: Sage.

Flaskas, C. (1997) 'Engagement and the Therapeutic Relationship in Systemic Therapy.' *The Journal of Family Therapy 19*, 263–282.

Flaskas, C. (2009) 'Narrative, Meaning-Making, and the Unconscious.' In C. Flaskas and D. Pocock (eds) *Systems and Psychoanalysis. Contemporary Integrations in Family Therapy.* London: Karnac.

Fonagy, P., Bateman, Anthony and Bateman, Alexandra, (2011) 'The Widening Scope of Mentalizing: A Discussion.' *Psychology and Psychotherapy: Theory, Research and Practice 84*, 1, 98–110.

Fonagy, P., Gergely, G., Jurist, E. and Target, M. (2004) *Affect Regulation, Mentalization and the Development of the Self.* London: Karnac.

Fonagy, P., Steele, M., Steele, H., Moran, G.S. and Higgit, A.C. (1991) 'The Capacity For Understanding Mental States: The Reflective Self in Parent and Child and Its Significance For Security of Attachment.' *Infant Mental Health Journal 12*, 3, 201–218.

Fredman, G. (2007) 'Preparing Our Selves for the Therapeutic Relationship, Revisiting "Hypothesizing Revisited".' *Human Systems: The Journal of Systemic Consultation and Management 8*, 44–59.

Fredman, G. (2011) 'Working with Networks: A Therapeutic Opportunity.' Conference delivered to Core Assets. Bromsgrove, U.K., February 2011.

Freedman, J. and Combs, G. (1996) *Narrative Therapy: The Social Construction of Preferred Realities.* New York: W.W. Norton.

Frost, N. and Parton, N. (2009) *Understanding Children's Social Care: Politics, Policy and Practice.* London: Sage.

Frost, N. and Stein. M. (2009) 'Editorial: Outcomes of Integrated Working with Children and Young People.' *Children and Society 23*, 315–319.

George, C., Kaplan, N. and Main, M. (1985) 'Adult Attachment Interview.' Unpublished manuscript, University of California, Berkeley.

Gerhardt, S. (2004) *Why Love Matters – How Affection Shapes a Baby's Brain.* London and New York: Routledge.

Gilligan, R. (1997) 'Beyond Permanence? The Importance of Resilience in Child Placement Practice and Planning.' *Adoption and Fostering 21*, 1, 12–20.

Gilligan, R. (2001) *Promoting Resilience: A Resource Guide on Working with Children in the Care System.* London: British Agencies for Adoption and Fostering (BAAF).

Gilligan, R. (2007) 'Spare time activities for young people in care: What can they contribute to educational progress?' *Adoption and Fostering 3*, 1, 92–99.

Gilligan, R., (2008) 'Promoting Resilience in Young People in Long-term Care – The Relevance of Roles and Relationships in the Domains of Recreation and Work.' *Journal of Social Work Practice: Psychotherapeutic Practice in Health, Welfare and the Community 22*, 1, 37–50.

Golding, K. (2003) 'Helping Foster Carers, Helping Children Using Attachment Theory to Guide Practice.' *Adoption and Fostering 28*, 3, 64–73.

Golding, K. and Picken, W. (2004) 'Group Work for Foster Carers Caring for Children with Complex Problems.' *Adoption and Fostering 28*, 1, 25–37.

Goodman, R. (1997) 'The Strengths and Difficulties Questionnaire: A Research Note.' *Journal of Child Psychology and Psychiatry 38*, 5, 581–586.

Goodman, R. (2001) 'Psychometric Properties of the Strengths and Difficulties Questionnaire (SDQ).' *Journal of the American Academy of Child and Adolescent Psychiatry 40*, 1337–1345.

Gordon, D.A., Arbuthnot, J., Gustafson, K.E. and McGreen, P. (1988) 'Home-based Behavioural-Systems Family Therapy With Disadvantaged Juvenile Delinquents'. *The American Journal of Family Therapy 16*, 243–255.

Greenwood, P.W. (2004) 'Cost-effective violence prevention through targeted family interventions.' *Annals of the New York Academy of Sciences 1036*, 201–14.

Hackett, S. (2001) *Facing the Future: A Guide for Parents of Young People Who Have Sexually Abused.* Lyme Regis: Russell House Publishing.

Hackett, S. (2004) *What Works For Children and Young People with Sexually Harmful Sexual Behaviours?* Barkingside: Barnardos.

Hackett, S. (2006) 'Towards A Resilience Based Intervention Model For Young People With Harmful Sexual Behaviours.' In M. Erooga and H. Masson (eds) *Children and Young People Who Sexually Abuse Others: Current Developments and Practice Responses.* London: Routledge.

Harker, R.M., Dobel-ober, D. and Berridge, D. (2004) 'More Than the Sum of its Parts? Inter-professional Working.' *Education of Looked After Children 18*, 179–193.

Hart, A. and Thomas, H. (2012) 'Controversial Attachments: The Indirect Treatment of Fostered and Adopted Children via Parent Co-therapy.' *Attachment and Human Development 2*, 3, 306–327.

Hawes, J. (1996) *A White Merc with Fins.* Vintage: London.

Hayden, C. (2005) 'More Than A Piece of Paper?: Personal Education Plans and "Looked After" Children in England.' *Child and Family Social Work 10*, 4, 243–252.

Hek, R., Aiers, A., Hughes, N. and Morris, K. (2010) *Promoting Best Outcomes for Children and Providing Best Support for Carers – A Review of Selected Literature for Foster Care Associates.* Bromsgrove: iCRIF.

Henderson, N. (2003) 'Hard-wired to Bounce Back.' *The Prevention Researcher 10*, 1, 1–7.

Henggeler, S.W., Letourneau, E.J., Chapman, J.E., Borduin, C.M., Schewe, P.A. and McCart, M.R. (2009) 'Mediators of Change For Multisystemic Therapy With Juvenile Sexual Offenders.' *Journal of Consulting and Clinical Psychology 77*, 451–462.

Henggeler, S.W., Melton, G.B., Brondino, M.J., Scherer, D.G. and Hanley, J.H. (1997) 'Multisystemic Therapy With Violent and Chronic Juvenile Offenders and Their Families: The Role of Treatment Fidelity in Successful Dissemination.' *Journal of Consulting and Clinical Psychology 65*, 821–833.

Henggeler, S.W., Melton, G.B. and Smith, L.A. (1992) 'Family Preservation Using Multisystemic Therapy: An Effective Alternative to Incarcerating Serious Juvenile Offenders.' *Journal of Consulting and Clinical Psychology 60*, 953–961.

Henggeler, S.W., Melton, G B., Smith, L.A., Schoenwald, S.K. and Hanley, J.H. (1993) 'Family Preservation Using Multisystemic Treatment: Long-term Follow-up to a Clinical Trial With Serious Juvenile Offenders.' *Journal of Child and Family Studies 2*, 283–293.

Henggeler, S., Pickrel, S. and Brondino M. (1999) 'Multisystemic treatment of substance-abusing and dependent delinquents: outcomes, treatment fidelity and transportability.' *Mental Health Services Research 1*, 3, 171–84.

Henggeler, S.W., Rodick, J.D., Borduin, C.M., Hanson, C.L., Watson, S.M. and Urey, J.R. (1986) 'Multisystemic Treatment of Juvenile Offenders: Effects On Adolescent Behavior and Family Interactions.' *Developmental Psychology 22*, 132–141.

Henggeler, S.W. and Sheidow, A. (2012) 'Empirically Supported Family-based Treatments for Conduct Disorder and Delinquency in Adolescents.' *Journal of Marital and Family Therapy, 38*, 1, 30–58.

HM Government (2004) *Every Child Matters: Change for Children.* Nottingham: DfES Publications.

Howe, D. (2005) *Child Abuse and Neglect. Attachment, Development and Intervention.* Basingstoke: Palgrave Macmillan.

Howe, D. (2010) 'Child Abuse, Neglect and Trauma: Attachment, Development and Interventions.' Presentation given at the Action for Children Conference, York, 9 February.

Howe, D. and Fearnley S. (1999) 'Disorders of Attachment and Attachment Therapy.' *Adoption and Fostering 23*, 2, 19–13.

Huffman, K. (2012) 'The Developing, Aging Neocortex: How Genetics and Epigenetics Influence Early Developmental Patterning and Age-related Change.' *Frontiers in Genetics 3*, 212. Available at: www.ncbi.nlm.nih.gov/pmc/articles/PMC3473232/ [accessed 18 May 2013].

Hughes, D. (1997) *Facilitating Developmental Attachment.* New York: Jason Aronson.

Hughes, D. (2004) 'An Attachment-based Treatment of Maltreated Children and Young People.' *Attachment and Human Development 6*, 3, 263–278.

Hughes, D. (2006) *Building the Bonds of Attachment – Awakening Love in Deeply Troubled Children* (2nd ed.) London: Jason Aronson.

Hughes, D. (2007) *Attachment-focused Family Therapy.* London: W.W. Norton and Company Ltd.

Hughes, D. (2009) 'Principles of Attachment and Intersubjectivity.' In A. Perry, *Teenagers and Attachment: Helping Adolescents Engage With Life and Learning.* London: Worth Publishing.

Hughes, D.A. (2011) *Attachment-focused Family Therapy Handbook.* New York and London: W.W. Norton and Company Ltd.

Hunter, M. (2001) *Psychotherapy with Young People in Care – Lost and Found.* Hove and New York: Brunner-Routledge.

Hycner, R. (1991) *Between Person and Person: Toward a Dialogical Psychotherapy.* New York: The Gestalt Journal Press Inc.

Ironside, L. (2004) 'Living a Provisional Existence – Thinking About Foster Carers and the Emotional Containment of Children Placed in Their Care.' *Adoption and Fostering 28*, 4, 39–49.

Jackson, S. (2004) 'Educating Children in Residential and Foster Care.' *Oxford Review of Education 20*, 3, 267–279.

Jackson, S. and Martin, P. (1998) 'Surviving the Care System: Education and Resilience.' *Journal of Adolescence 21*, 569–583.

Jernberg, A. (1979) *Theraplay.* San Francisco: Jossey-Bass.

Kaufman, G. (1992) *Shame – the Power of Caring.* Vermont: Schenkman Books, Inc.

Kegerreis, S. (1995) 'Getting Better Makes It Worse: Obstacles To Improvement in Children With Emotional and Behavioural Difficulties.' In J. Trowell and M. Bower (eds) *The Emotional Needs of Young Children and Their Families.* London: Routledge.

Kelly, C., Allan, S., Roscoe, P. and Herrick, E. (2003) 'The Mental Health Needs of Looked after Children: An Integrated Multi-agency Model of Care'. *Clinical Child Psychology and Psychiatry 8*, 3, 323–335.

Khan, T.J. (2013) 'Medicaid and Children in Foster Care.' Center for Health Care Strategies, March 2013 State Policy Advocacy and Reform Center. Available at: http://childwelfaresparc.com/2013/03/25 [accessed 30 June 2013].

Khan, T.J., and Chambers, H. J. (1991) 'Assessing reoffense risk with juvenile sexual offenders.' *Child Welfare 70*, 3, 333–345.

Klein, M. (1959) 'Our Adult World and its Roots in Infancy.' In M. Masud and R. Khan (eds) *Envy and Gratitude and Other Works 1946–1963.* London: The Hogarth Press.

Klein, N.C., Alexander, J.F. and Parsons, B.V. (1977) 'Impact of Family Systems Intervention on Recidivism and Sibling Delinquency: A Model of Primary Prevention and Program Evaluation.' *Journal of Consulting and Clinical Psychology 45*, 469–474.

Kobau, R., Sniezek, J., Zack, M.M., Lucas, R.E. and Burns, A. (2010) 'Well-being Assessment: An Evaluation of Well-being Scales for Public Health and Population Estimates of Well-being among US Adults.' *Applied Psychology: Health and Well-being 2*, 3, 272–297.

Kohut, H. (1977) *The Restoration of the Self.* New York: International University Press.

Krenke, I., Aunola, K., Nurmi, J. (2009) 'Changes in Stress Perception and Coping During Adolescence: The Role of Situational and Personal Factors.' *Child Development 80*, 1, 259–279.

Lambert, M. J. and Ogles, B.M. (2004) 'The Efficacy and Effectiveness of Psychotherapy.' In M.J. Lambert (ed.) *Bergin and Garfield's Handbook of Psychotherapy and Behavior Change* (5th ed.). New York: Wiley.

Laming, Lord (2003) *The Victoria Climbié Inquiry Report.* London: The Stationery Office.

Laming, Lord (2009) *The Protection of Children in England: A Progress Report.* London: The Stationery Office.

Landsverk, J.A. and Slymen, D.J. (2004) 'Placement movement in out-of-home care: patterns and predictors.' *Child Youth Services Review 26*, 185–206.

Langstrom, N. and Grann, M. (2000) 'Risk For Criminal Recidivism Among Young Sex Offenders.' *Journal of Interpersonal Violence 15*, 855–871.

Larner, G. (2000) 'Towards A Common Ground in Psychoanalysis and Family Therapy: On Knowing Not To Know.' *Journal of Family Therapy 22*, 61–82.

Larner, G. (2009) 'Intersecting Levinas and Bion: The Ethical Container in Psychoanalysis and Family Therapy.' In C. Flaskas, and D. Pocock, *Systems and Psychoanalysis, Contemporary Integrations in Family Therapy.* London: Karnac.

Leve, L.D., Harold, G.T., Chamberlain, P., Landsverk, J.A., Fisher, P.A. and Vostanis, P. (2012) 'Practitioner Review: Children in Foster Care – Vulnerabilities and Evidence-based Interventions That Promote Resilience Processes.' *Journal of Child Psychology and Psychiatry 12*, 1197–1211.

Liabo, K., Gray, K. and Mulcahy, D. (2013) 'A Systematic Review of Interventions To Support Looked-After Children in School.' *Child and Family Social Work 18*, 3, 341–353.

Lichtenberg, J. and Slap, J. (1973) 'Notes On the Concept of Splitting and the Defense Mechanism of the Splitting of Representations.' *Journal of the American Psychoanalytic Association 21*, 4, 772–787.

Littell, J.H. (2005) 'Lessons from a systematic review of effects of multisystemic therapy.' *Children and Youth Services Review 27*, 445–463.

Littell, J.H., Popa, M. and Forsythe, B. (2005) 'Multisystemic Therapy For Social, Emotion, and Behavioral Problems in Youth Age 10–17.' *Cochrane Database of Systematic Reviews*, 3, CD004797. Available at: www.ncbi.nlm.nih.gov/pubmed/16235382 [Accessed 18 May 2013].

Lobatto, W. (2013) 'The Art of Leading and Following – A Workplace Tango.' *Journal of Social Work Practice: Psychotherapeutic Approaches in Health, Welfare and the Community 27*, 2, 133–147.

Laming, Lord (2009) 'The Protection of Children in England: A Progress Report.' London: The Stationery Office.

Luke, N. and Sebba, J. (2013) *Supporting Each Other: An International Literature Review On Peer Contact Between Foster Carers.* Oxford: The Rees Centre.

Macdonald, G. and Turner, W. (2005) 'An Experiment in Helping Foster-carers Manage Challenging Behaviour.' *British Journal of Social Work 35*, 8, 1265–1282.

Mackewn, G. (1997) *Developing Gestalt Counselling.* London: Sage.

Maclay, F. (2006) 'Surviving the System as a Foster Carer.' *Adoption and Fostering 30*, 1, 1–14.

Maclay, F., Bunce, M. and Purves, D.G. (2006) 'Surviving the system as a foster carer.' *Adoption and Fostering 30*, 1, 29–38.

Mahoney, J.L., Cairns, B.D. and Farmer, T.W. (2003) 'Promoting Interpersonal Competence and Educational Success Through Extracurricular Activity Participation.' *Journal of Educational Psychology 95*, 2, 409–418.

Maslow, A.H. (1943) 'A Theory of Human Motivation.' Originally published in the *Psychological Review 50*, 376–390.

Mason, B. (1993) 'Towards Positions of Safe Uncertainty.' *Human Systems: The Journal of Systemic Consultation and Management 4*, 189–200.

Masten, A.S., Best, K.M. and Garmezy, N. (1990) 'Resilience and Development: Contributions From the Study of Children Who Overcame Adversity.' *Development and Psychopathology 2*, 425–444.

McAuley, C. and Trew, K. (2000) 'Children's Adjustment Over Time in Foster Care: Cross-informant, Stability and Placement Disruption.' *British Journal of Social Work 30*, 9, 1–107.

McCann, L. and Pearlman, L.A. (1990) 'Vicarious Traumatisation: A Framework for Understanding the Psychological Effects of Working with Victims.' *Journal of Traumatic Stress 3*, 1, 131–149.

McCluskey, U., Hooper, C-A. and Bingley Miller, L. (1999) 'Goal-corrected Empathic Attunement: Developing and Rating the Concept of an Attachment Perspective.' *Psychotherapy 36*, 1, 80–90.

McDermid, S., Holmes, L., Kirton, D. and Signoretta, P. (2012) *The Demographic Characteristics of Foster Carers in the UK: Motivations, Barriers and Messages for Recruitment and Retention.* Loughborough/London/Canterbury: The Childhood Wellbeing Research Centre.

McDonald, P.S., Burgess, C. and Smith, K. (2003) 'A support team for foster carers: the views and perceptions of service users.' *British Journal of Social Work 33*, 6, 825–32.

Meltzer, H., Gatward, R., Corbin, T., Goodman, R. and Ford, T. (2003) *The Mental Health of Young People Looked After By Local Authorities in England: Summary Report.* London: HMSO.

Mercer, J., Pennington, R.S., Pignotti, M. and Rosa, L. (2010) 'Dyadic Developmental Psychotherapy is not "evidence-based": Comments in response to Becker-Weidman and Hughes.' *Child and Family Social Work 15*, 1, 1–5.

Milligan, I. (2011) 'Resisting risk-averse practice: the contribution of social pedagogy.' *Children Australia 36*, 4, 207–13.

Minnis, H. and Devine, C. (2001) 'The Effect of Foster Carer Training On the Emotional and Behavioural Functioning of Children.' *Adoption and Fostering 1*, 44–54.

Morgan, K. and Baron, R. (2011) 'Self Efficacy in Foster Carers.' *Adoption and Fostering 35*, 1, 18–31.

Murray, L., Tarren-Sweeney, M. and France, K. (2011) 'Foster Carer Perceptions of Support and Training in the Context of High Burden of Care.' *Child Family Social Work 16*, 2, 149–158.

Nelson, P., Tabberer, S. and Chrisp, T. (2011) 'Integrated Working in Children's Centres: A User Pathway Analysis.' *Practice: Social Work in Action 23*, 5, 293–310.

Northwest Institute for Children and Families (2007) *Mockingbird Family Model: Project Evaluation.* Available at: www. mockingbirdsociety.org/images/stories/docs/MFM/nwicf_2007–5_report.pdf [accessed 18 May 2013].

NICE and SCIE (2010) *Promoting the quality of life of looked-after children and young people.* Public Health Guidance PH *28*. Available at: http://guidance.nice.org.uk/ph28 [accessed 18 May 2013].

NICE (2013) *Educating Looked after Children and Young People.* Available at: http://pathways.nice.org.uk/pathways/looked-after-babies-children-and-young-people [accessed 30 June 2013].

Ofsted (2012) *The Impact of Virtual Schools on the Educational Progress of Looked After Children.* Available at: www.ofsted.gov.uk/resources/120165 [accessed 18 May 2013].

Ogden, T. (1982) *Projective Identification and Psychotherapeutic Technique.* Northvale, New Jersey and London: Jason Aronson.

O'Sullivan, A. and Westerman, R. (2007) 'Closing the Gap: Investigating the Barriers to Educational Achievement for Looked after Children.' *Adoption and Fostering 31*, 1, 13–20.

Parsons, B.V. and Alexander, J F. (1973) 'Short-Term Family Intervention: A Therapy Outcome Study.' *Journal of Consulting and Clinical Psychology 41*, 195–201.

Perls, F., Hefferline, R.G. and Goodman, P. (1951) *Gestalt Therapy – Excitement and Growth in the Human Personality.* London: Souvenir Press.

Perry, B. (2002a) Principles of Working with Traumatized Children. Available at: www.scholastic.com/teachers/article/principles-working-traumatized-children [accessed 15 May 2013].

Perry, B. (2002b) The Impact of Abuse and Neglect on the Developing Brain. Available at: http://teacher.scholastic.com/professional/bruceperry/abuse_neglect.htm [accessed 15 May 2013].

Perry, B., Pollard, R., Blakely, T., Baker, W. and Vigilante, D. (1995) 'Childhood trauma, the neuro-biology of adaptation and "use-dependent" development of the brain: How "states" become "traits".' *Infant Mental Health Journal 16*, 4, 271–291.

Piescher, K.N., Schmidt, M. and Laliberte, T. (2008) 'Evidence-based Practice in Foster Parent Training and Support: Implications for Treatment Foster Care Providers.' Centre for Advanced Studies in Child Welfare, University of Minnesota School of Social Work. Available at: www.cehd.umn.edu/ssw/cascw/attributes/PDF/EBP/EBPFPTrainingSupportComplete.pdf [accessed 15 May 2013].

Pignotti, M. and Mercer, J. (2007) 'Holding Therapy and Dyadic Developmental Psychotherapy Are Not Supported and Acceptable Social Work Interventions: A Systematic Research Synthesis Revisited.' *Research on Social Work Practice 17*, 4, 513–519.

Pinkerton, J. and Dolan, P. (2007) 'Family Support, Social Capital, Resilience and Adolescent Coping.' *Child and Family Social Work 12*, 3, 219–228.

Pithouse, A.J., Lowe, K. and Hill-Tout, J. (2004) 'Foster Carers who Care for Children with Challenging Behaviour: A Total Population Study.' *Adoption and Fostering 28*, 3, 20–30.

Pocock, D. (2009) 'Working With Emotional Systems: Four New Maps.' In C. Flaskas and D. Pocock *Systems and Psychoanalysis, Contemporary Integrations in Family Therapy.* London: Karnac.

Price, E. (2003) 'The 'Coherent Narrative'. Realism, Resources and Responsibility in Family Permanence.' In C. Archer and A. Burnell *Trauma , Attachment and Family Permanence: Fear Can Stop You Loving.* London and Philadelphia: Jessica Kingsley Publishers.

Price, J.M., Chamberlain, P., Landsverk, J., Reid, J.B., Leve, L.D. and Laurent, H. (2008) 'Effects of a Foster Parent Training Intervention on Placement Changes of Children in Foster Care.' *Child Maltreatment 13*, 1, 64–75.

Registered Homes Act (1984) London: The Stationery Office.

Richardson, J. and Joughin, C. (2000) *The Mental Health Needs of Looked After Children.* London: The Royal College of Psychiatrists/Gaskell.

Robertson, A.S. (2006) 'Including parents, foster parents and parenting caregivers in the assessments and interventions of young children placed in the foster care system.' *Children and Youth Services Review 28*, 2, 180–193.

Rocco-Briggs, M. (2008) '"Who Owns My Pain?" An Aspect of the Complexity of Working With Looked After Children.' *Journal of Child Psychotherapy 34*, 2, 190–206.

Rosenthal, R. and Jacobson, L. (1968) *Pygmalion in the Classroom.* New York: Holt, Rinehart and Winston.

Rowland, M.D., Halliday-Boykins C.A., Henggeler, S.W., Cunningham, P.B. *et al.* (2005) 'A Randomised Trial of Multisystemic Therapy With Hawaii's Felix Class Youth.' *Journal of Emotional and Behavioural Disorders 13*, 13–23.

Rubin, D.M., O'Reilly, A.L., Luan, X. and Localio, A.R. (2007) 'The Impact of Placement Stability on Behavioral Well-being for Children in Foster Care.' *Pediatrics 119*, 2, 336–44.

Rushton, A. and Minnis, H. (2002) 'Residential and foster family care.' In M. Rutter and E. Taylor (eds) *Child and Adolescent Psychiatry* (4th ed.). Oxford: Blackwell.

Rutter, M. (1999) 'Resilience concepts and findings: implications for family therapy.' *Journal of Family Therapy 21*, 2, 119–144.

Rutter, M. (2007) 'Resilience, Competence, and Coping.' *Child Abuse and Neglect 31*, 3, 205–9.

Ryff, C.D., Singer, B.H. and Dienberg-Love, G. (2004) 'Positive Health: Connecting Well-being and Biology.' *The Royal Society, 359*, 1383–1394.

Sackett, D.L., Straus, S.E., Richardson, W.S., Rosenberg, W. and Haynes, R.B. (2000) *Evidence Based Medicine: How to Practice and Teach EBM.* (2nd ed.). New York: Churchill-Livingstone.

Schaeffer, C. M. and Borduin, C.M. (2005) 'Long-term Follow-up to a Randomized Clinical Trial of Multisystemic Therapy with Serious and Violent Juvenile Offenders.' *Journal of Consulting and Clinical Psychology 73*, 445–453.

Scherr, T.G. (2007) 'Educational Experiences of Children in Foster Care: Meta-Analyses of Special Education, Retention and Discipline Rates.' *School Psychology International 28*, 4, 419–436.

Schofield, G. (2001) 'Resilience and family placement. A lifespan perspective.' *Adoption and Fostering 25*, 3, 6–17.

Schofield, G., (2002) 'The Significance of A Secure Base: A Psychosocial Model of Long-term Foster Care.' *Child and Family Social Work 7*, 4, 259–272.

Schofield, G. and Beek, M. (2005a) 'Providing A Secure Base: Parenting Children in Long-term Foster Family Care.' *Attachment and Human Development 7*, 1, 3–25.

Schofield, G. and Beek, M. (2005b) 'Risk and *Resilience* in Long-term Foster-care.' *British Journal of Social Work 35*, 8, 1283–1301.

Schofield, G. and Beek, M. (2006) *Attachment Handbook for Foster Care and Adoption.* London: BAAF.

Schofield, G. and Beek, M. (2009) 'Growing Up in Foster Care: Providing A Secure Base Through Adolescence.' *Child and Family Social Work 14*, 3, 255–266.

Schore, A. (2003) 'The Human Unconscious: The Development of the Right Brain and its Role in Early Emotional Life.' In V. Green (ed.) *Emotional Development in Psychoanalysis, Attachment Theory and Neuroscience – Creating Connections.* Hove: Routledge.

Schore, A.N. (1994) *Affect Regulation and the Origin of the Self.* Hillside, NJ: Lawrence Erlbaum Associates Inc.

Schore, A.N. (2001) 'Contributions from the Decade of the Brain to Infant Mental Health: An Overview.' *Infant Mental Health Journal 22*, 1–2, 1–6.

Sebba, J. (2012) *Why do people become foster carers? An International Literature Review on the Motivation to Foster.* Oxford: REES Centre. Available at http://reescentre.education.ox.ac.uk/research/publications/ [accessed 17 May 2013].

Selekman, M.D. (1997) *Solution-focused Therapy with Children: Harnessing Family Strengths for Systemic Change.* New York and London: The Guilford Press.

Sellick, C. (2006) 'From Famine to Feast. A review of the foster care research literature.' *Children and Society 20*, 1, 67.

Sellick, C. and Howell, D. (2004) 'A Description and Analysis of Multi-sectoral Fostering Practice in the United Kingdom.' *British Journal of Social Work 34*, 4, 481–499.

Sexton, T. and Turner, C.W. (2010) 'The Effectiveness of Functional Family Therapy For Youth With Behavioral Problems in A Community Practice Setting.' *Journal of Family Psychology (JFP): Journal of the Division of Family Psychology of the American Psychological Association (Division 43) 24*, 3, 339–48.

Sharland, E. and Taylor, I. (2007) 'Interprofessional Education in Qualifying Social Work. Research Review for SCIE.' Available at: www.scie.org.uk/publications/misc/ipe.asp [accessed 16 May 2013].

Shepperd, S., Doll, H., Gowers, S., James, A., *et al.* (2009) *Alternatives to inpatient mental health care for children and young people (Review).* The Cochrane Collaboration, John Wiley and Sons Ltd. Available at: www.update-software.com/BCP/WileyPDF/EN/CD006410.pdf [accessed 17 May 2013].

Siegel, D. (1999) *The Developing Mind.* New York: Guilford Press.

Siegel, D. and Hartzell, M. (2004) *Parenting from the Inside Out.* New York: Penguin Group.

Sinclair, I., Gibbs, I. and Wilson, K. (2004) *Foster Carers: Why They Stay and Why They Leave.* London: Jessica Kingsley.

Sloper, P. (2004) 'Facilitators and Barriers for Co-ordinated Multi-agency Services.' *Child: Care, Health and Development 30,* 6, 571–580.

Sprince, J. (2000) 'Towards an Integrated Network.' *Journal of Child Psychotherapy 26,* 3, 413–431.

Sroufe, L.A. (1997) Psychopathology as an outcome of development.' *Development and Psychopathology 9,* 2, 251–66.

Staines, J., Farmer, E. and Selwyn, J. (2011) 'Implementing a Therapeutic Team Parenting Approach to Fostering: The Experiences of One Independent Foster-care Agency.' *British Journal of Social Work 41,* 2, 314–332.

Stallard, P. (2002) *Think Good Feel Good – A Cognitive Behaviour Therapy Workbook for Children and Young People.* Chichester: Wiley.

Steele, H. (2003) 'Holding Therapy Is Not Attachment Therapy: Editor's Introduction to this Invited Special Issue.' *Attachment and Human Development 5,* 219–220.

Stern, D. (1985) *The Interpersonal World of the Infant.* London: Karnac Books.

Stott, L. (2006) 'Holding It All Together: Creating Thinking Networks.' In K.S Golding, H.R. Dent, R. Nissim and L. Stott (eds) *Thinking Psychologically About Children Who Are Looked After and Adopted. Space for Reflection.* Chichester: John Wiley and Sons Ltd.

Stout, B.D. and Holleran, D.J. (2012) 'The Impact of Evidence-based Practices on Requests for Out-of-Home Placements in the Context of System Reform.' *The Journal of Child Family Studies (2013) 22,* 311–321.

Sundell, K., Hansson, K., Lofholm, C.A., Olsson, T., Gustle, L.H. and Kadesjo, C. (2008) 'The Transportability of MST To Sweden: Short-Term Results from A Randomized Trial of Conduct Disordered Youth.' *Journal of Family Psychology 22,* 550–560.

Sundet, T. and Torsteinsson, V.W. (2009) 'Thinking Through Togetherness: Developmental Metaphors and Systemic Thinking.' In C. Flaskas and D. Pocock *Systems and Psychoanalysis, Contemporary Integrations in Family Therapy.* London: Karnac.

Swick, K.J. (2007) 'Empower Foster Parents Toward Caring Relations with Children.' *Early Childhood Education Journal 34,* 6, 393–398.

Thomas, N. (1997) *When Love is Not Enough: A Guide to Parenting Children with RAD –Reactive Attachment Disorder.* Ashland, OH: Atlas Books.

Tomm, K. (1987a) 'Interventive Interviewing: Part I. Strategizing as a Fourth Guideline for the Therapist.' *Family Process 26,* 3–13.

Tomm, K. (1987b) 'Interventive Interviewing: Part II. Reflective Questioning as a Means to Enable Self-healing.' *Family Process 26,* 167–183.

Tomm, K. (1988) 'Interventive Interviewing: Part III. Intending to Ask Lineal, Circular, Strategic or Reflexive Questions?' *Family Process 27,* 1–15.

Utting, W. (1997) *People Like Us: The Report on the Review of Safeguards for Children Living Away from Home.* London: The Stationery Office.

Vacca, J.S. (2008) 'Breaking The Cycle of Academic Failure For Foster Children — What Can the Schools Do to Help?' *Children and Youth Services Review 30,* 9, 1081–1087.

van der Kolk, B. (2005) 'Developmental Trauma Disorder – Towards A Rational Diagnosis For Children With Complex Trauma Histories.' *Psychiatric Annals 35,* 5, 401–408.

Varela, E.R. and Vernberg, E.M. (2003) 'Developmental Perspectives on Post-traumatic Stress Disorder.' *The Prevention Researcher 10,* 2, 4–6.

Waldron, H.B., Slesnick, N., Turner, C.W., Brody, J.L. and Peterson, T.R. (2001) 'Treatment Outcomes For Adolescent Substance Abuse At 4- and 7-Month Assessments.' *Journal of Consulting and Clinical Psychology 69,* 802–813.

Walker, M. (2004); 'Supervising practitioners working with survivors of childhood abuse: countertransference; secondary traumatisation and terror.' *Psychoanalytic Practice, Individuals, Groups and Organisations 10,* 2 173–193.

Walker, J. (2008) 'The Use of Attachment Theory in Adoption and Fostering.' *Adoption and Fostering 32,* 49–57.

Ward, H., Jones, H., Lynch, M. and Skuse, P. (2002) 'Issues Concerning the Health of Looked After Children.' *Adoption and Fostering 26,* 4, 1–11.

Ward, T. and Stewart, C.A. (2003) 'The *Treatment* of Sex Offenders: Risk Management and Good Lives.' *Professional Psychology, Research and Practice 34,* 353–360.

Warman A., Pallet, C. and Scott, S. (2006) 'Learning From Each Other: Process and Outcomes in the Fostering Changes Training Programme.' *Adoption and Fostering 30,* 3, 17–28.

Welsh Office (1999) *Building for the Future – A White Paper for Wales – CM4051.* Norwich: The Stationery Office.

Weyts, A. (2004) 'The Educational Achievements of Looked After Children: Do Welfare Systems Make A Difference To Outcomes?' *Adoption and Fostering 28,* 3, 7–19.

Whenan, R., Oxlad, M. and Lushington, K. (2009) 'Factors Associated With Foster Carer Well-being, Satisfaction and Intention to Continue Providing Out-of-Home Care.' *Children and Youth Services Review 31,* 7, 752–760.

White, M. (1995) *Re-authoring Lives: Interviews and Essays.* Adelaide: Dulwich Centre Publications.

White, M. (2006) 'Working With Children Who Have Experienced Significant Trauma.' In M. White and A. Morgan (eds) *Narrative Therapy with Children and Their Families.* Adelaide: Dulwich Centre Publications.

Wilson, J. (1998) *Child Focused Practice: A Collaborative Systemic Approach.* London: Karnac Books.

Wilson, K. and Evetts, J. (2006) 'The Professionalization of Foster Care.' *Adoption and Fostering, 30,* 1, 39–47.

Wilson, K., Petrie, S. and Sinclair, I. (2003) 'A Kind of Loving: A Model of Effective Foster Care.' *British Journal of Social Work 33,* 8, 991–1003.

Winnicott, D.W. (1971) *Playing and Reality.* London: Tavistock Publishers.

Woodcock, J. (2009) 'Love and Hate and the Oedipal Myth: The Perfect Bridge Between the Systemic and the Psychoanalytic.' In C. Flaskas and D. Pocock *Systems and Psychoanalysis, Contemporary Integrations in Family Therapy.* London: Karnac.

Worling J.R. and Curwen T. (2000) 'Adolescent Sexual Offender Recidivism: Success of Specialised Treatment and Implications for Risk Prediction.' *Child Abuse and Neglect 24,* 965–982.

Yontef, G.M. (1993) *Awareness, Dialogue and Process – Essays on Gestalt Therapy.* New York: The Gestalt Journal Press Inc.

Yuen, A. (2007) 'Discovering Children's Responses to Trauma: A Response-based Narrative Practice.' *International Journal of Narrative Therapy and Community Work 4,* 3–18.

Zetlin, A.G., Weinberg, L.A. and Shea, N.M. (2006) 'Improving Educational Prospects for Youth in Foster Care: The Education Liaison Model Intervention.' *School and Clinic 41,* 5, 267–273.

Ziegenhain, U. (2004) 'The Contribution of Attachment Theory to Early Prevention and Professional Training.' *Educational and Child Psychology 21,* 1, 46–58.

Zolli, A. and Healy, A.M. (2012) *Resilience: Why Things Bounce Back.* London: Free Press.

Subject Index

Author Index